SHAKESPEARE'S HOMELAND

SHAKESPEARE'S HOMELAND

SKETCHES OF STRATFORD-UPON-AVON
THE FOREST OF ARDEN AND
THE AVON VALLEY

BY

W. SALT BRASSINGTON, F.S.A.

AUTHOR OF " HISTORIC WORCESTERSHIRE," " THE HISTORY
OF THE ART OF BOOK-BINDING," ETC., ETC.

WITH

OVER SEVENTY ILLUSTRATIONS BY

HENRY J. HOWARD AND SIDNEY HEATH

LONDON : J. M. DENT & CO.
NEW YORK : E. P. DUTTON & CO.
1903

FOREWORDS

In the following sketches the Author has endeavoured to record his impressions of the country around Stratford-on-Avon, and especially to collect local traditions connected with our ever living Poet, William Shakespeare, a considerable portion of whose life was spent in the Vale of the Red Horse.

Each sketch is complete in itself. The first seventeen chapters deal with places directly associated with Shakespeare. Chapters eighteen, nineteen, and twenty are short accounts of relics and portraits of the Poet, and Shakespeare Celebrations. The remaining twenty-one chapters relate chiefly to places within easy reach of Stratford-on-Avon.

The aim of the Author being to write a book that may be interesting and useful to many visitors to the district, no attempt has been made to deal with the subjects in a scientific manner.

CONTENTS

		PAGE
INTRODUCTION		xiii

CHAP.

I. THE CRADLE OF THE POET'S FAMILY . .		1
II. THE LORDS OF ARDEN		6
III. ASTON NEAR BIRMINGHAM, AND THE POET'S ANCESTORS		11
IV. THE HOME OF SHAKESPEARE'S GRANDFATHER, ROBERT ARDEN		16
V. SNITTERFIELD, HOME OF THE POET'S ANCESTORS .		26
VI. THE POET'S COURTSHIP . . .		36
VII. SHAKESPEARE'S JOURNEY TO WORCESTER . .		42
VIII. CHARLECOTE, HOME OF THE LUCYS . . .		50
IX. A JOURNEY TO LONDON		62
X. SHAKESPEARE'S STRATFORD HOMES . . .		71
XI. STRATFORD-UPON-AVON CHURCH . . .		81
XII. A WALK TO CLIFFORD CHAMBERS . . .		91
XIII. THE FAT ALE WIFE OF WINCOT . . .		101
XIV. POOR YOUNG SOMERVILE		105
XV. KING JAMES'S MASTER OF THE ORDNANCE .		109
XVI. THE SHAKESPEAREAN VILLAGES . . .		113
XVII. EVESHAM AND THE PLAYERS . . .		131
XVIII. SHAKESPEAREAN RELICS		140
XIX. PORTRAITS OF SHAKESPEARE . . .		145
XX. SHAKESPEARE CELEBRATIONS, 1769 . .		157
XXI. THE SOFT FLOWING AVON . . .		177
XXII. PRINCELY WARWICK AND THE NEVILLES .		192
XXIII. S. MARY'S CHURCH, WARWICK . . .		204

CONTENTS

CHAP.		PAGE
XXIV.	Leicester Hospital, Warwick . . .	210
XXV.	Kenilworth	214
XXVI.	Gibbering Ghosts, Hobgoblins and Witches .	224
XXVII.	Compton Wynyates	229
XXVIII.	The Campden Wonder	237
XXIX.	The Legend of Winchcombe . . .	246
XXX.	Loxley and Robin Hood	251
XXXI.	Henley-in-Arden	254
XXXII.	Alcester	259
XXXIII.	Ettington and Halford Bridge . . .	263
XXXIV.	Cavaliers and Roundheads at Stratford-on-Avon	271
XXXV.	Cavaliers and Roundheads: The Battle of Edge Hill	277
XXXVI.	A Visit to Gloucestershire . . .	280
XXXVII.	A Ramble in the Forest of Arden . .	296
XXXVIII.	Guild of the Holy Cross . . .	307
XXXIX.	Home of the Washingtons . . .	315
XL.	Around Meon Hill	320
XLI.	Churches in the Neighbourhood of Stratford .	328
Index	353

LIST OF ILLUSTRATIONS

The Newly-Discovered Portrait of Shakespeare. Reproduced
in facsimile by kind permission of the Trustees of the
Memorial Museum, Stratford-on-Avon . . *Frontispiece*

	PAGE
Gate House, Kenilworth Castle	xiii
The Abbey, Tewkesbury	xiv
The River Walk, Leamington	xvii
Shakespeare Memorial, Stratford-on-Avon . . .	xix
Cottage at Clifford Chambers	xx
Knowle Church	3
Aston Cantlow Church	9
The Arden Tomb in Aston Parish Church . . .	12
Cottages at Wilmcote	16
Wilmcote	19
Oak Settle at " The Swan," Wilmcote . . .	23
Cottages at Tiddington	29
Snitterfield Church	33
Shottery Manor House	36
Anne Hathaway's Cottage	39
Dovecote at Shottery	41
Charlecote	51
Shakespeare's Birthplace at Stratford . . .	71
Room wherein Shakespeare was born . . .	72
The Kitchen, Shakespeare's Birthplace . . .	78
Holy Trinity Church, Stratford-on-Avon . . .	80
Stratford Church from the River Avon . . .	83
Interior, Stratford Church	87

	PAGE
The Old Rectory, Clifford Chambers	93
Gable of Old Rectory, Clifford Chambers	96
Gable of Manor House, Clifford Chambers	99
Facsimile of Entry in Quinton Church Register	102
Porch, Wotton Wawen Church	107
Bidford	113
"Nine Men's Morris"	120
"Beggarly" Broom	125
"Papist" Wixford	127
Norman Gateway, Evesham	132
Pershore Bridge	138
Mill at Guy's Cliff	176
The Avon in Winter	177
Clopton Bridge from the Swan's Nest	179
At Luddington	184
Welford-on-Avon	186
Ruin of Archway, Evesham	187
The Abbey Gates, Tewkesbury	188
Tewkesbury from the Severn	190
Mill Street, Warwick	193
Warwick Castle from the River	197
The Market Place, Warwick	200
A Bit of Warwick	206
Leicester Hospital, Warwick	210
Kenilworth Castle—The Banqueting Hall	215
Kenilworth Banqueting Hall	219
Kenilworth Church Doorway	223
Compton Wynyates	231
At Chipping Campden, the Market Place	239
At Chipping Campden	243
Henley-in-Arden	254
The Bell Inn, Tewkesbury	281

LIST OF ILLUSTRATIONS

	PAGE
At Broadway	283
A Quaint House at Tewkesbury	286
The Warwick Chantry in Tewkesbury Abbey	287
Tomb of Hugh le Despencer	289
Tomb of John Wakeman, Tewkesbury Abbey	291
High Street, Tewkesbury	293
The Tower of Hampton-in-Arden Church	296
Porch and Gates of Solihull Church	303
Berkswell Church	305
Guild Hall and Almshouses in 1901	306
Guild Chapel and Grammar School	309
Old Court, Sheep Street, Stratford-on-Avon	314
Manor House, Sulgrave	315
The Harvard House	318
Burton Dasset Beacon	345

GATE HOUSE, KENILWORTH CASTLE

INTRODUCTION

WHERE SIX COUNTIES MEET

WHEN one of the sweetest of Elizabethan poets took
pen in hand to describe his native England, he found
it impossible to write pleasantly about places without
giving their personal associations. Whenever he was
able to localise an incident Michael Drayton did so;
but where history, or his knowledge of it, failed, he
made up for lack of interest by personifying hills, vales,
and rivers, as classic poets long ago were wont to do.
In "Poly-Olbion," Severn and Avon become coy nymphs;
Malvern—"Manly Malvern"—a giant; and the smaller
hills sweet maids. This, although allowable in charming poetry, in sober prose would be out of place: yet
the difficulty experienced by Drayton when writing his
great topographical poem still confronts the writer who
would describe a landscape. Unless some human
interest can be introduced, his picture fails to please,

his descriptions are obscured by the " sweet smoke " of mere verbage, and his work is dull and monotonous. Directly he introduces incidents he begins to claim attention, the smoke lifts, the characters stand forth in their true and natural colours.

It is the people whose lives are associated with the place that make the story interesting. Though now a peaceful district, the home of an industrious and energetic race engaged in agricultural pursuits, or manufacture, the Midlands in former times were the scene of stirring events, and of many battles.

The castles of Warwick, Kenilworth, Tamworth, Dudley, and Maxtoke remind us of the days of chivalry : the Cathe- drals of Worcester, Lichfield, Gloucester, and Coventry : the noble churches of Stratford, Warwick, Tewkesbury, Tred- ington, and Brailes are monuments to the piety and love of religion cherished by our forefathers.

The Abbey Tewkesbury

The great build- ings in the busy streets of Birmingham bear witness to the commercial enterprise of Warwickshire men whose pleasant homes are scattered throughout the district.

From Tamworth in the north to Long Compton in the south, Warwickshire stretches fifty miles in length ; and east to west, from Rugby to Alcester, the shire covers full thirty miles.

Staffordshire, Derbyshire, Leicestershire, Northamptonshire, Oxfordshire, Gloucestershire and Worcestershire are her neighbours. It may be truly said that no other place has played a more important part in England's history :—

> " The foremost place, as fame doth attest,
> Belongs to our mid-country." [1]

The roll of great names extends from heroic Guy, Earl of Warwick, to famous Joseph Chamberlain of Birmingham, and includes those of the fairest lady— Lady Godiva—and the greatest poet—William Shakespeare.

Should we stand upon the ramparts of Tamworth Castle to view the Tame flowing towards the German Ocean, we must think of the fort which King Alfred's daughter, Ethelfreda, built beside the river there, and of the many changes which have passed since our English forefathers first established themselves in seagirt Britain.

The three spires of Lichfield's Gothic fane recall memories of the missionary labours of S. Chad among our Saxon ancestors; and in later times of " Fanatic Brooke," who stormed the fair Cathedral, and fell before the rifle of " Dumb Dyott"; of Dr Johnson trudging off to London with David Garrick to earn fame and fortune, and returning to stand in its market-place to do penance for an act of filial disrespect.

Should we repair to Kenilworth, and wander beneath the great fragments of the lordly palace, we are reminded of John of Gaunt, " time-honoured Lancaster "; of Robert Dudley, the magnificent entertainer of

---

[1] John Cotton, " Songs and Sentiment."

Queen Elizabeth; and of those "princely pleasures" made world famous by the novels of Sir Walter Scott.

We may repair to Leafy Leamington with memories of Ruskin, Dr Jephson and Lord Lansdowne; or we may travel along the broad road beneath the speading arms of oak and elm, to the little town of Stratford-on-Avon, and from the Shakespeare Memorial tower gaze over the vale of the Red Horse, the Avon valley, the vale of Evesham and the Severn valley; the fairest landscape in all England, full of memories of the past. Here Celt and Roman, English and Norman, King and Barons fought for possession or for freedom. There, upon the slopes of Edge Hill, the forces of King Charles and Cromwell met in deadly strife, and yonder on Evesham's battlefield Simon de Montfort fell before the victorious army of King Henry.

Westward, hidden behind intervening hills, lies Worcester's loyal city, with its great Cathedral, enshrining the tomb of King John, and full of memories of Saints, Princes, Bishops, and of the last battle of that great struggle wherein usurping Cromwell drove out the Stuart King.

Nearer home we see the red tiled roof and dark timbers of the house which sheltered the greatest genius the world has ever known—SHAKESPEARE THE IMMORTAL, and also the fair church wherein his body lies entombed—a church, cathedral-like in proportions and arrangements, beautiful in every detail, and associated with the worship of God for many centuries.

We may visit the busy haunts of men, tread the crowded streets of towns, or steal away along sequestered lanes where trees arch overhead, and the

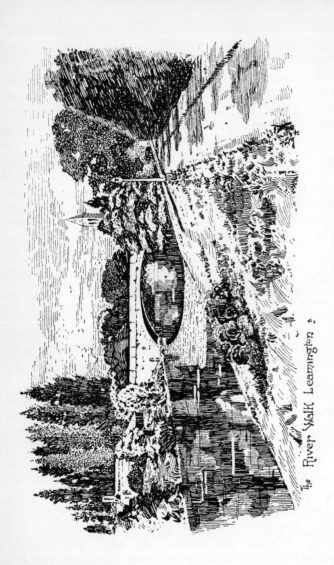

The River Walk Leamington s.

only sounds are wild birds' songs, and the ploughman's merry note: but wherever we go we find traces of the past history of the land.

SHAKESPEARE MEMORIAL, STRATFORD-ON-AVON

The very names of the villages often remind us of men famous in English history; Preston Bagot, Welles-bourne Hastings, Compton Verney, Naunton Beauchamp and Baddesley Clinton preserve the names of famous owners of the soil: while such names as Alcester and Chesterton carry the mind back to the days of ancient Rome; Wooton Wawen to those of Saxon, and Beau-desert to those of Norman Conquerors.

In brief, the district teems with associations of ages past, associations interesting in themselves, and important when considered in relation to one another, and to the history of the English race.

Cottage at
Clifford Chambers

SHAKESPEARE'S HOMELAND

CHAPTER I

THE CRADLE OF THE POET'S FAMILY

A REMOTE farm house in the parish of Temple Balsall, and on the borders of Wroxhall, twelve miles north of Stratford-on-Avon, little known and seldom visited, has an interest greater than is attached to many more famous places.

Oldediche, Olditch, or Woldiche, was the home of the Shakespeare family long before any of the name settled at Stratford-on-Avon. On high ground, near the southern boundary of Temple Balsall, stands a tiny hamlet, composed of two farm houses, and a couple of cottages. This hamlet was anciently known as Woldiche, or Oldediche; it was here, and in one of the farm houses, that the Poet's ancestors were living at the end of the fourteenth century. The house must have been many times repaired since those days, and was considerably altered in the sixteenth century, but it still retains many of its ancient features : especially noteworthy is the pre-Reformation plan of the house. It is a dwelling of ample size, betokening its former owners to have been people of substance. The Hall, now divided into two rooms, was spacious, and the parlour opening out of it, of fair dimensions, and richly panelled, possibly in the Tudor period. In the upper storey, a curious passage way, called the oratory or prayer room, with niches in the walls, may be seen. There is also a dark hole in the thickness of the wall at the back of the prayer room, said to be a priest's hiding place.

The front of the house has been modernised, the old timbers removed, and red brick substituted : fortunately the house still has an old-world appearance within, and there can be little doubt that this substantial homestead was the cradle of the Warwickshire Shakespeares five hundred years ago, and that Adam Shakespeare of Oldediche, who is mentioned in the Baddesley Clinton muniments, lived within its walls.

The present occupier of the farm states that the property belonged to his great-grandfather, from whom the tradition that the Shakespeares once lived in the house, has been handed down from generation to generation till the present day. This is most valuable information because none of the Poet's numerous biographers appear to have been aware of the tradition, or to have associated his ancestors with this place until Mr W. B. Bickley, the transcriber of the Register of the Guild of Knowle, communicated the fact to the Birmingham papers.

There is no doubt that the habitation is an ancient one. The early members of the Shakespeare family, whose names are recorded in the Register of S. Anne of Knowle, in Warwickshire, are said to be of Woldediche or Temple Balsall, the parish wherein Olditch is situated. The first name on the Shakespeare pedigree, as it now stands, is that of "Adam de Oldediche" who died in 1414. Adam was the ancestor of the Baddesley Clinton branch, from which the Poet was not descended. This has been fairly proved by the Rev. Father Norris in his interesting book on Baddesley Clinton, but nevertheless Adam of Woldediche most probably was the progenitor of William Shakespeare.

In the Register of the Guild of Knowle under the year 1457 we find a pious entry for the prayers of the faithful on behalf of Richard Shakspere and Alice his wife of Woldiche. From this entry it is clear that Richard and Alice had departed this life before the year 1457.

From the same source, *i.e.* the Knowle Guild Book,

Knowle
Church

we find in 1486 among the brethren and sisters of the fraternity, the names of Thomas Shakspere and Alice his wife of Balsale; and we gather from the same book that Thomas had died before 1511. It is probable that Thomas and Alice had a son John, who was the father of Richard Shakespeare of Snitterfield, the Poet's grandfather, who died about 1560, leaving several children, of whom John, the Poet's father, was the youngest.

The migration of the family from their ancient home

at Olditch has been partly traced, and it is absolutely certain that some of the earlier members held land on military tenure.   Recent researches in the British Museum have brought to light a fact of some importance, that is, that Thomas (?) Shakspere occupied a house at Westminster in proximity to the King's Court, and that he paid a considerable rent for it. It is therefore probable that he held an appointment under the Crown, and was indeed one of the adherents of Henry of Richmond.   We may be sure that he was rewarded by the victorious Earl after the battle of Bosworth Field, although up to the present time no record of a special grant to him has been found.   It is clearly stated in the grant of arms in the Heralds' College that John Shakespeare's "parents and late grandfather were for their valiant and faithful service advanced and rewarded by that most prudent King Henry the Seventh of famous memorie, sythence whiche tyme they have continued at those partes in good reputation and credit."

Mary Arden's ancestor for a similar service received a like reward, but on a larger scale.   Now, as a record of the grants to the Ardens is known, and that to the Shakespeares is not, it has been assumed that the Herald inaccurately ascribed Henry of Richmond's reward as given to the Ardens alone, and claimed as an honour for his own family by John Shakespeare. The words of the original document however have no uncertain ring about them, and from the facts that are known it is fairly certain that Thomas Shakespeare received a reward from the Royal Tudor in proportion to his merits and social position.

PROBABLE DESCENT OF WILLIAM SHAKESPEARE FROM ADAM OF OLDITCH.

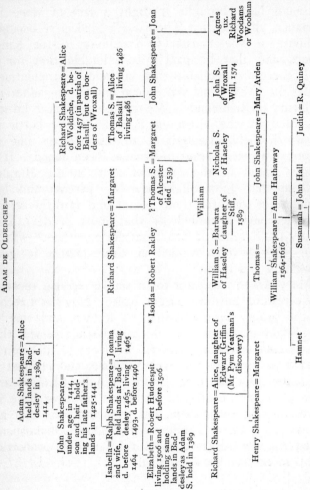

ADAM DE OLDEDICHE =

Adam Shakespeare = Alice held lands in Baddesley in 1389, d. 1414

John Shakespeare = under age in 1414, son and heir holding his late father's lands in 1425-1441

Richard Shakespeare = Alice of Woldiche, d. before 1457 (in parish of Balsall, but on borders of Wroxall)

Thomas S. = Alice of Balsall living 1486
living 1486

John Shakespeare = Joan

Isabella = Ralph Shakespeare 2nd wife, held lands at Baddesley 1465, living d. before 1493, d. before 1496
1464

Joanna living 1465

Richard Shakespeare = Margaret

? Thomas S. = Margaret of Alcester died 1539

Nicholas S. of Haseley

John S. of Wroxall Will, 1574

Agnes ux. Richard Woodams or Wooham

Elizabeth = Robert Huddespit living 1506 and d. before 1506 holding same lands in Baddesley as Adam S. held in 1389

* Isolda = Robert Rakley

William

William S. = Barbara of Haseley daughter of —— Stiff, 1589

Richard Shakespeare = Alice, daughter of Edward Griffin (Mr Pym Yeatman's discovery)

Thomas =

John Shakespeare = Mary Arden

Henry Shakespeare = Margaret

William Shakespeare = Anne Hathaway 1564-1616

Hamnet

Susannah = John Hall

Judith = R. Quiney

Thomas Nash = Elizabeth = Sir John Barnard d. s. p.

Ralph had no sons, and his estate in Baddesley was divided between these two daughters. This branch of the Shakespeares at an end.

* Ralph had no sons, and his estate in Baddesley was divided between these two daughters. This branch of the Shakespeares at an end.

CHAPTER II

THE LORDS OF ARDEN

CENTURIES before the Shakespeares settled in Warwickshire the Ardens held the proud position of proprietors of the midland forest land. Dugdale believed that in the time of Alfred the Great and Edward the Elder, Rohand was the Saxon lord of Warwick. His only daughter, Felicia, married Guy, son of Seward, Lord of Wallingford, who became Lord, or Earl of Warwick in the right of his wife.

"Earl" Guy was the famous champion whose prowess forms a subject of romance. Guy had a son, Reynbourne, who was stolen and carried into Russia: one of the Earl's train, "a gallant knight, Sir Heraud de Arderne," went in search of the Earl's son, who, when found, married the Lady Leonetta, King Athelstan's daughter. From this marriage descended, after four generations, Wygot, "a potent man, and a great warrior in the time of Ethelwold"; he married Ermenild, sister of Leofric, Earl of Mercia, husband of the famous Lady Godiva.[1]

Wygot and Ermenild had a son, Ailwyn, who held the post of Vice-Comes of Warwickshire under his uncle, Leofric, in the time of Edward the Confessor; and his son, Turchill de Arden, held fifty-two lordships in Warwickshire at the time of the Norman invasion.

[1] Dugdale uses the title "Earl" though in Saxon times that title was scarcely understood.

6

He had married for his second wife his kinswoman, Leverunia, heiress of the Earls of Mercia, and became ancestor of the Comptons of Compton Wynyates; the Bracebridges of Kingsbury; the Ardens of Park Hall; and consequently of William Shakespeare.

Many of Turchill's possessions were taken from him by William Rufus and bestowed upon one of the Beaumont family, Henry Newburgh, first Norman Earl of Warwick. Turchill had a daughter, Margaret, by his first wife, the Countess of Perche. Probably in order to secure for himself and his heirs the quiet possession of the lands and honours wrested from the Ardens, Henry married Turchill's daughter Margaret. Turchill, stripped of his honours, retired to the remote woodlands,

> " Where nightingales in Arden sit and sing
> Among the dainty dew-empearled flowers."

The part of the country chosen for his retreat appears to have been northward of Stratford, towards Tamworth and Coleshill, the manors of Curdworth, Minworth, Barston, Great Packington, etc.

The ramifications of the Arden pedigree are most intricate, for the Ardens appear to have been a prolific race, and mated with most of the noble families in the Midlands. A Sir Henry de Arden living in the time of Henry IV. had manors at Park Hall, Castle Bromwich, Pedimore, and lands in Curdworth, Minworth, and Aston, which his son Sir Ralph conferred on his mother. The family first took sides against the house of Lancaster, at the beginning of the Wars of the Roses; for this cause, Robert Arden was attainted in 1452. In the Harlean MSS. (1167 F. 57) it is stated that "Robert Arden of Park Hall, in the parish of Curdworth, attainted by Henry VI., the usurping

King, because he took part with Richard, Duke of York, true heir to the crown, was cruelly executed at Ludlow."

Robert Arden had seven children; but his son Walter is the only one of whom we have any certain knowledge. Walter was buried in the church of S. Peter and S. Paul at Aston juxta Birmingham, where his monument may still be seen. His wife was Eleanor, second daughter and co-heiress of John Hampden of Buckinghamshire. Walter and Eleanor had six sons: John, Thomas, Martin, Robert, Henry, William; and four daughters. Thomas, who is believed by George R. French to have been the second son, was grandfather of Mary Arden, wife of John Shakespeare. Walter Arden is commemorated in Aston church by a monumental brass, and a portrait in a stained glass window, described by Dugdale. The old window was destroyed, but a new one copied from Dugdale's drawing has been inserted.

Walter's eldest son, John, married Alice, daughter of Sir Richard Bracebridge of Kingsbury, under most romantic circumstances. It appears that John Arden, being then under age, was kidnapped by Richard Bracebridge, who also claimed descent from Turchill de Arden. The result of this kidnapping was that a feud arose between the Bracebridges and the Ardens; it was at length settled by arbitration, Sir Simon Mountford of Coleshill and Sir Richard Bingham being arbitrators. It was determined that the marriage should be solemnised between John and his sweetheart in February 1472-3. A jointure of two hundred marks was settled upon the bride, and for the trespass done by Sir Richard Bracebridge in so taking away the young gentleman, he agreed to give Walter Arden the best horse that could by him be chosen in Kingsbury Park.

Walter Arden's second son, Thomas, is mentioned in the will of his father in 1502, and in that of his brother, the before-named Sir John, in 1526. He is described as of Aston Cantlow, from 1501 to 1547, and he purchased lands at Snitterfield in 1501. We

ASTON CANTLOW CHURCH

do not know the name of his wife, but his son was Robert Arden of Wilmcote, in the parish of Aston Cantlow, Shakespeare's grandfather.

The old house at Park Hall is a moated mansion situated in the parish of Erdington, not far from the great Chester road, and within an easy walk of the magnificent chase of Sutton Coldfield. The district has become a suburb of Birmingham, and the fact that Aston was the mother-church of the district will account for the Ardens being buried within its walls. Their tombs, and those of the Erdingtons, have been carefully renovated within the last twenty years, forming the chief adornments of the Erdington Chapel, rebuilt for their reception. From the coincidence that the Park Hall family were buried at *Aston* juxta Birmingham, and a cadet of the same house lived and was buried at *Aston Cantlow* near Stratford, some confusion has arisen. The immediate ancestors of William Shakespeare, that is, his grandfather and probably his great-grandfather were buried at Aston Cantlow, but his great-great-grandfather had his last resting-place at Aston juxta Birmingham.

The name Aston is of fairly common occurrence, so common indeed, that each Aston has to be differentiated : and thus we have Aston near Birmingham, Aston Cantlow, Steeple Aston, Aston Subedge, etc.

Branches of the Arden family were early settled in Oxfordshire and Staffordshire, and it is probable that the Oxfordshire branch made an alliance with Sir Thomas More, the great Lord Chancellor. The Arden arms appear upon his tomb in Chelsea church, and are there in right of his second wife, Alice, widow of one of the Middletons. She was, we have strong reasons to believe, one of the Oxfordshire Ardens. That a kinswoman of Shakespeare's mother was wife of the saintly Sir Thomas is a fact at least worthy of record, if of nothing more.

In modern times the Ardens have still kept up their ancient reputation and mated with some of the nobles of our land, so that the blood which flows in the veins of our modern nobility may be traced back to those old Saxon Lords, who ruled in the wild forest districts which gave them their name.

CHAPTER III

WE may recapitulate some of the facts recorded in the previous chapter :—

In the fifteenth century the Ardens were established at that corner of Warwickshire which lies between Birmingham and Sutton Coldfield, at Park Hall, Pedimore, and Nechells. Their chief place of burial appears to have been the ancient church of S. Peter and S. Paul of Aston juxta Birmingham. Park Hall is situated between Castle Bromwich and Water Orton, near to the river Tame; the house was moated and surrounded by a large park : Pedimore, situated on the opposite side of the river, about two miles away, had an extensive moat also ; and Nechells the third mansion was pleasantly placed, its lands now form a district of Birmingham and the manor house, like those of Park Hall and Pedimore, has disappeared.

In the reign of Richard II., Sir Henry Arden was living at Park Hall, and his descendant Sir John, Esquire of the body to Henry VII., married Alice, daughter of Richard Bracebridge of Kingsbury.

Sir Walter Arden of Park Hall was William Shakespeare's great-great-grandfather, Robert Arden of Wilmcote being descended from the second son of Sir Walter.

The main line was continued by Sir John already

mentioned, whose son, Sir Thomas, married Mary, daughter of Sir Thomas Andrews of Cherwilton. Their son, William Arden, married Elizabeth, daughter of Edward Conway of Ragley, a family long settled at Luddington near Stratford-on-Avon. Their son, Edward Arden, was attainted by Queen Elizabeth in Shakespeare's lifetime.

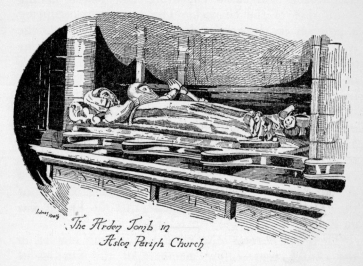

The Arden Tomb in
Aston Parish Church

Of the Poet's direct ancestor, Sir Walter, it is recorded that by his will made in June 1502 he bequeathed his body to be buried in the church of S. Peter and S. Paul at Aston, near to Birmingham, and to the Vicar of Aston for his mortuary and his Tythes forgotten, his best ox, and at his burial twelve pounds of wax, and lights and six torches to be borne by six poor men, each to have a black gown for that service, also a trentall of masses to be sung for his soul, also for the souls of his father and mother, and all

Christian souls; constituting Eleanor his wife executrix, and Edward Belknap, John Bracebridge and John Boteler of Solihull overseers thereof (Dugdale).

This Walter Arden and his wife had a brass in the middle of the chancel; an engraving of it is given in Dugdale. Their effigies were also displayed in a window of the north aisle, destroyed but again produced from Dugdale's engraving, and placed in the south side of the chancel. The monument occupying a position on the north side of the chancel, under the western arch, is of earlier date, and possibly represents Sir Thomas Arden of Nechells, who lived in the time of Richard II., or more probably Sir Henry, who was living in the same reign. The tomb appears to have been made up, and has been several times removed; one side of it, and the effigy of the knight, are of alabaster, the other side, and the effigy of the lady, are of freestone, and her costume is of later date. There can be no doubt, however, from the wild boar carved at the knight's feet, and the arms of Arden on one of the shields, engraved in Dugdale, that the knight was an Arden.

There are several other altar tombs, with effigies, in the church representing members of the families of Erdington and Holte. A large monument on the south wall of the Erdington Chapel was erected to the memory of Sir Edward Devereux, ancestor of Viscount Hereford. Sir Edward's wife was Katherine, daughter of Edward Arden of Park Hall, attainted in 1584, and sister to Mrs Somervile of Edstone. The Devereux monument appears to have been erected by the widow; and among other coats of arms, that of Arden is conspicuous.

The Poet's mother's descent from this great family

of Arden, one of the most distinguished in the Midlands, must have had a distinct influence upon the career of her son, whose knowledge of the characters introduced into his plays, came to him almost by intuition from his earliest years.   The pride of ancestry inbred in those of ancient lineage, whose forefathers from time immemorial have taken a leading part in the affairs of their country, comes naturally to a scion of an ancient house. This trait in the character of Shakespeare is easily discoverable in many of his writings : like Horace he scorns the vulgar, and drives them from him.   Nevertheless he was by no means blind to the merits of honest shepherds, homely swains, and the true nobility of labour :—

> " Ah, what a life were this ! how sweet! how lovely !
> Gives not the hawthorn bush a sweeter shade
> To shepherds, looking on their silly sheep,
> Than doth a rich embroidered canopy
> To kings, that fear their subjects' treachery !
> O, yes it doth ; a thousand-fold it doth."

It cannot be too strongly insisted upon that from his knightly ancestors Shakespeare derived qualities which could never have been possessed by the unlettered son of a rustic butcher of ignoble descent.   On the contrary the facts, as we now know them, prove that while on his mother's side the Dramatist came from an ancient family of knights, his father's was also ancient, and though less distinguished, equally honourable. The sturdy English yeomen, in time of peace tilling the land which their swords defended in war time, were as brave and as proud of their family descent as any knight could possibly be of his.   Tradition would certainly play an important part in the formation of character, and the Poet would have heard many tales of the doings of his own ancestors upon the battle field and in the councils of the land.

It may seem strange to seek Shakespeare's noble ancestry under the smoky canopy of the capital of the Midlands, yet in that great town are preserved the best monuments of this feudal race.

At a later time, when Birmingham began to show signs of increasing industry, and other families possessed the Ardens' lands, a magnificent Jacobean mansion was built by Sir Thomas Holte on the hill hard by the parish church of Aston.   Aston Hall compares favourably with Hardwick House, Hatfield, Charlecote, or any other of the great halls of that period.   Though not so large as some of those mentioned, it is still almost perfect in all its arrangements, and while the surroundings have changed, and a town has been built upon the park, the Hall itself remains much as it was nearly three hundred years ago.

It has often been said that Washington Irving took this mansion as his model for "Bracebridge Hall."   To-day the house, though no longer inhabited, serves the purpose of a museum, and is the property of the Corporation of Birmingham.   It should be one of the most valued possessions of that great Corporation, and it is satisfactory to know that the hardware town so far values its inheritance that Aston Hall is carefully preserved from the ravages of time.   It may be noted in passing as a curious fact that while the ancestors of Shakespeare are buried in the parish church of Aston, an old clock said to have belonged to him is preserved to this day in the museum in the long gallery of Aston Hall, within a bow shot of the burial place of his ancestors.

COTTAGES AT WILMCOTE

CHAPTER IV

THE HOME OF SHAKESPEARE'S GRANDFATHER, ROBERT ARDEN

EVERY fact relating to Shakespeare has special interest at the present time, when so many detractors of the Warwickshire Bard are endeavouring to prove that he was a poor, illiterate fellow, about whom little is known, and that little not very creditable. Being convinced that these critics are led astray by want of exact local knowledge, and that their theories are founded upon false premises, the writer has for some time been trying to clear up many obscure points connected with the Poet's ancestry.

The importance of full and exact particulars regarding the homestead of Shakespeare's maternal grandfather must be evident to anyone at all acquainted with the subject; and the sentiment attached to that most picturesque farm house called " Mary Arden's Cottage," is at once apparent. Either the story now told about it is untrue and unworthy of credence, or it is true, and of more than common import.

The home of the Poet's mother, the gentle Mary Arden, to whose noble lineage, if to anything hereditary, the Poet owed his genius, cannot fail to be of the greatest interest, and in this respect ranks only second to the birthplace in Henley Street.

The evidence, both documentary and architectural, is almost conclusive that " Mary Arden's Cottage " is the house once occupied by the Arden family.   From the inventory of goods belonging to Robert Arden at the time of his death, it is clear that his place of abode was not a mansion, but simply a farm house of a type common in the Midlands, and in fact over the greater part of England in the days of the Tudor sovereigns.

These old farm houses, the residences of smaller landowners, consisted of a hall, or living-room, of one storey, divided into bays by massive timbers supporting the roof.   At one end was a building of two storeys, the lower room being sometimes a kitchen, or a sitting-room when the kitchen happened to be arranged at the other end.[1]   The upper chamber, or solar (the sunny room), was reached by a staircase leading from the living-room.   In smaller houses a window opening into the hall was provided in the solar so that the master of the house might be able to see what was taking place beneath.

The larger farm houses and manors were usually provided with a gallery at one end of the hall, next to the solar, and instead of a window there was a

---

[1] From some indications of a great chimney and an oven, it is possible that the kitchen was at the opposite end of the house to the solar in the case of " Mary Arden's Cottage."

B

doorway giving access to the gallery from the upper
room.   The manor house at Solihull may be cited as
an example of the style of house we are endeavouring
to describe.

Close to these farm houses, but not adjoining, were
the barns, stables, and outbuildings : these, as well as
the house, were protected by the moat, enclosing the
square or rectangular area, whereon the buildings stood.
Sometimes, where a supply of water was abundant,
there was on one side a pond serving both as a fish
pond, and also as a defence to another series of buildings, stables and cattle sheds.

The old homestead at Wilmcote was planned in this
way, and remains one of the finest specimens of a
mediæval, timber-built, farm house now to be found near
Stratford.   That it should have been so little altered
is somewhat wonderful, considering its antiquity and
the proximity of the railway to the village.

Having learned something of the arrangement of a
Warwickshire farmstead in the fifteenth century, we
may now become better acquainted with Robert Arden's
house and its furniture.

A spacious hall, hung round with tapestry ("peyntid
clothes") whereon quaint figures were depicted, furnished
with two long tables, several oaken benches, a cupboard
for plate, two oak chests and a little table with shelves :
such was the living room of Robert Arden of Wilmcote.
The kitchen had a store of all kinds of cooking utensils
in brass and pewter, candlesticks, basins, and chafing
dishes : the best chamber provided with comfortable
beds and substantial furniture was also hung round
with tapestry.   The barns well stocked with corn ; the
stables and farm buildings with horses, colts, oxen, cows,
and calves ; and in the pastures near the house a flock

of fifty sheep, all betokened that the owner was a well-to-do yeoman.[1]

MARY ARDEN'S COTTAGE, WILMCOTE

With the increase of luxury in the sixteenth century the old habits of life were changed generally, and

[1] These particulars are known to us from the inventory of Robert Arden's goods, taken after his death in 1556.

through the Midlands farm houses were altered in accordance with the advanced ideas of the time. The hall, which had served both as a living-room during the day, and by night as the sleeping place of the family and servants (except the master, mistress, and honoured guests, who occupied the solar), was then divided into two storeys, and into several rooms both above and below.

This alteration was effected in the old house at Wilmcote about the year 1597, and fortunately, except for occasional repairs, it has remained substantially the same to this day, the stout oak timbers having withstood the wear and tear of three centuries. The exterior is practically the same as when Robert Arden's remains were carried thence to be buried in the ancient church at Aston Cantlow, the chief differences being that the walls are now covered with "rough-cast" plaster, which has preserved the timber beneath; three dormer windows have been inserted in order to admit light to the bedrooms formed in the roof of the old hall; and the necessary chimneys to the several additional fire-places have been built. With these exceptions the house is little changed, though the surroundings are much altered.

In course of time the barns and stables, having fallen into decay, were renewed, in some instances additions made, and in others, portions were swept away. Some of the old farm buildings yet remain, and are easily distinguished from the modern structures. The moat has been almost filled up, and a modern road passes between the house and one portion of this water defence.

Quite recently, in 1899, when the house was under-going repair, the plaster over the end of the dormer window furthest from the solar, was found to have the date 1597 worked upon it. This discovery, together with the structural alterations evident in the interior, warrants the conclusion that the hall was converted into a building of two storeys in that year: the fine oaken beams and joists then inserted, being neatly wrought, are easily recognised from among the older and rougher wooden framing of the original house.

So far, documentary evidence supports the theory that Robert Arden lived in a house similar to that now claimed to be his, but there is yet wanting the testimony of muniments of title to establish the claim without dispute.

Halliwell-Phillipps examined the deeds of Stave-all Farm, which now includes the house in question, and saw that the abstracts of title did not go back to the days of Elizabeth; he then found another set of deeds relating to an adjoining property and therefrom drew a conclusion believed by the present writer to be incorrect.

At various times during the last three centuries the Wilmcote properties have changed hands; sometimes the house appears to have gone with one farm, and sometimes with another. This threw Halliwell off the right scent.

A special clause in the Act of Parliament regulating Shakespeare's Birthplace Trust provides that should the house at Wilmcote ever come into the market it may be purchased by the Trustees. Evidently those who framed this Act did not share the doubt expressed by Halliwell-Phillipps.

Wilmcote, although distant from Stratford only three miles, being an isolated village with no main road through it, is little visited. It lies about a mile to

the west of the great highway connecting Stratford
with Birmingham.   Passing out of the town along this
road one is soon in the open country.   To the right
lies Clopton House, backed by a tree-covered hill : to
the left is the hamlet of Bishopton with its neglected
spa, whose waters are said to surpass in medicinal
qualities those of Royal Leamington.   So highly is
Bishopton water esteemed by some that a project has
been formed for laying pipes from the spa to Stratford,
and building a hydropathic establishment on the hill
above the town.   Should this scheme be carried out,
it will undoubtedly cause Stratford-on-Avon to become the resort of those who are seeking to restore
their failing health by means of honest water and
fresh air.

A little further on the road is crossed by a line now
known as "The King's Lane," an old highway from
Warwick,   through   Snitterfield   and   Bishopton,   to
Shottery.   It is said that King Charles II. passed this
way when seeking refuge at Long Marston after the
battle of Worcester, hence the name, but the tradition
is rather discounted by the fact that formerly some one
named King occupied a farm house near the lane.

From   this   point   the   road   ascends   to   the   "Dun
Cow" inn, a place of Shakespearian association.   The
turn to Wilmcote is now almost in sight, and in less
than a mile we pass the station on the G.W.R., beyond
which "Mary Arden's Cottage" is situated.

The by-road we have to traverse rejoices in the
name of "Feather-bed Lane," probably because it was
so badly made.   It is not a very ancient road, and
within living memory was little more than a bridle path.
Halliwell-Phillipps has preserved an interesting note in

reference to this place as it was in the early part of
the nineteenth century: the facts being communicated
to him by a Stratford friend who wrote as follows:—

"When my father was married in November 1804,
he brought my mother in a post-chaise to the top of
this lane, intending to drive through it into the village,

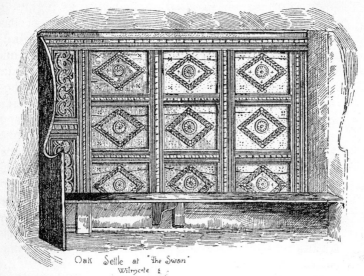

Oak Settle at "The Swan"
Wilmcote

but it was so soft, adhesive, and muddy, that he found
it impossible to do so: it runs through Starve-all[1]
Farm, which then possessed the same kindred qualities,
and I have heard that its name originated in its tendency
to starve all who sought to obtain a living upon it.
But all this is now altered, the land having years ago
been thoroughly drained and put in good order."[2]

[1] Starve-all appears to be a corruption of Stave Hall, a name signifying that the house had a *hall*, and probably a post near it indicating a
ford or passage across a brook.

[2] Halliwell-Phillipps, "Outlines," vol. 2, page 201.

The present writer when talking one day to a
Wilmcote man (November 1898) heard Mary Arden's
Cottage referred to as Starve-all, and a place called the
Ashbies was said to be "near the canal, on the Stratford side of Feather-bed Lane." Halliwell-Phillipps,
who did not thoroughly sift this matter, states "the
exact site of the real Ashbies is unknown, but it must
have been within a very short distance of the above-
mentioned farm, *i.e.* Starve-all." He then proceeds to
quote from various abstracts of title which refer to the
land of John Shakespeare bounding a certain field called
the "meadow piece" on the west side, which would
pretty well agree with the locality of the Ashbies as
now determined.[1]

The present owner, G. E. Smith, Esq., of Stratford-
on-Avon, states that in the time of his great-grandfather
the house was said to be the one owned by the Ardens.
In the will of Robert Arden the bequest to his youngest
daughter Mary is "all my lande in Willemecote, cawlide
Asbyes, and the crop upone the grounde sowne and
tylled as itt is; and viiil xiiis and iiiid of money to be
payed over ere my goodes be devydide."

In this will there is no mention of a bequest of a
house to Mary, but to his widow and his daughter

---

[1] "The continuous descent of the Ashbies estate after the time of
the Lamberts is unknown, but it is found in the latter part of the
seventeenth century in the hands of one Clement Edkins, who owned
'three-quarters of one yard-land, and one messuage and one yard-land
and four acres,' at Wilmcote in 1699; these properties being described
as 'the lands late of one John Smith, deceased.' It appears from an
indenture of 1725 that the three-quarters of the yard-land had been
purchased by Smith in 1668 from Adam Edkins, and hence it may be
inferred that the other estate, the description of which is identical with
that given of Ashbies in 1589 and 1597, had also belonged to the last-
named individual." (Halliwell-Phillipps, ii. 205.)

Alice, Robert Arden bequeathed his copyhold in Wilmcote, on condition that the widow should allow Alice
quietly to occupy half with her. This implies that the
widow and her youngest unmarried daughter were to
live in the homestead together. That the widow did
so is evident from her will dated 1579, wherein she is
described as of Wilmcote, and whereby she bequeathed
her farm stock and household goods to various persons.

The Arden house and " three-quarters of yard-land "
was, according to Halliwell ("Outlines," vol. 2. 205)
owned by Adam Edkins in 1668. This statement is
doubtless correct though the inference drawn from it
may not be so. It may be remembered that Robert
Arden's fourth daughter, Katherine, married Thomas
Edkins of Wilmcote, and consequently it appears that
her descendants for some time retained possession of
this portion of the family estate. As for the Asbies, the
inheritance of Shakespeare's mother, this farm consisted
of 86 acres of land of various kinds, arable, meadow,
and pasture, possibly with a house; it does not follow
that that house was the family dwelling.

While there is nothing to prove that the Asbies was
the farm house now bearing Mary Arden's name, there
are many circumstances pointing to the conclusion that
the old house at Wilmcote which is still left to us, is
actually the one in which her father lived. Probably
the matter could be settled definitely if access could be
had to the Court-rolls and other records of the Manor
of Aston Cantlow.

CHAPTER V

In our walks through Shakespeare's Country it is now time for us to visit Snitterfield,[1] a pleasant upland village about three miles from Stratford. Taking the Warwick Road we shortly pass S. Gregory's Church, a handsome building designed by the younger Pugin, and worthy of the reputation of that artist. Within its walls the little Roman Catholic community of Stratford assemble for divine service. To the left of this Church a road and footpath lead to Welcombe House, one of the country seats of Sir George Trevelyan, occupying the site of Welcombe Lodge, formerly belonging to Shakespeare's friends the Combes.

Much of this ground was unenclosed in Queen Elizabeth's time, though an attempt to enclose it was made towards the end of Shakespeare's life: and as a freeholder he had a considerable interest in this matter, which indeed has given us one of the most interesting biographical touches relating to his latter days. In November 1614 the Poet's cousin Greene went up to London, and on the 17th of that month called on "cosen Shakespere" and "went to see him how he did." "He (Shakespeare) told me that they (the Combes) assured him they ment to inclose no further than to Gospel Bush, and so upp straight (leaving out part of the

---

[1] Snitterfield probably means "Snipefield."

Dyngles to the field) to the gate in Clopton hedg, and take in Salisbury's peece : and that they ment in April to svey the land and then to give satisfaccion, and not before : and he and Mr. Hall say they think yr. will be nothing done at all."

This matter of the enclosure was one in which the local landowners led by William Combe, the Poet's friend, were opposed by the Corporation of Stratford, representing the popular interest : for if the commons were enclosed the poor would suffer.   It is clear, I think, that Shakespeare backed the Corporation in their endeavour to befriend the poor.

The hills around Welcombe bear traces of ancient occupation.   Here is a rounded eminence called "Spyford," upon which a windmill once stood, though in ancient times, if we may judge by the name, its purpose was a less peaceful one.   Here are the " Dingles," a curious ravine, whether the work of nature, or of man, it is somewhat hard to determine.   Hard-by Welcombe House a mound, crowned by a little tower, is worthy of notice : it is a tumulus, and, as far as we know, unexplored.   The name Welcombe points to a British origin, and perhaps signifies " the valley of the well" : there is a spring there to this day.

It was a likely place for an early settlement as it is protected on the east by the river Avon, and has a steep escapement towards the river.   Three miles to the north an ancient road, the Marraway, crosses the country towards the Avon, which it reached at Charlecote and Wellesbourne ford.   Along this road the men of Mercia marched to attack the warriors of Wessex, and a fearful battle is said to have taken place hereabout.   Sir Henry Taylor has celebrated this in his stirring ballad :—

" By Wellesbourne and Charlecote ford
At break of day I saw a sword.
Wessex warriors, rank by rank,
Rose on Avon's hither bank ;
Mercia's men, in fair array,
Looked at them from Marraway :
Close and closer ranged they soon,
And the battle joined at noon.

By Wellesbourne and Charlecote Lee
I heard a sound as of the sea,
Thirty thousand rushing men—
Twenty thousand met by ten."

Between Hampton Lucy and Stratford there were probably two fords, one opposite Welcombe, and the other at Alveston ; the latter is still in use. The Marraway comes through Norton Lindsey and passes Snitterfield on the east, crosses the present Warwick Road, and becomes merely a footpath through the fields. It points, however, to Hampton Lucy, and thence probably ran on to join the Fosse Way.

But we have somewhat overshot our mark, and must follow the Warwick Road past "The Hill," the residence of A. D. Flower, Esq.

The Warwick Road along which we pass resembles a drive through a park, rather than a public highway. An avenue of lofty trees shades the well kept road : on the left the land rises to the Welcombe Hills, and on the right the meadows extend to the banks of the winding river. We soon reach the drive to Welcombe House, where the Dingles come down to the road, and at a little over a mile from Stratford take the Chain-turning leading past Ingon to Snitterfield.

The lofty Obelisk on the hill commemorates two brothers, Robert Needham Philips, and Mark Philips,

the first member of Parliament for Manchester, former
owners of the estate.   We are now approaching Ingon,
a farm which Shakespeare bought.   His father, John
Shakespeare, for many years cultivated land hereabout,
indeed wherever we wander in the neighbourhood of

Cottages at Tiddington

Stratford we are certain to find traces of the Poet or
his family: proving that they were an energetic race,
and by no means the illiterate, unimportant, and indigent
people they are sometimes stated to have been.

Ingon is in fact one of the most beautiful spots in
the district, and the Poet's holding consisted of one
hundred and seven acres of land, with common rights,
a most desirable estate.   There is also in Snitterfield
sufficient evidence to prove that the Shakespeares were
men of substance, and probably of "worship" in the
county.

It may be interesting here to collect a few facts about
the Shakespeares of Snitterfield.

In 1543 Richard Shakspere of Snytfelde received a
legacy from Thomas Atwode, *alias* Tailour, of Stratford,
of four oxen then in his keeping.   In 1560 Agnes, the
widow of Robert Arden of Wilmcote, granted a lease
to her brother, Alexander Webbe, of two messuages
with a cottage in Snitterfield, with a yard and a half of
arable land thereunto belonging, then in the occupation of Richard Shakespeare, John Henley, and John
Hargreve (? Heritage).

Richard Shakespeare disappears after 1560, he probably died about the end of that year; his wife is
believed to have been one of the Webbe family.   The
farm he occupied has not been identified with certainty,
but it probably lay on the north side of Warwick Lane,
and he held land under Robert Arden of Wilmcote.
He had three sons : John, the Poet's father, who married
Mary, his landlord's daughter ; Thomas, who married
and had a son (John?), and Henry, whose wife's
christian name was Margaret.   Henry had two children,
a son and a daughter, James and Joanna : both of whom
died in infancy.

John Shakespeare appears to have farmed some land
at Snitterfield, and his son William purchased the one
hundred and seven acres before mentioned.

Tradition assigns to the Shakespeares a farm near
the Church, on the right-hand side of the highway
towards Lushcombe, and the fields called Burman and
Red Hill.   Halliwell-Phillipps believed that the Poet's
Uncle Henry tilled these fields, and occupied a house
there, some fragments of which remained in a neighbouring barn at the end of the nineteenth century.

Mr W. H. Bryan, a saddler, dwelling in a cottage a

little to the north of the Church, has preserved an old oak cupboard, upon the door of which is a design in small brass nails,—

	I BOVGHT IT		
1582	I SAWED IT	15 MAY 83	WILLIAM SHAKESPERE.[1]
JVNE	I CARVED IT		
	I NAILED IT		

BORN APRIL 23, 1564.

Whether William Shakespeare is answerable for this inscription we cannot say, but, like the bricks in the chimney mentioned by the Poet (2 Henry VI. Act 4, scene 2), the nails are there to testify to the fact to this day.[2]

Tradition associates the old Snitterfield homestead with the famous poaching affair at Fulbrook. For Shakespeare, it is said, dodged the keepers who were sent by Squire Lucy to protect the deer in Fulbrook

[1] The history of the cupboard, as given by its present owner, runs as follows :—It was originally in the house of John Shakespeare, at a farm house now destroyed, but formerly standing in a field to the north-east of the Church. When this house was pulled down, the cupboard passed into the possession of two men, who lived in a cottage about two hundred yards distant from the farm. The men grew old, and the cottage was pulled down. Mr W. H. Bryan's grandfather then bought the cupboard, and built it into the wall of his own house. In course of time this house was also rebuilt and the old cupboard removed into an out-house as a piece of useless lumber ; there it remained for some years, until a visitor one day remarked that it was a curious old piece of furniture, and advised the owner to have it cleaned and put in his house. The process of cleaning soon revealed the inscription. What had been useless lumber, was now regarded as a priceless relic by its owner. See also Chapter xviii.

[2] The cupboard has been mentioned here because many inquiries have been made about it. The author can only advise those who may be interested to go to Snitterfield and see it for themselves.

Park, and took refuge in the farm occupied by his grandfather, and afterwards by his uncles. Be this tradition false or true, it is but one of many to the same effect. These facts remain: the Poet's grandfather, father, and uncles lived at Snitterfield, and tilled land there: consequently it follows that the feet of William Shakespeare were familiar with the lanes and field-paths between Stratford-on-Avon and this village. That the place was dear to him and that he often stayed there follow as corollaries. His love of Snitterfield is sufficiently evinced by his purchase of many acres of land in that parish. The ancient Church, standing in its grove of trees on the hill-side, must have been a perfectly familiar object to him, and probably also some of the old cottages in the district were standing in his time.[1]

The deer-stealing episode is rather strengthened by the fact that Shakespeare's relatives lived at Snitterfield in proximity to the park at Fulbrook, and within sight of Sir Thomas Lucy's house, for from the hills at Snitterfield the turrets of Charlecote are visible. There is no more beautiful district in the neighbourhood of Stratford than that to the north-west of the Warwick road, where the rolling hills of Welcombe and Snitterfield descend to the green meadows through which the Avon flows. The views from various points in the village are both extensive and charming, so much so that the place has become a favourite abode of several ancient and wealthy families, whose pleasant seats peep out from among shrubberies and coppices.

After a ramble through the village we may return either over the Welcombe hills, or by the Stratford reservoir and Lower Clopton, and so along the steep

[1] For an account of Snitterfield Church see Chapter xli.

SNITTERFIELD CHURCH

C

descent of King's Lane to the Birmingham road which leads us back to Stratford.

On the brow of Rowley hill, overlooking Stratford-on-Avon, and adjoining the Welcombe estate, it is proposed (1903) to build a large Hydropathic Hotel, upon part of the land assigned to the Corporation when the commons were enclosed.

Shottery Manor House.

CHAPTER VI

THE POET'S COURTSHIP

A NARROW path leads from Chestnut walk, through allotment gardens and fields, from the town of Stratford-on-Avon to the tiny village of Shottery, scene of Shakespeare's courtship, and consequently one of the most famous spots on earth. In these fields the ridges and furrows, denoting the ancient system of cultivation, remain to remind us of the manners of former days, and of the desire which Shakespeare felt to become a landed proprietor before these common fields were enclosed and sold. On the left of the path, just outside the village, stands an ancient farm, Shottery Manor, with walled garden and picturesque dove-cote. Here and there a group of cottages with whitewashed walls and thatched roofs carry the mind back to the days of old : while other groups of modern cottages somewhat

36

rudely thrust themselves upon our notice. Surely in this little hamlet nothing obtrusively modern should be permitted, and the utilitarian spirit of the age should be banished from the precincts of a place associated with the Poet's early experience of Love's Young Dream.

On the sloping bank of a little brook stands a long, low farm-house; a yeoman's dwelling of great antiquity, and exceedingly picturesque. It is now divided into two dwellings, that furthest from the road being occupied by the custodian's family, while the other portion is shown to the public. In the kitchen, now the chief room of the house, the Hathaways and their descendants have lived for generations down to our own time.

We well remember one of these, good old Mrs Baker, who had seen and shaken hands with Sir Walter Scott, and received at the door of that ancient room many celebrities, and nearly all the literary people of England and America, Poets, Statesmen, and Scholars of her time.

In the pages of the sad story, *Asphodel*, Miss Braddon has left us a vivid picture of Mrs Baker in her prime. The writer remembers, when a boy, being taken to visit Anne Hathaway's Cottage, and seeing Mrs Baker, who exhibited her Family Bible wherein her descent was recorded, and hearing her explain it. Years afterwards he heard the same words from her lips, and a few months later stood beside the grave in the Cemetery of Stratford-on-Avon in reverent silence while the funeral service was read over the remains of that kindly old woman, whose ancestors claimed alliance with Shakespeare.

In the Cottage there is a rare store of old furniture, inherited by Mrs Baker, and sold by her to the Trustees of Shakespeare's Birthplace.

Among the relics retained is the famous " Shakespeare's courting-settle," an ancient high-backed seat of a kind usually found in farm houses of the Tudor period. The sentimental interest attached to this rough wooden seat is second to none, and always recalls memories of the happy days when Shakespeare wooed Anne Hathaway.

Ascending the narrow time-worn stairs that have creaked beneath the tread of thousands of pilgrims, we find the " little chamber " wherein the great Elizabethan bedstead of the Hathaway family is still preserved. We may notice the old mattress of plaited rushes, of a kind now seldom seen, but formerly most common : [1] even the sheets of home spun linen, with rich old ornament of drawn thread, remain in their accustomed place. The panels upon the back of the bed are inlaid with arabesque designs in box and other woods.

This relic of a bygone age, interesting as it is from an antiquarian point of view, becomes doubly so when we realise its associations.

The Cottage, probably repaired and considerably altered by John Hathaway (I H) in 1697, as appears by a stone let into one of the chimneys, is believed to be the one occupied by John Hathaway, the archer, who is mentioned in a muster roll of Henry VIII. The property appears to have gone by the name of the " Hewlands " and was in the possession of the Earl of Warwick in 1590, Joan Hathaway, widow, paying thirty-three shillings and four pence and a heriot to the lord. (Halliwell-Phillipps, " Outlines," vol. 2, p. 190.)

Deductions drawn by Halliwell-Phillipps from evidence which he examined one is not always ready to accept

---

[1] This form of mattress was often represented beneath the carved effigies of Knights and Ladies in the Middle Ages.

as correct. While credit must be given to that industrious and ardent Shakespearian scholar, who, more
than any other man, collected and recorded facts about

ANNE HATHAWAY'S COTTAGE

Shakespeare, it is notorious that his enthusiasm often led
him to conclusions we cannot always agree with, as in
this instance where he is dubious.

The description given in Latin in a MS. in the
Staunton collection, now destroyed, may be translated
as follows:—

"John Hethewey holds by copy of the court given the 20th day of April in the 34th year of the reign of Henry VIII., one messuage and ½ a virgate of land, lying in Shottery called Hewland, and one messuage and one virgate of land lately in the occupation of Thomas Perkyns, and one toft and ½ a virgate of land called Hewlyns with its appurtenances, holding the same for himself and his heirs according to the custom of the manner aforesaid, paying thence in rent per annum 33 shillings and 8 pence with suit of court and fine, and heriot [1] when it occurs."

In 1610 the Hathaways purchased the estate from William Whitmore and John Randoll, who had obtained a grant of the manor of old Stratford from James I. Bartholomew Hathaway's purchase was subject to the chief rent before mentioned. In 1624 John Hathaway died and bequeathed the property he had acquired in 1610 to his son John, and the house and a portion of the land continued in the possession of the family till 1838. The male line of the Hathaways became extinct by the death of another John in 1764. At the commencement of the nineteenth century the house belonged to William Taylor, a descendant of the Hathaways, who sold it in 1838 to Thomas Barnes for £345. It was bequeathed by him to Mr William Thompson of Stratford-on-Avon, who, in May 1892, sold it to the Trustees of Shakespeare's Birthplace for £3000, exclusive of furniture.

Mrs Baker, *née* Taylor, who for so many years resided in the house, was descended from the Hathaways collaterally, and her son and his family still (1902) live in the house so long and interestingly associated with their family.

[1] A heriot is a payment, generally in kind, payable at the death of a tenant to the lord of the manor.

During a period of three hundred years the old house has often been repaired and altered. The chief entrance is said to have been on the north side, where a doorway may still be seen. It would have been approached by a path leading into the village of Shottery from the Alcester Road. The beams upon the ceiling of the chief living room bear the initials I. H., E. H., I. B. 1697. This date agrees with the date on the chimneys, and as before stated, points to an extensive alteration. Probably before that time the house had a large hall of one story, which was then divided into two stories in exactly the same way as the Arden house at Wilmcote. If this is so, the large room, now occupied by Mr Baker, once would have formed a portion of the hall, the hearth being in the middle of the floor in about the same position as the present fireplace. This, however, must be taken merely as a suggestion, since we have no actual proof of the interior having been altered in this manner.

Dovecote at Shottery.

CHAPTER VII

"The perfect ceremony of love's rite."—*Sonnet* 23.

THE Poet tells us that he had been here and there and "shown himself a motley to the view." Had we no further proof than his writings it would be fair to conclude that Shakespeare was a traveller, for he speaks of places in the tone of one who has visited them, yet we have external evidence of Shakespeare having visited few places. Documents of unimpeachable authority prove that he went to both London and Worcester.

In 1582 Shakespeare was living at Stratford, and was espoused to Anne, daughter of Richard Hathaway, of Shottery. Richard Hathaway died before July 9th, 1582, consequently in November of that year Anne was an orphan. She was older by seven years than her betrothed, and we may be sure possessed personal charms sufficient to have attracted the attention of William Shakespeare.

In those days a form of betrothal ratified in the presence of relatives was considered tantamount to a marriage, and it happened frequently that the ecclesiastical part of the ceremony was not completed till absolutely necessary for the legitimation of a child. It was only from 1558, the year in which Queen

42

Mary died, that the Catholic faith, and the Catholic rites, had been superseded by those of the Reformed religion. Religion was then in a state of transition, and people, especially those of the Midland counties, had a lingering affection for the old forms, and a covert dislike of the new. Moreover a public betrothal was then considered to be a binding ceremony, carrying with it conjugal rights: this is no haphazard statement, but rests upon legal evidence of the highest authority.

Professor Dowden summarises the case as follows, "The ceremony of wedlock may have been preceded by precontract, which according to the custom of the time and place, would have been looked on as having the validity of marriage though as yet unsanctified by ecclesiastical rites."[1]   Charles Knight[2] aptly quotes the betrothal of Florizel and Perdita, in the sheep-shearing scene in "The Winter's Tale" (Act IV. Scene iv. line 402, etc.), where the young couple are betrothed in the presence of witnesses. The whole of this scene breathes the sweet fragrance of the Midland festivals, such as the Poet must have witnessed many times on the hills about his native town, or on the Cotswolds. To quote Professor Dowden again, "It may be added that the words 'wedded wife' were at this time in no way tautological; a woman duly espoused might be a wife though the priestly benediction had not yet been bestowed."

Here it may be noted that the evidence of the age of Shakespeare's wife—seven years his senior—rests solely on the inscription upon her gravestone.

[1] E. Dowden, "William Shakespeare, A Biography," Edition 1843, page 213.

[2] C. Knight, "Introduction to Shakespeare," Edition 1893, page 9.

Had William Shakespeare been the reprobate some of his biographers would have us believe he would scarcely have made a journey from Stratford-on-Avon to Worcester to bind himself to a woman whom he had dishonoured. This journey shows signs of having been deliberately planned, and systematically carried out in every detail. The bridegroom being a minor was required by law to provide sureties, who must be present with him at the time of the execution of the bond. The sureties were his friends and neighbours, and accompanied him from Stratford to Worcester. One of these was Fulk Sandells, the overseer, or executor, of Richard Hathaway's will, and the representative of the Hathaway family. Fulk Sandells took with him to Worcester the seal of Richard Hathaway, and with it sealed the bond.

These facts are surely enough to throw a new light on the subject of Shakespeare's marriage. It is unfortunate that so many of the biographers should have misunderstood this episode of their hero's career. Even Mr Sidney Lee takes a pessimistic view of the affair, being apparently influenced by the fact that the bridegroom's family were conspicuously absent from the proceedings

A little consideration will easily account for this. The family pride of Shakespeare's mother and father might be sufficient to make them stand aloof from an alliance between their eldest son and the daughter of their more humble neighbour, the farmer of Shottery, while the youth's spirit, being of no common kind, brooked not parental interference. But it may be pointed out that Anne's mother, though living, also took no part in the affair.

That the marriage may have estranged Shakespeare

from his family and friends for a time is possible, nay probable, but that he was guilty of any dishonourable action towards the woman he chose to marry is highly improbable.

In the Bishop of Worcester's Registry in the Edgar Tower, hard by the Cathedral, two documents of enormous importance from a Shakespearian point of view, are preserved. The first is an entry in the Register Book of marriage licences. The entry is in Latin, and may be translated as follows :—" 1582, item on the 27th of November a like licence (of matrimony) was issued to Wm. Shaxpere and Anna Whateley of Temple Grafton."

This entry being in Latin the bride's name is in the accusative case, and the final "m" of Annam has been mistaken by the clerk for a "w." This mistake has led to the statement that a licence was granted to a certain William Shakespeare to marry a certain Anne Whateley. The error is at once obvious when the original register and bond are examined. This bond, also at Worcester, is dated 28th of November 1582, and the bride's name is recorded as " Anne Hathwey, of Stratford."

That the entries " Anne Hathwey of Stratford " and " Anna Whateley of Temple Grafton" refer to one and the same person there cannot be a doubt, because no other licence for the marriage of William Shakespeare is recorded in the Register. There remains only the difficulty of the bride's place of abode ; she would rightly be described as of Stratford, Shottery being a hamlet of that place. No one has yet been able to discover why she should have been described by the Bishop's Registrar as of Temple Grafton. Two hypotheses, however, may be advanced :—

1. Temple Grafton is a clerical error for Stratford-on-Avon.
2. That though Anne's home was properly at Shottery, yet after her father's death she may have been staying with friends at Temple Grafton.

The latter is possible, because the alliance with the headstrong youth of Stratford may have caused anxiety to the widow Hathaway, and the girl might have been sent from home. The first conjecture rests on the assumption that the whole entry of the bride's name and place of abode is an error of the clerk who transcribed the entry from *rough notes* into the Register.[1] Of course it is possible that the labours of some future student may be rewarded by the discovery of the key to this mystery. Should this occur, indeed it is not a remote possibility, this most interesting event in Shakespeare's life may be still further elucidated.

It is within living memory, and since the publication of Halliwell-Phillipps' "Outlines of the Life of Shakespeare," that the discovery of the entry in the Bishop's Register was made, though the existence of the bond was known to Halliwell-Phillipps.

On an autumn morning, while mist yet obscured the distant landscape, a little cavalcade set out from Stratford in the direction of Worcester. The roads in those days, being neither so numerous or in such good repair as they are now, a journey of twenty-four miles from Stratford to Worcester and back presented many difficulties. The country was then unenclosed, and great tracts of common and waste land extended over the whole district. We may follow the travellers westward

[1] The whole of this subject has been most ably treated by Mr Joseph Hill in his edition of Burgess' "Historic Warwickshire."

as they ascend to the higher ground outside the town. They may have gone either to Bidford or to Alcester; in any case they must have crossed the river Arrow. If the road through Alcester was chosen they would make for Inkberrow or Flyford Flavell, but if they passed through Bidford they would then go by way of the Lenches.

Supposing the road to Alcester was selected, the more probable route, Billesley and its old Hall would soon be passed on the right, and a descent made down Red Hill through a deep, time-worn cutting still to be seen on the right of the present road, across the fields and meadows to a bridge over the Arrow, and the first halt would be made for a stirrup cup at the Inn at Alcester.

Passing through the town the road keeps south-west to the village of Arrow, an ancient settlement near Ragley Park.   Very soon the party would reach Cook-hill, where a magnificent prospect would meet their gaze.   Behind, the wooded meads of Arden's pleasant vale, watered by the streams of Avon and Arrow: before them the valley of the Severn, dotted over with villages and pleasant farms, with the distant ridge of Malvern clearly outlined against the sky.

The next halting-place would be Inkberrow.   Passing through richly cultivated fields, the road still points westward, past Flyford Flavell and Spetchley, with its fine park and mansion-house.   A few miles more, and the last hill before the gate of Worcester is reached, and the road descends to Sidbury.

Although Worcester had in ancient times been visited by kings and armies, it had yet to earn its reputation for loyalty in time of peace and war, and the road that Shakespeare passed over had not then been stained with the blood of the Cavaliers and Roundheads, nor had the great battle been fought which decided the fate of the nation. The travellers were, however, approaching a fortified city, encompassed by high stone walls having gates at intervals. They would pass the old Commandery, a venerable institution still standing. They would approach Sidbury gate, pass under its Gothic archway, and regard its massive circular towers, and so clatter through the ill-paved streets to an inn in the neighbourhood of the Cathedral. Having dismounted they would repair to the Bishop's Registry, and having stated their business, would be told to call next day to complete the matter.

The Registrar, having duly noted particulars for the Latin entry, which we still may read, would bid his clients good-afternoon ere they departed to amuse themselves until the morrow. They would at least gaze at the exterior of the grand old Cathedral and its monastic buildings, they would probably enter the fane, and stand beside the tomb of King John. " At Worcester shall his body be interred, for so he willed it," are Shakespeare's own words with reference to this monarch.

The entry being dated on the 27th November (old style) and the bond on the 28th, it is evident that the contracting parties were in Worcester on those days. They must therefore have remained the night and probably returned to Stratford in the afternoon of the following day.

Seven years before the date of Shakespeare's visit " our most victorious and sovereign Lady, Queen Elizabeth," visited Worcester, coming from Hartlebury Castle, where she had rested the night before. It was Saturday between seven and eight of the clock when her Majesty came riding on her palfry towards the city,

" and in the confines of the liberties of the same city,
being at Salt Lane end, Mr Christopher Dighton and
Mr Richard Spark, bailifs of the said city, Mr Thomas
Heywood and Mr John Coombs, aldermen of the
same, and Mr George Warberton, high chamberlain
of the city aforesaid, together with one Mr William
Bellu, supplying the place and room of Sir John
Throckmorton, recorder of the said city, together with
others to the number of twelve persons who had been
bailifs, all in scarlet gowns faced with black satin, and
the residue of the 24 in murrey in grayne gowns, and
all the 48 in violet in grayne gowns." [1]

The Bishop of Worcester at the time of Shakespeare's visit was John Whitgift, a man of exemplary
life, who during a short period ruled over the Midland
diocese. That Shakespeare had friends in Worcester
is highly probable : even in the list of names given
above we recognise several familiar in Stratford, as
well as in the faithful city. The church formed a
bond between the two places, Stratford being in the
diocese, and the Bishop having possessions in the
town.

[1] " Worcester in Olden Times." John Noake, page 172.

D

CHAPTER VIII

SHOULD anyone be visiting Stratford-on-Avon, and feel interested in the romantic stories and associations of Shakespeare's boyhood, he would naturally wish to pay an early visit to Charlecote Hall, one of the finest Elizabethan mansions in England, scene of the Poet's alleged escapade with the deer of Sir Thomas Lucy.

The way to Charlecote lies across the Clopton Bridge, turns sharply to the left skirting the Avon, to the little village of Tiddington, whence it turns to the right just before passing Alveston new church, and passes the grounds of Baraset House beneath an avenue of lofty trees, and then descends to the meadows near the river. About half a mile further on Little Ham Bridge comes into view, and here we may pause to look for "Hiron's Hole," the scene of a gruesome tragedy.

The story goes that on the 4th of November 1820, Mr William Hiron, a gentleman of Alveston, was murdered by four men, who mistook him for another gentleman whom they had intended to rob.

The spot where Hiron's head fell is marked by a slight depression in the ground, which, according to popular belief, if filled up during the day, will reappear next morning. The cause of this phenomenon may well be left to the inquiring reader to discover, but the local explanation is, "It is the work of spirits."

CHARLECOTE

The murderers were discovered and subsequently hanged at Warwick in 1821. The curious in these matters may find a monument to Mr Hiron in Alveston old church, and at the Shakespeare Memorial a copy of a tract giving a detailed account of the whole affair.[1]

After leaving Hiron's Hole, and its grim associations, the handsome park gates of Charlecote soon come into view;[2] shortly before reaching this gate we may notice a remarkably fine oak tree having the straightest branches of any tree in Warwickshire; these branches are said to be equal in number to the weeks in the year. A footpath near leads to the house and village. Over the gates we see the arms of the Lucy family carved in stone, a red shield bearing three pike, or lucies, between golden crosslets.

Near the lodge the road takes a sharp turn to the right, and then to the left, skirting the park boundary for about a mile. The main road continues to the village of Wellesbourne, but the lane to the left (four miles from Stratford) winds round by the chief entrance to the park, where a carriage-drive leads directly to the picturesque gate-house, designed by that celebrated architect, John of Padua.

The present mansion was built by Sir Thomas Lucy in 1558, and except for some additions made about 1833, remains much the same as it was in the days of Queen Elizabeth.

Time has dealt kindly with Charlecote Hall, its old walls being toned and mellowed by age: its turrets and

[1] An account of the trial of the murderers was published in the local newspapers at the time, and reprinted in pamphlet form in 1899 by J. Morgan, Stratford-on-Avon.

[2] At certain seasons, upon payment of a small fee, carriages are allowed to pass through this gateway to the Hall.

gables still remain as the original builders left them. But within the mansion many changes have been made : the place has been considerably modernised and refitted. The great hall, however, contains interesting family portraits : and the library a suite of beautiful ebony furniture, inlaid with sea-horse ivory, given by Queen Elizabeth to the Earl of Leicester in 1575, and brought from Kenilworth.

We do not wish to descant upon modern marble tables, or sideboards of carved oak : these are things of yesterday, and we are looking for things of the distant past.

At the beginning of the nineteenth century, when Washington Irving visited Warwickshire, the ancient furniture had disappeared. He had hoped to find the stately elbow-chair in which the country squire of former days " was wont to sway the sceptre of empire over his rural domains," and in which his imagination had pictured Sir Thomas Lucy sitting when the recreant Shakespeare was brought before him. But, alas! the old furniture had vanished.

The main front of the house, planned in the shape of the letter E, a compliment to the Queen, is flanked by two wings having graceful octagonal turrets at the outer corners. The central limb of the E is formed by a handsome porch of two stories, which adds grace and dignity to the façade.

Over the door the arms and initials of the Virgin Queen may still be seen, and in the spandrels the initials of Sir Thomas Lucy, who is said to have hastily built it, before the Queen's visit to Warwickshire.

It was on the 24th of August 1572 that Queen Elizabeth arrived at Charlecote on her royal progress from lordly Warwick to Compton Wynyates. The great Queen and her magnificent train pale in their splendour before a greater figure, who must, we assuredly believe, have been present at Charlecote on that day.

There was living in Stratford-on-Avon in the year of grace 1572 a seven year old boy, son of the chief Alderman [1] of that town. Would not the leading inhabitant of the neighbouring borough, as of duty bound, have ridden over to pay homage to his royal mistress, and would not all Stratford have followed the worthy Alderman to see the brave show as it passed along the lanes towards the Hall?

It has been supposed that Shakespeare witnessed the princely entertainments at Kenilworth Castle in 1575, but the Queen also visited Kenilworth in 1566, 1568 and 1572, and in the latter year passed within four miles of Shakespeare's Stratford home. It requires no stretch of the imagination to suppose that the Poet saw the Queen on that occasion, when we know that his father held the most honourable public appointment in a town less than four miles distant from the scene of her entertainment by the supposed original of "Justice Shallow."

Thirteen years after the event just recorded, tradition has it that William Shakespeare went to Charlecote on a less honourable errand, namely, to steal Squire Lucy's deer. One cannot believe that Shakespeare ever was a thief, though we may incline to the opinion that he hunted deer in the neighbourhood, on Squire Lucy's land. The contention that there was not a deer park at Charlecote at that time is of no importance, because there may have been, and probably were, deer in the

---

[1] On Sept. 5th, 1571, John Shakespeare was elected chief alderman of Stratford-on-Avon, a position which he held till Sept. 3rd, 1572. Adrian Quiny was bailiff.

Forest of Arden : *i.e.* upon the commons and unenclosed lands in Warwickshire.   Parks were places for hunting deer found in the forest, and driven into the enclosure.

The author of " As You Like It " was familiar with the ways of wild deer—

> " Come, shall we go and kill us venison ?
> And yet it irks me, the poor dappled fools,
> Being native burghers of this desert city,
> Should in their own confines, with forked heads
> Have their round haunches gored."
> "As You Like It," II. i. 21.

This passage shows the writer to have been well skilled in hunting lore.   The " forked heads " most probably refer to the antlers of the deer themselves, not to any instrument used by the hunter.

In the days of Queen Elizabeth the pastime of hunting was conducted somewhat after the following manner.   When the huntsman had selected a deer he would charge the herd, dividing it into two parts, then charge the part in which was the selected beast, and so repeating the manœuvre until the stag was isolated. Should the animal attempt to rejoin the herd he would be gored by the *forked heads* of his brethren, who would soon discover the victim.   The unfortunate stag would thereupon start, seeking shelter from his tormentors, and so, driven by the beaters, enter the enclosed park, where the hunting—a cruel pastime—went on.[1]

So much for the royal sport of hunting timid deer.

> " a poor sequestered stag
> That from the hunter's aim had ta'en a hurt "

[1] This description of Elizabethan sport is based upon notes on the above quotation from " As You Like It," made by the Rev. C. J. Wilding, Vicar of Arley, who, when a boy, actually took part in this description of hunting : and now maintains, against all critics, this interpretation of the phrase " forked heads."

had escaped, but being wounded was therefore not
allowed to rejoin his companions :[1] and so formed a
subject fitting for the " melancholy Jacques " to moralise
upon, being but a type of frail humanity.

Let us now turn to the Star Chamber business.
Justice Shallow, who " wore a dozen white lucies in his
coat," is thereby identified with Sir Thomas Lucy,
whose coat of arms displays, not twelve, but three
white lucies, or pike. It would not have been politic
to satirise the squire openly, so, still more to throw an
opponent off the scent, Justice Shallow's estates lie in
Gloucestershire, on the Cotswolds : in an opposite
direction from Stratford to those of Sir Thomas Lucy
at Charlecote. The allusion, not in the quarto of 1602,
and only in the later editions, is clearly a topical one.

But was this the matter which made Justice Shallow
wroth, and banished Shakespeare from Stratford ?
Possibly the clue may be found in the " Merry Wives
of Windsor," Act I. Scene i.

> " *Shallow*. Knight, you have beaten my men, killed my deer and
> broke open my lodge.
> *Falstaff*. But not kissed the keeper's daughter.
> *Shallow*. Tut, a pin ! this shall be answered.
> *Falstaff*. I will answer it straight. I have done all this."

Perhaps this explains the whole business. Shakespeare himself speaks through the mouth of Falstaff.
There had been some hunting adventure of the kind
hinted at, and the keeper's daughter seems to have
played an important part in it : possibly that of informer.

However this may be, the local legends have no reference to a lady ; a strange omission seeing that the hero
of the adventure himself alludes to one.

[1] Deer will not allow a bloodstained, or wounded comrade to rejoin the herd.

Perhaps the earliest allusion to the Charlecote incident yet found is in one of Sir Hans Sloane's MSS. at the British Museum, a document written during Shakespeare's lifetime—a treatise apologetical for hunting by Thomas Gibson. Part 1, c. 1605. Part 2, c. 1614. The treatise abounds with abuse of the players of the day, and in several instances seems to point emphatically to Shakespeare, connecting him with the offence of poaching.[1]

There is no doubt that the deer-stealing tradition is of some antiquity, and was well established in the neighbourhood at the commencement of the eighteenth century. It is mentioned by Rowe, Shakespeare's earliest biographer: and noted by Archdeacon Davies, Vicar of Sapperton, in Gloucestershire, who died there in 1708.

According to this worthy the youth " was much given to all unluckiness in stealing venison and rabbits, particularly from Sir Thomas Lucy, who had him oft whipped, and sometimes imprisoned; and at last made him fly his native county to his great advancement. But his revenge was so great that he is his Justice Clodpate : and he calls him a great man, and that in allusion to his name, he bore three louses rampant for his arms."

In the same century it was also reported that Shakespeare shot the deer to provide venison for his marriage feast : and in our own time we have been told that he sold the venison and gave the money to the poor.

To make the story still more circumstantial the site of the deer-barn at Fulbrook, where the slaughtered deer was hidden, is still shown, and a house in Waterside, the " Black Swan," bears the reputation of having

[1] See a letter by Mr E. J. L. Scott, *Athenæum*, June 6, 1896.

sheltered Shakespeare when he fled across the river from Sir Thomas Lucy's men.

A lonely Inn, the "Dun Cow," on the Birmingham Road, is the reputed rendezvous of the Poet and his companions after their poaching expeditions: and it is said that the venison was cooked before the ample fireplace of that old Inn. This is traditional only.

Every one is familiar with the lampoon on Sir Thomas Lucy—a poor performance, quite unworthy of the author of "Hamlet" and "Venus and Adonis,"—the whole ballad is undoubtedly a forgery, though possibly the first part is of greater antiquity than the remainder.

> "A parliamente member, a justice of peace,
>   At home a poor scare-crow, at London an asse;
>   If lowsie is Lucy, as some volke miscalle it,
>   Then Lucy is lowsie, whatever befall it,
>   He thinks himself greate,
>   Yet an asse is his state
>   We allowe by his ears but with asses to mate;
>   If Lucy is lowsie as some volke miscalle it,
>   Sing lowsie Lucy, whatever befall it."

The phrase "a parliament member" is not older than Charles II.'s time, and on the authority of Thomas de Quincey "quite unknown in the colloquial use of Queen Elizabeth."

Charles Knight, whose judgment is usually sound, had little doubt that the regret expressed by Rowe in his life of Shakespeare (1709-10) that the ballad was lost, "was productive not only of the discovery, but of the creation of the delicious fragment." By-and-by more was discovered, and the entire song was found in a chest of drawers that formerly belonged to Mrs Dorothy Taylor, of Shottery, near Stratford, who died in 1778, at the age of eighty. Malone published the song, which seems to have been given to him by John Jordan, the wheelwright poet of Stratford.

It is now time to leave the old home of the Lucys, and journey onwards, but before doing so we may attempt to climb the tumble-down stile, an ingenious contrivance, often productive of merriment.   Charlecote, thanks to the good taste of recent members of the Lucy family, is still most picturesque, a typical Warwickshire village; its cottages overgrown with ivy, and other creeping plants; roses and honeysuckle clustering round the porches, and sweet old-fashioned flowers luxuriating in the fruitful gardens.

In the new church at Charlecote lie buried under marble tombs the remains of former owners of the estate, and the effigy of Sir Thomas Lucy in attitude of prayer, vividly recalls the days of good Queen Bess. We can regard the features of the man who here entertained the Queen, and possibly in after years persecuted Shakespeare.   Old views of this church represent it as a small edifice, with a tiny bell-cote.   It was enlarged and finally rebuilt in the nineteenth century. The churchyard retains many old tombstones.   It was here that Washington Irving wrote his chapter on " The Stout Gentleman," while his friend Leslie sketched.

A lane turning to the left along the park fence leads to the neighbouring village of Hampton Lucy, celebrated for " a bank whereon the wild thyme blows,"—Scar Bank, a green slope on the further side of the Avon, sacred to the memory of fairy dancers, as the old folk maintain.

In this village we may pause to see the church, a fine building enlarged and restored by Sir Gilbert Scott in a style reminding us of French rather than English models.

From Hampton Lucy the road passes through some open fields to a narrow, winding lane, joining the main road from Stratford to Warwick at the second milestone from the former town. We return and our pilgrimage to Charlecote is done. The memories of its past glories will be long impressed upon the mind, as well as the sylvan beauties of this part of leafy Warwickshire.

CHAPTER IX

A JOURNEY TO LONDON

In the sixteenth century a traveller from Stratford-on-Avon to London would have found the city of Oxford a convenient resting-place. The whole journey would probably have taken two or three days to accomplish. Oxford, thirty-eight miles distant from Stratford, may be reached by several routes. One over Edge Hills to Banbury, another by way of Shipston and Long Compton, and this being the shorter was probably the one most familiar to the Poet.

A traveller along either road passes from the Avon valley across a ridge of hills separating its fertile fields from those of the Thames valley, and it is only by taking one of these routes and viewing the Warwickshire plains from the surrounding hills that one is able to realise the nature of the country in which Shakespeare was born and spent the earlier part of his youth.

The Avon valley, in late geological periods, formed the bed of a vast sea or lake, and the site of Stratford must have been one of the deepest depressions beneath the surface of the waters. Geologists tell us that the nearest land was at Malvern. That great inland sea is now represented by the Severn and its tributary, the narrow thread of the silver Avon. When the settlers first made their appearance in this country the heights were chosen by them for their dwelling-places, and we

find almost the only prehistoric remains of any importance upon the summit of the wind-swept hills separating
the Avon from the Thames valley.   A few time-worn
and weather-beaten stones, the Rollrights, remain the
only monuments of prehistoric man in this district.

In all probability the traveller in the days of
Elizabeth would take much the same route as the
wayfarer in the days of Victoria.   The road, however,
has been improved : of old, before stage-coaches ran, its
state must have been very rough, rendering a journey
either in summer or winter a rather formidable undertaking.   Yet there were compensating circumstances,
the land being unenclosed, the greensward beside the
road was pleasant to horseman or pedestrian.   In these
days it is but a half day's ride from Stratford to Oxford
for a cyclist, indeed the whole distance to London is
often completed in twelve hours.   We know how
quickly the Gunpowder Conspirators made the journey
on horseback, and that in the days of Elizabeth or
James I. the distance could be covered in a day.

Let us now attempt a brief descripton of the journey.
Having said good-bye to his family, the Poet would
mount his horse and ride over Clopton Bridge. We say,
" mount his horse " advisedly, having little sympathy
with those who believe that the son of the Bailiff of
Stratford trudged to London on foot.

The old Manor House of Alveston, the remains of
the ancient hermitage, and a few cottages would soon
be passed, and at three miles the village of Atherstone
be reached.   On the right, across the fields is pleasant
Clifford with the mansion of the Raynesfords and its
familiar associations : a little further is Alscot, where at
that time the Hunckes were lords of the manor.   By
a gentle decline the horseman passed into the valley

of the Stour, leaving on his right Alderminster, Whitchurch, and Preston. Very soon Lower Etting-ton, the seat of the Shirleys, is reached, and then Halford Bridge is passed on the left. At the present time there is a curious milestone by the lodge leading to Ettington. The inscription upon it, though modern, is somewhat quaint :—

> " Six miles to Shakespeare's town whose name
> Is known throughout the earth.
> To Shipston four, whose lesser fame
> Boasts no such Poet's birth."
>   1871.

Ettington can claim one of the oldest deer-parks in the country, and its owners, the Shirleys, have dwelt on that spot probably since Saxon times, and boast of not a few warriors in their line, though perhaps they are best known by the fame of one who was a poet,[1] a Londoner bearing their name.

Of these old warriors we may say :—

> " Their bones are dust,
> Their swords are rust,
> Their souls are with the Lord, we trust."

Shakespeare, who came of a fighting family, has been careful to record the names of several of his neighbours in his historical plays, and passing Etting-ton, as he must have done many times, these lines in "Henry IV." would occur to him :—

> " *P. Henry*. Hold up thy head, vile Scot, or thou art like
> Never to hold it up again ! the spirits
> Of valiant *Shirley*, Stafford, Blunt, are in my arms."[2]

---

[1] James Shirley, the poet and dramatist, was born in 1596, and he perished from fatigue on the day of the great fire of London, October 29th, 1666. He was consequently Shakespeare's contemporary, though only a youth when his great master and neighbour died.

[2] "1 Henry IV." Act V. Sc. iv.

In the same way in "Henry V." his neighbours, the Getleys (or Ketly) receive acknowledgment from him :—

> " *K. Henry*. Where is the number of our English dead?
>   Edward the duke of York, the earl of Suffolk,
>   Sir Richard Ketly, Davy Gam, esquire." [1]

The way still points southward past Newbold, and at the top of a hill eight miles from Stratford, crosses the great Fosse Way, the Roman road to Leicester. From this point we see the tapering spire of Tredington, mother church of the district. Spacious, strong and well preserved, Tredington church contains many pre-reformation features, and the parsonage house, though rebuilt, and shorn of its glories, recalls memories of one of the finest specimens of domestic architecture in the neighbourhood.

It is but a short ride from Tredington to Shipston-on-Stour, a clean little market town of little note and interest.

All this time we have been skirting the river Stour and passing latterly through Worcestershire.

A mile from Shipston the road again enters Warwickshire. On the left is Barcheston, a manor belonging to the Willingtons in Henry VIII.'s time. Sir William Willington, a wealthy wool stapler, had a family of daughters for whom he provided husbands among the foremost men in the county, so at this day most of the barons of Warwickshire quarter the arms of Willington. Brailes lies four miles to the left, and we are quickly passing Weston House, an ancient seat of the Sheldons, and now the seat of Earl Camperdown. After passing the park at Weston the road enters the valley among the hills and presently the beautiful village of Long

---

[1] " Henry V." Act IV. Sc. viii.

E

Compton is reached.   A curious legend, told by Selden illustrative of Tithes is told of this place [1] :—

" For the practice of payment among Christians, both *Britons* and *Saxons* ; might we believe the common tale of that *Augustine*, the first Archbishop of *Canterbury* Province, his coming to *Cometon* in *Oxfordshire*, and doing a most strange miracle there ; touching the establishing of the doctrine of due payment of Tithes, we should have as certain and express authority for the ancient practice of such payment, as any other Church in *Christendome* can produce.   But as the tale is, you you shall have it, and then censure it.   About the year (they say) DC. *Augustine* coming to preach at *Cometon*, the Priest of the place makes complaint to him, that the Lord of the Mannor having been often admonished by him, would yet pay him no Tithes.   *Augustine* questioning the Lord about that default in devotion ; he stoutly answered, That the tenth Sheaf doubtless was his that had interest in the nine, and therefore would pay none. Presently *Augustine* denounces him excommunicate, and turning to the Altar to say Mass, publiquely forbad, that any excommunicate person should be present at it, when suddenly a dead Corpse, that had been buried at the Church door, arose (pardon me for relating it) and departed out of the limits of the Church-yard, standing still without, while the Mass continued.   Which ended, *Augustine* comes to this living dead, and charges him in the name of the Lord God to declare who he was.   He tells him, that in the time of the *British* State he was *hujus villæ Patronus*, and although he had been often urged by the Doctrine of the Priest to pay his Tithes, yet he never could be brought to it ; for which he died, he sayes, excommunicate, and was carried to Hell.

[1] J. Selden, " The History of Tythes." MDCXVIII.

Augustine desired to know where the Priest that excommunicated him, was buried : this dead shewed him the place ; where he makes an invocation of the dead Priest, and bids him arise also, because they wanted his help. The Priest rises. *Augustine* asks him, if he knew the other that was risen : he tells him, yes ; but wishes he had never known him : for, (saith he) he was in all things ever adverse to the Church, a detainer of his Tithes, and a great sinner to his death, and therefore I excommunicated him. But *Augustine* publickly declares, that it was fit mercy should be used towards him, and that he had suffered long in Hell for his offence (you must suppose, I think the Author meant Purgatory) wherefore he gives him absolution, and sends him to his grave, where he fell again into dust and ashes. He gone, the Priest new risen, tells, that his Corpse had lien there about C.LXX. years ; and *Augustine* would gladly have had him continue upon earth again, for instruction of Souls, but could not thereto intreat him. So he also returns to his former lodging. The Lord of the Town standing by all this while, and trembling, was now demanded, if he would pay his Tithes ; but he presently fell down at *Augustines* feet, weeping and confessing his offence ; and receiving pardon, became all his lifetime a follower of *Augustine*."

In the centre of the village the road turns to the left and ascends the hill to the bleak uplands on the Oxfordshire border, but before passing from the valley the ancient church, the scene of the legendary romance of S. Augustine just quoted, and after the church the village inn with its sign of the lion may be visited. Some few years since some friends of the writer were staying at Long Compton and persuaded the landlord to allow them to restore the ancient sign of the Red Lion. Like the famous inn sign at Bettys-y-coed painted by David Cox, the sign of this inn was painted by a well-known artist, one of the guests.   It is on record that the land-lord of the Red Lion celebrated the occasion in a right jovial manner.

A stiff climb and we reach a point on a hill top above Compton between the Little and the Great Rollright. Like Stonehenge, though not nearly so extensive, these monoliths have for many centuries attracted the atten-tion of antiquaries.   They were as famous in the days of Elizabeth as they are now, indeed it is highly probable that in the sixteenth century the monoliths were far more perfect than at present.   The Whispering Knights, two stones standing a little apart from the main circle, have long formed a subject for romantic tales, and are represented in ancient drawings of the Rollrights.

These so called "Druidical remains" undoubtedly belong to a period when the inhabitants of Britain worshipped the sun, and although possibly at a later date burials may have been made here, the stones were originally erected as a Temple of the Sun.

The face of the country has changed, no longer is the wayfarer surrounded by green fields and smiling hedgerows, the land is bare and barren looking, hedges are few and stone walls general, while here and there a clump of ragged fir trees rear their gaunt arms against the sky.   The mournful note of the lapwing alone disturbs the silence of the lonely fells.   We have passed from the Forest of Arden to the Feldon.   Here and there a deep valley hides itself among the dun coloured hills, and the road now and again descends, but more generally a course high up among the hills appears to have been chosen.

There is nothing of great interest between Long

Compton and Woodstock: but Woodstock is a name to conjure with. It is but a few miles from the home of the fair Rosamund—now replaced by the palace of the Duke of Marlborough—to the City of Spires and learning, where the surrounding county is more fertile. All these scenes which we have briefly described were known to Shakespeare, and his mind must have been affected by them just as the mind of any observant traveller is affected at the present day.

The Poet would enter Oxford by the broad way of S. Giles, and then pass under the gate leading to the Corn Market, and his tired horse would slacken pace as it neared its journey's end—the Crown Inn, where mine host Davenant and his jolly wife were waiting to receive an honoured and ever welcome guest.

With the romantic traditions of Shakespeare and the Davenants we cannot now deal, but, apart from the tradition, the bare statement that he was accustomed to stay at Oxford, remains as an accepted fact.

The second half of the journey would probably be varied according to circumstance or the mood of the traveller. Sometimes the way would be taken through Dorchester and Nettlebed to Windsor, but there is a tradition that another road was occasionally selected leading through a portion of Buckinghamshire. At a little place on this road Shakespeare is said to have encountered the Watch, and thereby to have given immortality to Dogberry and Verges. These incidents, however, are too far afield for our present purpose, and we must shortly return to Warwickshire, but before doing so it may be well to record that the writer has made the journey from Stratford to London and back by road, in order to acquaint himself with the scenes which were familiar to Shakespeare.

At the present time it is possible for anyone caring to do so to stay at the inns, traditionally the identical hostelries, at which Shakespeare stayed: the Crown at Oxford, about the identity of which, however, there is some dispute; the Star and Garter at Windsor; and another old inn at Grendon, the place famous as the abode of that wonderful parish official, Master Dogberry.

How the journey ended we may surmise; the Poet entered London, under one of the gates now destroyed, and, towards the latter part of his life at least, would finally draw rein before his house at Blackfriars, beneath the shadow of old S. Paul's and within sight of the Globe Theatre, across the Thames at Southwark.

CHAPTER X

SHAKESPEARE'S STRATFORD HOMES

WHATEVER else is uncertain about the life of our Poet, there is no doubt that he spent many years in Stratford: and we know that during that period Shakespeare lived in at least three houses. The place of his birth undoubtedly was his father's house, and that house, we have no reason to dispute, was the fine timber-framed tenement in Henley Street, now National property.

Theorists have from time to time set up rival claims for a house in Greenhill Street, the Brook House in Waterside, and even the old rectory at Clifford Chambers: but there is little reason, and less fact, to bolster up these theories. On the other hand there is absolute proof that John Shakespeare lived in Henley Street, and carried on his business of wool stapler and glover in the premises now so well known all over the world.

The long timber-framed house, with its gables and dormer windows, and its garden and back premises running down to the old Guild-Pits, appears to have been built before the suppression of the Guild whose prosperity materially influenced the growth of the town: many substantial houses being built upon land belonging to the fraternity, granted on easy terms to certain

ROOM WHEREIN SHAKESPEARE WAS BORN

people.   The Birthplace is no mean cottage, it is a commodious town house, suitable for an alderman and chief magistrate.   It appears that John Shakespeare occupied these premises continuously from the time of his son's birth, and even before then, until his own death in 1601.   His eldest son inherited the paternal freehold, and left it to the members of his family: the details of the transfer of the estate from one possessor to another are known with certainty from the year 1556, the year in which John Shakespeare bought the property, to the present time.   These absolute facts sufficiently attest the respectable position of the Shakespeares in Stratford: John Shakespeare's house being one of the better class, not, as is popularly supposed, a poor cottage. The forest of Arden supplied the timber for its construction, well matured oak, tough enough to last a thousand years.

The fact then stands that the earliest years of the Poet's life were passed in his father's Stratford home, and this old house may well be regarded as one of the world's shrines.

From the time of his marriage to the year 1598 Shakespeare lived partly in London, and partly in Stratford, but his wife and family had their home in the latter town. Of course it is possible that during fifteen years Mrs Shakespeare lived in more than one house, but we find that after the purchase of New Place the Poet's cousin, Thomas Greene, alias Shakespeare, made his home with the family.

Greene was a lawyer, and held the honourable position of Town Clerk of Stratford. He appears to have been a bachelor, and was a man of some property, owning the estate now known as Avonbank. Probably Mrs Shakespeare lived under the same roof as the Town Clerk before they removed to New Place, and this supposition is strengthened by a passage in Langbain's "Lives of the Poets." The only house answering to the description given in that book was the house of Thomas Greene, the Poet's cousin.

Even in those days the house by the church was a place of some importance, and had belonged to the Guild.[1] In the fifteenth century the schoolmaster

[1] House of S. Mary in "le Oldtown" A.D. 1412-13. The master of the Guild allowed 4s. annual rent to the schoolmaster as long as he kept a school in the house of S. Mary. ("Guild Accounts," page 12.)

was allowed to live there, and at an earlier period it appears to have been either the residence of an official, or of some of the monks of Worcester : the manor then belonging to the Benedictine monastery of that place. The passage in Langbain is of great interest, and is worth quoting in full : it appears only in the edition corrected by an editor and published without date, but probably about the year 1699.

WILLIAM SHAKESPEARE

"He was born and buried in *Stratford*-upon-*Avon* in *Warwickshire*. I have been told that he writ the Scene of the Ghost in *Hamlet* at his House which bordered on the Charnel-House and Church-Yard. He was both Poet and Player ; but the greatest Poet that ever trod the Stage. I am of Opinion, in spight of Mr *Johnson*, and others from him, that though perhaps he might not be that Critic in Latin and Greek as *Ben* : yet that he understood the former, so well as perfectly to be Master of their Histories, for in all his Roman Characters he has nicely followed History, and you find his *Brutus*, his *Cassius*, his *Anthony*, and his *Caesar*, his *Coriolanus*, etc., just as the Historians of those times describe 'em. He died on the 23rd April, 1616, and is buried with his Wife and Daughter in *Stratford Church* aforesaid, under a Monument on which is a Statue leaning on a cushion."

It is evident from Greene's diary that when his cousin was contemplating settling down in Stratford he was obliged to make arrangements for removing from New Place to his own house in the Old Town. The tenant occupying the house was unwilling to leave just then, and Greene notes that this did not much matter because he could arrange to remain at New Place for another year.

The inference to be drawn from this memorandum in Greene's diary is that the Poet found it difficult to sever his connection with the theatre and his company of players, though he did return to Stratford in the year 1609 and took up his abode with his family at New Place, which he had so far repaired and improved as to make it the most important house but one in the town; the old College, where his friend John O'Combe lived, being the largest residence in Stratford at that period. Other entries in the diary refer to the rebuilding by the Corporation of a wall between Greene's property and the churchyard. This leaves no doubt that the present "Avonbank" was the estate owned by Robert Greene, since the churchyard wall was the boundary between the two. Langbain's words, "which bordered on the Charnel-house," clearly refer to Greene's house, the charnel-house being on the north side of the chancel.

There is every reason to believe that during the intervals of a busy life in London Shakespeare for many years returned to Stratford in the summer months, spending his holidays with his family in the pleasant old house beside the river. Of all places in the world this quiet spot was the most suitable for the Poet to compose his chief work. The churchyard scene in Hamlet, with all its pathos and humour, was probably a transcript from real life, though the scene was transferred from Stratford in Warwickshire to Elsinore in Denmark. The grave-diggers are no Danes, but Warwickshire clowns: their humour and philosophy is so natural that one can scarcely believe it to be purely imaginary. That the neighbourhood of the churchyard should have suggested the ghost scene in "Hamlet" is also highly probable, and one may picture the Poet writing in one of the old rooms with a window facing the church where he was baptised, and watching the fantastic shadows in the moonlit churchyard.

The third house, about which the most sceptical person has no doubt whatever, is New Place. Here Shakespeare lived from the time of his retirement from London till his death in 1616. It was but a short period, but certainly an extremely pleasant one : the Poet having been able to realise his ambitious dreams. There is no doubt that he had a strong desire to return to his native town and hold an honourable position among his friends. For a brief period the fortunes of the family had been under a cloud, and it was legitimate for the most energetic member to desire to retrieve the position at one time almost lost. That Shakespeare did this, and more than this, is a sufficient proof of his energy and talent. It is also a proof that his talents were recognised and rewarded by his contemporaries.

The words of Rowe, the Poet's first biographer, in reference to this are very definite :—"The latter part of Shakespeare's life was spent, as all men of good sense will wish theirs may be, in ease, retirement, and the conversation of his friends." This period of contentment appears to have commenced about 1609, certainly not later than 1611.

Those who know how pleasantly time passes in a country town for those who have means, inclination, and health to enjoy it, will realise the sweets of this last age.—The sunny garden of New Place, with smooth green lawn, beds bright with flowers, and prospects of river, meadows, and distant hills : the old church tower, with tapering spire visible among the trees : the constant

callers, always hospitably received, willing to play a game
of bowls on the green in the summer time, or sit around
the fire and chat in winter: the satisfaction of being
able to help with one's means in forwarding anything
for the public weal, such as the repair of highways, to
which fund it is recorded that Shakespeare contributed
in 1611.

When John Leland made his famous itinerary of
England he came in due course to Stratford, and noted
the chief buildings in the town. In Birmingham also
he records that he saw a fair mansion-house of timber—
the old Crown House—a building still in existence, and
although now in the heart of the busy city, a notable
house, and a substantial one. Leland remarks of New
Place:—

"this Hugh Clopton builded also by the north syde
of this chappell a praty house of bricke and tymbre."

Sir Hugh Clopton, Stratford's great benefactor, built
this pleasant house, and a century after his time New
Place had come by purchase to one of the Underhills,
who sold it to Shakespeare for £60.

New Place then being in need of repair the Poet restored his future home. It had a frontage towards the
chief street of the town, and a side entrance from Chapel
Lane, into a little green courtyard. Beyond the courtyard was the "great garden," still one of the most
beautiful open spaces in the town. It is pleasant to
think of the Poet passing his last years in this beautiful
spot, surrounded by his relatives and friends, and visited
by some of his kindred spirits, members of the famous
coterie of the Mermaid.

In 1675 New Place was repurchased by the Cloptons,
and practically rebuilt. In 1759 the house was pulled
down by that eccentric cleric, the Rev. Francis Gastrell

Prebend of Lichfield: who had previously cut down Shakespeare's mulberry tree which grew in the little courtyard before mentioned. Gastrell left Stratford

THE KITCHEN, SHAKESPEARE'S BIRTHPLACE

execrated by the townspeople, and all that remains of New Place may be seen in a few pits, excavated by Halliwell-Phillipps, a part of the foundation walls, a portion of a groined arch, and a couple of wells. This is all that is left of the house in which the Poet died, except some timber framing built into the highest story of the adjoining house.

HOLY TRINITY CHURCH, STRATFORD-ON-AVON

CHAPTER XI

STRATFORD-UPON-AVON CHURCH

CATHEDRAL-LIKE, beautifully situated beside the Avon,
hoary with antiquity, the resting-place of the world's
greatest poet, the parish church of Stratford-upon-
Avon is one of the most interesting and picturesque
of all the stately fanes of England. That Shakespeare
lies buried here is true, yet the church of Stratford
was built ages before the Poet's ancestors settled in
Warwickshire. In the dim Saxon times a church and
monastery were founded probably upon or near the
site of the present structure. When Shakespeare
bought a lease of part of the tithes, and obtained a
proprietorship in the collegiate church, he certainly
evinced an interest in its welfare, and possibly prevented its destruction : in this sense only can it be
called Shakespeare's Church.

Little is known about the structure previous to the
thirteenth century, though apparently there are traces
of Norman work incorporated in the Early English
masonry.

About a hundred years later, that is roughly speaking
about the year 1300, the church underwent considerable reconstruction; in 1325 Thomas Cobham, Bishop
of Worcester, granted an indulgence to all contributing
to the repair of the church, and in 1331 the south
aisle was rebuilt, and in it was placed an altar to

F

S. Thomas of Canterbury. A chantry was founded which in course of time became a college, owning the advowson of the parish church. This chantry owed its existence to the munificence of John de Stratford, Archbishop of Canterbury, who was consecrated archbishop in 1323. The altar stone of this chapel is now used as the high altar of the church.

The next reconstruction took place in the fifteenth century, when Dean Balsale rebuilt the chancel as it at present stands, the work being completed by his successor Collingwood: to this period must be assigned the handsome clerestorey, the north porch, and the west window: the last additions being made in the early years of the sixteenth century.

Upon entering the porch remains of holy water stoups may be noticed on the east and west sides. The great oaken doors, richly carved, the small wicket with grotesque bronze head and heavy ring, popularly supposed to be a sanctuary knocker, at once prepare the visitor to expect a richly decorated church within. Though shorn of its original ornaments the fine proportions of the church remain. The lofty nave, lighted from above by large clerestorey windows, and flanked by wide aisles with handsome traceried windows, reminds one of a cathedral church; and the chancel, seen through the double arches of the central tower, heightens the effect. The extreme length of the church from east to west is 197 feet, the nave with aisles is 68 feet broad, and the transepts stretch from north to south 89 feet.

At the west end, near the door, the ancient Registers, containing entries of Shakespeare's baptism and burial, are on view together with an old picture of the church

STRATFORD CHURCH FROM THE RIVER AVON

as it was in the early part of the nineteenth century, a chained book, and other objects of interest.

The north aisle now contains the monuments of the Clopton family. A portion of this aisle was originally used as a Lady chapel, and contained three altars served by the priests of the Guild. The eastern portion is now a pew belonging to Clopton House. The monument of Sir Hugh Clopton is believed to be a cenotaph, because the knight dying in London was buried in the church of S. Margaret, Lothbury, and this tomb, though prepared for him, never received his remains. The altar tomb beneath the window has the carved effigies of William Clopton, Esq., and his wife, Anne, daughter of Sir George Griffith, Knight; William Clopton was a contemporary of Shakespeare, and died in 1592. Against the east wall is a large and handsome monument to George Carew, Earl of Totness, and his Countess, Joyce Clopton, daughter of William Clopton before mentioned. Several mural tablets to the memory of the Cloptons are to be seen upon the walls, and a small inscription records that Sir Arthur Hodgson caused this chapel and the monuments to be restored in 1892. A helmet and the tattered remnants of a banner still hang above the tomb, being all that is left of the funeral ornaments formerly displayed over the family monuments. The window in the Clopton chapel contains fragments of ancient glass, but the lower portion has been lately filled with some good modern glass to the memory of Lady Hodgson.

The second window towards the left commemorates one of the sons of Sir Arthur and Lady Hodgson; and the third window is a memorial to Frederick Pritchard, M.R.C.S., and his wife and son.

The south aisle had an altar dedicated to S. Thomas of Canterbury; the site is now occupied by part of the organ, and near it is the old font in which Shakespeare was baptised. A window in this aisle has been filled with stained glass to the memory of a brave young officer, Richard Fordham Flower, once captain of the Stratford-on-Avon Volunteers, and subsequently lieutenant in the Warwickshire Imperial Yeomanry, who was killed in action in South Africa in August 1900. At the western end of the south aisle may be noticed the colours of the Warwickshire Militia, raised in 1811.

On the south side of the nave, against the first column from the east, stands the pulpit; a handsome, and very ornamental one of green marble with statues in white marble. These represent S. Ambrose, S. Augustine, S. Gregory, S. Jerome, and S. Helena. The inscription around the pulpit is as follows:—
"In Dei gloriam et in memoriam Helena Faucit MDCCCC. A.D."

The pulpit was the gift of Sir Theodore Martin, whose desire to commemorate his accomplished wife has been the means of securing this beautiful piece of ecclesiastical furniture for the collegiate church of Stratford-upon-Avon. It is by far the most costly and elaborate of all the ornaments in the church, but there is no reason to doubt that in course of time the venerable structure will gleam with marble and brilliant colours. Indeed the pulpit is in some measure the forerunner of a movement destined to produce a better taste in ecclesiastical art. In the middle ages even small country churches were generally most tastefully decorated with mural paintings: these wall paintings were obliterated after the Reformation. The restoring architects of the nineteenth century

INTERIOR, STRATFORD CHURCH

when removing the whitewash usually destroyed the
paintings, being entirely satisfied when they had un-
covered the stonework beneath the plaster; stonework
which the original builders never intended to leave
bare.   Unfortunately the church of Stratford has been
almost stripped of any trace of colour, yet in one or
two places small remnants of the once gorgeous wall
paintings remain, but, as there is an awakening sense of
appreciation of colour, we may expect to see frescoes re-
introduced before long.   When that much to be desired
time arrives the pulpit will be found to harmonise entirely with its surroundings.

Before passing to the transepts the visitor should
notice a handsome carved door leading to the belfry
staircase, and upon the wall beside it the remains of
an ancient painting, now, alas, almost obliterated.   The
north transept is divided by a screen and the northern
portion is used as a vestry.   The south transept in
modern times has been fitted up as a chapel for occasional services.   The south window contains some good
modern stained glass purchased with money contributed
by American visitors to the church.

The chancel was entirely rebuilt in the fifteenth
century : it is now divided from the tower by an oak
screen, and contains the ancient oak stalls with curiously
carved miserere seats, used by the canons of the collegiate church.   The windows are large and lofty, and
have been filled in modern times with stained glass.   It
is much to be regretted that no vestige of the original
glass mentioned by Dugdale now remains.   The most
noticeable feature of the chancel is the monument to
William Shakespeare, containing the well-known effigy
of the Poet.   The Shakespeare family vault is immediately below the monument, and upon the stones of the

floor within the altar rails are inscriptions to the Poet and members of his family.

Upon the east wall on the north side of the altar is the altar tomb with its canopy to the memory of Shakespeare's friend and neighbour, John Combe. Against the north wall, a little to the east of Shakespeare's monument is a finely carved, and sadly mutilated tomb of the founder of the chancel, Dean Balsale.

On the 23rd of April in each year the ceremony of decking the Poet's tomb is observed. Floral offerings are placed upon the stones above the vault. Year-by-year the offerings become more numerous, and the ceremony is growing in importance.

Every visitor to the church should not fail to take a quiet walk through the churchyard by the path skirting the river, where a row of gigantic elms casts long shadows over the moss-grown graves. The view obtained from this spot is indeed a beautiful one, scarcely to be matched in England. On the south side of the chancel there is an ancient raised tomb, sometimes called William Winter's seat. It was here that William Winter often sat when visiting Stratford towards the close of the nineteenth century, and here at midnight, in the pale moonlight, while the owls were hooting in the trees above, and the murmuring waters of the Avon flowed over the mill weir, he composed some of his charming descriptions of Stratford and the neighbourhood. Centuries before our time another poet and lover of the drama must often have wandered about this churchyard. No doubt his love for the venerable church and its peaceful surroundings influenced his mind when engaged upon the works which have immortalised his name, and must ever render the place of his birth and sepulture dear to every lover of English literature.

CHAPTER XII

To follow the footsteps of William Shakespeare as he travelled to and fro among his relatives and friends has often been attempted but never successfully achieved; probably because his biographers were not long resident in the midland shires, and studied the Poet's life from afar, instead of in the neighbourhood in which their hero lived. After a lapse of three centuries Warwickshire and the midland counties have become a Holy Land to Shakespeare votaries, and every village, every house, associated ever so remotely with Shakespeare is endowed with a new and lively interest. Yet it is doubtful if many more facts can now be unearthed, the period of time between the days of Queen Elizabeth and our own being so great. However, it cannot be out of place to describe some of the country around Stratford which hitherto has been dealt with only by historians of adjoining counties in ponderous and costly volumes, out of the reach of all except the wealthy.

Our English counties are not arranged in square blocks like the United States of America, and certainly bear no marked resemblance to a chessboard; their boundaries are irregular, but there is usually a reason, physical or historical, for all these peculiarities. In many instances a peninsular of land belonging to one

county will be found stretching far into another, and
dotted about are curious little detached portions.   This
is particularly the case in Worcestershire, Warwickshire,
and Gloucestershire.

It will be found generally that these isolated parts
formerly belonged to a noble, or a religious institution
in an adjoining county, and for convenience were
detached from the division to which they naturally
belonged, and recorded as part of the county in which
their owner lived, or was most powerful.

The portion of Warwickshire in which Stratford-on-
Avon is situated lies on the borders of Worcestershire,
Gloucestershire, and Oxfordshire; so, although William
Shakespeare was a Warwickshire lad, he had only to
take a little stroll from his father's door to be in
Gloucestershire or Worcestershire.   We may be sure
that in these adjoining counties we shall find traces of
England's greatest poet, yet it is singular how this
chance of making discoveries has been neglected.   It is
but a short walk from the Market Cross of Stratford-on-
Avon in Warwickshire to the village green of Clifford
Chambers in Gloucestershire, yet how few of the
visitors to Stratford have ever heard of the name of
Clifford.

The village lies about two miles to the south of the
town, and the path leading to it skirts the churchyard
of Holy Trinity, and at Mill Lane descends to a foot-
bridge across the Avon.   In going down the narrow
path it will be interesting to notice the flood-boards
on the mill wall, where it may be seen that the highest
flood on record ushered in the present century, the water
being at its greatest height at midnight, December 31,
1900.

An inscription on the north-west pier of the bridge

records that it was built in 1599, rebuilt in 1812 when Austin Warrilow was Mayor, and again rebuilt in 1867, C. F. Loggin being Mayor of Stratford at that time.[1]

This old foot-bridge must often have been crossed by the Poet and members of his family.   It seems that

The Old Rectory
Clifford Chambers ?

William Black realised this when he wrote *Judith Shakespeare*. "Let us cross the foot-bridge Prue, and go through the meadows and round by Clopton's bridge and so home." It was along this path that Judith passed to keep her tryst with the wizard at the

[1] Wheler's "History," p. 111, states that the bridge was built in 1590, and that in 1595 the corporation of Stratford covenanted, by deed under their common seal, with Sir George Carew, Knight of Clopton (afterwards Earl Totness), Sir Edward Greville, Knight of Milcote, Sir Baptist Hickes, Bart. of Campden, Hercules Raynsford, Esq. of Clifford, and others (at whose expense the bridge was erected), to keep it in perpetual repair.

stile by the Weir-brake, which is in Clifford, a parish in Gloucestershire.

A little lower down the river there was anciently a ford, with a road leading from it up the steep marl bank or cliff, which may have given the name of Clifford to the village.

The present footpath, however, passes under a railway embankment, and crosses the meadows to the foot of the hill where there is a short but steep ascent, and from the top an extensive view is obtained. To the north lies Stratford, backed by the wooded hills of Welcombe, with the mill and church in the foreground: the houses skirting the silver river which foams and tumbles over the lashers at the mill. In the middle distance the picturesque pile of the Shakespeare Memorial Buildings rises from the greensward and breaks the skyline: the beautiful gardens of "Avonbank," and the classic colonnade of an eighteenth century orangery help to complete an unrivalled landscape. There is an unique charm in the scene: the town nestles in a hollow beside the river, surrounded by rich pastures and verdant hills: the river, winding in a broad reach from the old, many-arched bridge to the ancient church, girds the birthplace and burialplace of Shakespeare with a silver zone, in which the trees and buildings are reflected.

Turning from this typical Warwickshire scene we see from the summit of the "Cross o' the Hill" over the plain of Worcestershire—the Severn valley—to the serrated ridge of the Malvern Hills, usually blue or purple in the distance, and to the Cotswold Hills in Gloucestershire. Half way across the valley rises the pleasant hill of Bredon, and to the south the heights of Ilmington, Meon and Broadway. Under a little hill, a mile to the south, the square, embattled tower of Clifford Chambers' Church peeps out from among a bower of trees.

> "Dear Clifford's seat (the place of health and sport)
> Which many a time hath been the Muse's quiet port." [1]

But to reach Clifford we must cross the fields till the highroad is reached, follow the road as it descends to a pretty timbered house on the right hand, which is in Gloucestershire, and the old mill on the left, which is in Warwickshire: this spot illustrates the curious division of county boundaries already referred to. After passing these houses you cross the ancient bridge of three arches which spans the Stour, and must then have one foot in Warwickshire whilst the other is in Gloucestershire.

If we continued along the road we should pass the site of the ancient castle of the Grevilles, ancestors of the present Earl of Warwick, Milcote Castle, of which no stone is now left standing above ground, and then to Weston-on-Avon and Welford. But the road we take turns to the left at the disused and weedy pound, past the "New Inn," where the village street begins. The road opposite the inn is the King's Highway to Mickleton, Campden, and Broadway; as pleasant a road as any in this part of England.

The village street is broad, and the cottages which fringe it picturesque and substantial. There is an air of comfort and respectability about the place which betokens a squire and rector of the good old school. The ancient timber-framed house adjoining the churchyard is the rectory where William Shakespeare's schoolmaster, Walter Roche, must have lived during a part

---

[1] Poly-olbion, fourteenth song.

of his life: and where John Shakespeare of Clifford must have been a frequent guest.

At the end of the village the great gates of the Manor House disclose the ancient home of the Raynsfords,

Gable of Old Rectory
Clifford Chambers

friends of Michael Drayton, and consequently, without doubt, of Shakespeare also.

An elaborate alabaster monument, and several brasses in the chancel of the church still remind us of the Raynsfords, one of whom married the lady celebrated in the sonnets of Michael Drayton. This lady ever held her poet in high esteem.

Now let us suppose that Drayton came to pay a visit to the Raynsfords at Clifford Manor House, we ndeed know he did so—for has he not recorded the fact in Poly-olbion?—he was a frequent visitor there. All the country round was known to him, the Vale of the Red Horse and Meon Hill were familiar to him. Meon,

> " destitute of nought that Arden can him yield:
> Nor of th' especial grace of many a goodly field."

He would have to pass along the roads we now pass along, though the commons were not enclosed and hedges were fewer than at present. On those occasions Drayton would naturally meet his friend William Shakespeare of Stratford-on-Avon, sometimes walking to see him at the house he occupied before he bought New Place, and afterwards at New Place. Shakespeare must also have walked over the Cross o' the Hill to Clifford : and so we see the Poet amid surroundings new to most of us.

But who was John Shakespeare of Clifford? Possibly the Poet's uncle or a near kinsman of his. It was not unusual for two brothers to bear the same Christian name, yet the relationship is not established with certainty.

John Shakespeare of Clifford married Julian Hobbins who died in 1608 : the Poet's father died in 1601. But in 1608 John Shakespeare of Clifford was living and made his will, leaving to the church of Clifford the bier " which I had made at my own proper cost and charges." A modern brass plate is now fixed on the old oak bier to record the history of this curious piece of parish furniture which may be the actual bier bequeathed by John Shakespeare, and at least is older than the oldest inhabitant can remember.

Besides the quaint brasses to the squires and dames of this sequestered village, and the richly carved ala-

G

baster figures, and the mural tablets, there are other interesting features belonging to Clifford Church—a seven-sided font of unusual form and great antiquity; an altar cloth of crimson velvet embroidered in gold and silver, said to have been part of the trappings used at the funeral of Catherine of Arragon, given as a perquisite to the then rector of Clifford, who was one of the officiating priests. The altar cloth is probably of Indian workmanship, and is said to have been an elephant cloth. There is also a cushion embroidered with the badges of Henry VIII.'s first Queen. Nor have we yet exhausted the diversity of rare items. There is a silver chalice, parcel gilt, the oldest known with a dated maker's mark except one. The figure of the Saviour on the Cross has been desecrated, also the inscription on the stem of the cup.

In the churchyard, between the village street and the western tower, shaded by trees and moss grown, may still be seen the tomb of a long-forgotten gipsy queen.

In 1885-86 the church was reverently repaired by the Rev. F. H. Annesley, under the advice of Mr John Cotton, an architect and archæologist of sound judgment and rare taste.

The Manor House of Clifford Chambers dates from pre-Reformation times. The manor having been church property the house was probably first built by the monks. It afterwards passed into the possession of the Raynsfords, the Dightons, and Annesleys: it is now occupied by Colonel Studdy.

Roger de Bulley gave the manor to the Abbey of S. Peter's, Gloucester. It had previously formed part of the possessions of the famous Brightric, who scorned the love of the Princess of Flanders who afterwards became the Queen of William the Conqueror.

Before leaving Clifford we must at least look at the Manor House from the field path leading across the park from Clifford to Atherstone-on-Stour. The house is venerable in appearance; the south-eastern front has lately been stripped of its plaster covering, revealing a

Gable of
Manor House
Clifford Chambers

handsome timber framework, and many blocked up windows, the oak mullions still retaining traces of the red paint which formerly decorated them.

The remains of the moat may still be seen; and the old, many timbered structure accords with the old world traditions which enrich its history. After the monks departed the wealthy squires took possession and added to the house as occasion required, but few additions have been made since the eighteenth century: it remains one of the finest specimens of an ancient manor house in the county, exactly the place to have been "The Muse's quiet port."

But as the setting sun gilds its many paned windows we must return to Stratford, passing by another mill, and a field path towards the Shipston Road, and so crossing Clopton Bridge back to the life and bustle of the little market town.

Note.—Three ways in which to reach Clifford :—

1. Over the Clopton Bridge, round by the Shipston Road, working to the right.
2. Up the tramway, over the bridge seen from the Clopton Bridge, where a very pretty view of the church is obtained.
3. The one indicated in this chapter, past Lucy's Mill and over the foot-bridge.

There is a footpath from the Manor House at Clifford across the fields, working to the left ; which comes out at the Mill in Warwickshire.

CHAPTER XIII

THE FAT ALE WIFE OF WINCOT

QUITE a little controversy has sprung up about the residence of Mistress Marion Hacket, who supplied Kit Sly, the tinker, with malt liquor. Marion Hacket, could she know it, would probably blush to find herself so famous. She is, however, one of the many topical allusions in Shakespeare, and has become thereby so celebrated that her name is now known even to the school boys and girls of England and America. Yet all she did was to supply Kit Sly with ale. The hand of the enchanter touched her, and, behold, Marion became world renowned.

Whether she lived at Wilmcote, the home of Shakespeare's grandfather, at Wilnecote near Tamworth, or at Wincot in Gloucestershire, matters little ; there is no doubt that the fat ale wife was no imaginary person, but a real and actual person who lived somewhere in the Midlands in the days of Queen Bess. The probabilities are in favour of the good woman having had her dwelling-place at Wincot, a hamlet of Clifford Chambers, where portions of a fine old house remain to this day.

About two miles along the road leading from Clifford to Chipping Campden a pathway across the fields to the left leads to the lone farm-house at Wincot. The house has been partly rebuilt, but retains some old rooms with great mullioned windows. On one side of the garden grow three mulberry trees traditionally said to have been planted by William Shakespeare. In the days of Elizabeth there were other houses besides this in the hamlet, and one of these may have been the inn. The Hackets lived in this neighbourhood, and the local traditions associate the place with the Poet, who indeed mentions two members of the family—Marion, the fat ale wife, and her daughter, Cicely.

Now it so happened that the position of Wincot made it much easier for the people living there to attend church at Quinton, rather than their own parish church at Clifford, and we find in the register of the former place a rather significant entry.

Elsewhere, p. 116, we have quoted the words of Sir Aston Cokain in reference to the "Wincot ale that foxed a beggar so," but Sir Aston Cokain lived quite long enough after the event to have made a mistake about the place referred to in the play. It should be borne in mind, also, that Kit Sly claimed to be a son of old Sly of Barton-on-the-Heath, which place lies some fifteen miles to the south-west of Stratford. The Gloucestershire Wincot is about ten miles distant from Barton-on-the-Heath and five from Stratford. This circumstance, taken together with the fact that people named Hacket lived at, or near Wincot, makes it most probable that Shakespeare's reference is to this place, rather than to Great Wilmcote, or Wilnecote in the north.

One point, however, should be noticed, although the name of Sly is found in the records of Stratford-on-Avon, the drunken tinker is no creation of Shakespeare, being mentioned in an older play, " The Taming of a Shrew," a play altered and partly rewritten by our Poet. The scene of the induction to the comedy is laid at the country house of a nobleman, who amused himself at the tinker's expense. Such an incident may very well have happened in the neighbourhood of Stratford, and it has therefore been suggested that Clopton House was the place in the Poet's mind when he recast the play: the introduction of the name " Wincot " further strengthens this theory, Clopton House being but a short three miles from the hamlet of Wilmcote, some-times called Wincote locally.

When writing comedy the Poet constantly indulges his fancy by introducing well-known names and treating them with poetic license.

Thus in " As You Like It " the Forest of Arden shelters lions and snakes amid groves wherein palm trees appear to grow as naturally as if the scene was placed in Africa instead of mid-England.

It is nothing to the Poet that there should be three

" Wincots "; the confusion of names is appropriate in a fairy tale—or in the realms of romance. The incident of the players is quite in keeping with the customs of the times: for in those days many nobles and wealthy men maintained a troupe of players who performed in the great halls of their mansions. The records of the period prove this, and the matter is brought sufficiently near home by the fact of Sir Thomas Lucy having at one time his own band of actors.

In most of the large country houses around Stratford a play must have been an amusement of fairly common occurrence, and Clopton, no less than Charlecote, may have afforded a home to the children of Thespis. Consequently there is nothing improbable in the guess that Shakespeare had Clopton House in his mind when he recast " The Taming of a Shrew."

However true all these premises may be they do not detract from the fact that the Hackets had their home on the Gloucestershire border at or near Wincot.

The entry in the Quinton register is most remarkable, the scribe apparently having the name Cicely in his mind at the time of writing, since he actually formed the letter " C " and then corrected to " S " for " Sarah," as is apparent in the photograph of the entry of the baptism given on a former page, " Sara Hacket, the daughter of Robert Hacket " (Nov. 21st, 1591).

CHAPTER XIV

WHEN Queen Elizabeth persecuted Catholics she did
so with a refinement of cruelty which was worse than
killing them outright, and it is not to be wondered at
that some of the persecuted turned against the hand
that made them tremble. One of the most pathetic
cases was that of John Somervile, of Edstone, near
Stratford-on-Avon. John Somervile married Margaret
Arden, a daughter of Edward Arden, of Park Hall, by
his wife Mary, daughter of Sir Robert Throckmorton,
of Coughton Court. Margaret Arden was therefore a
near kinswoman of Robert Arden of Wilmcote, who
traced his descent from the same ancestor. Somervile
was young, enthusiastic, and apparently of a weak mind.
For some reason, not too clearly known, Edward Arden
had offended the Earl of Leicester. The Throckmortons had suffered very considerably for religious and
political opinions, and these sufferings endured by his
relatives appear to have unhinged the mind of John
Somervile, who thereupon was possessed with a mad
craze to kill the Queen. Accordingly we find him
setting out for London, and making no secret of the
object of his journey. He proceeded as far as a village,
four miles from Aynho, near Oxford, where he told the
people of the inn that he intended "to shoot the
Queen with his dagg": whereupon with little to do

he was arrested, but before he could be tried he was found one morning strangled in prison. Alas! Poor young Somervile.

But the matter did not end there, he had left a wife and a father-in-law, and the vindictive Dudley soon found occasion to make away with Edward Arden, who was attainted and executed about the year 1584.

I have always thought that this affair of "Poor Young Somervile" and the execution of Edward Arden, the chief of the family of our Poet's mother, may have been one of the causes that led Shakespeare to go away to London about the year 1584-85. Shakespeare certainly belonged to a family which had incurred the displeasure of the reigning favourite, Leicester, and although only a remote kinsman of Edward Arden, he would naturally feel much sympathy for his relatives at Park Hall, Erdington.

Enough has been said of the sad affair of Somervile of Edstone, let us now pay a visit to the place in which he lived. The present Edstone Hall is a modern looking structure occupying the site of the older mansion, but the grounds have probably been little altered. Here lived William Somervile, the poet, who wrote one of the most charming poems on rural subjects, "The Chase"—

> "The chase I sing, Hounds, and their various breed."

A poem practical and pleasant, now little read though famous. The author,

> "Near Avona's silver tide
> Whose waves in soft meanders glide,"

passed the greater portion of his life, and now lies buried in the chancel of the venerable church at Wootton

Wawen. The plain slab covering his grave records that his death took place on July 15th, 1742.

William Somervile, one of a now neglected group of minor poets, whose works are purer reading than many of their brethren of the nineteenth century, may some day, perhaps, be again in fashion. The squire of Edstone allowed hospitality to exceed the bounds of prudence, and his intimate friend, William Shenstone, said of him, " I love Mr Somervile because he knows so perfectly what belongs to the flocci - nauci - nihili-pilification of money."

PORCH, WOOTTON WAWEN CHURCH.

The present entrance to the grounds of Edstone Hall is about five miles from Stratford on the Birmingham road, between Bearley and Wootton Wawen. The house can be seen from the Great Western Railway line between Bearley and Claverdon stations, and its situation is one of much beauty amid park-like land, undulating and well-wooded.

We seem to breathe the particularly fresh and invigorating air of this pleasant place when reading the poems of its former owner, who loved the rural surroundings, and delighted in country life and field sports.

The sad story of his ancestor, now an almost forgotten incident in the annals of our country, affected the author of "The Chase" but little, yet in the days of Queen Elizabeth the tragic fate of the owner of Edstone Hall was discussed by people of every class far beyond the Warwickshire border. The fact of the family connection between the Somerviles and Shakespeare, and that the two families were near neighbours, is sufficient to justify the assumption that the great dramatist was acquainted with the victim of Elizabeth's religious persecution, and this assumption is strengthened by a passage in the third part of "King Henry VI." Act V. Scene i, where Sir John Somervile is represented as coming before the walls of Coventry as a partizan of Henry.

"*The Earl of Warwick.* Say Somervile, what says my loving son ?
                                        And by the guess, how nigh is Clarence now ?
      Somervile.   At Southam I did leave him with his forces,
                            And do expect him here some two hours hence."

In this scene Shakespeare shows knowledge of Warwickshire, and the district no less than of the local men of note, who were then strutting their brief hour upon the stage of history. Though at the period of the play there was probably no Sir John Somervile, that Christian name was evidently familiar to him in connection with the family of Somervile. The localities mentioned in the scene referred to are, Dunsmore, Daintry (Daventry), Southam and Warwick. These references clearly prove that the author knew the distances from Coventry to the four neighbouring towns, and is a local allusion of great significance.

CHAPTER XV

THE question has often been asked what part did Shakespeare play in that extraordinary business known by the familiar name of "The Gunpowder Plot." The answer has been uniformly a negative one, but those who have studied the life of Shakespeare most closely have always seen that the Poet must have been in some way affected by the plot. The part he played during the Essex rebellion is better known, but we may never know exactly how his sympathies would be affected. From the number of isolated facts, connected with his neighbours' affairs, it is possible by inductive methods to throw a good deal of light upon Shakespeare's feelings and conduct towards his friends.

It is perfectly certain, for instance, that William Shakespeare was acquainted with the owner of the largest house in the parish in which he was born, and since that person was closely related to Sir Walter Raleigh, one of the little company of wits who frequented the Mermaid tavern, it follows naturally that anything affecting either his friend or his neighbour must have interested him considerably.

In that grim fortress, the Tower of London, the Master of the Ordnance to King James I. had an official residence known as the Brick Tower: but his Majesty's officer seldom lived there. The Brick Tower was occupied by a state prisoner, Sir Walter Raleigh, whose act of gallantry won the heart of Queen Elizabeth, and whose fruitless endeavours to bring back gold from the New World exasperated James I.

In his prison Sir Walter held a little court of men of intellect and letters, a formidable rival to that at Whitehall. The uncrowned King was visited by some of the greatest and best people in England: Ben Jonson, Lord Bacon, Selden, Heriot, Hues, Prince Henry, and possibly Shakespeare, were among the company in those rooms.

Yet why should we thus associate the Brick Tower, in the Tower of London, with William Shakespeare of Stratford-on-Avon? The answer is a simple one, and the association closer than might be expected. The Master of the Ordnance at that time was George Carew, Earl of Totness, a Devonshire man, and cousin to Sir Walter. His Countess was Joyce Clopton, heiress of those Cloptons whose name will ever be associated with Stratford. Shakespeare lived in a house of their building in Stratford, and his heirs resold it to a member of the same family.[1]

The Earl of Totness and William Shakespeare were neighbours in the country, and must have been acquaintances in town. The wits who frequented the Brick Tower were Shakespeare's cronies, and although we have no record of the Poet having visited Sir Walter, there is every probability of his having done so.

After Shakespeare's retirement from the stage, about

---

[1] The Earl and Countess of Totness lie buried in the Clopton vault in Stratford Church: and their effigies in marble, adorned with gold and colours, lie stretched upon the altar tomb beneath a canopy of curious workmanship, within a few paces of Shakespeare's resting-place in the sanctuary.

the time he was settling in Stratford, the Gunpowder Plot was hatched, and in the hatching of it Clopton House came into prominence. The noble Earl of Totness was then in town; his country house was left in the charge of servants. One day there rode up to the door a little cavalcade, a gentleman and his retinue. The gentleman explained that he was a friend of the Earl's, and had received permission to stay at Clopton for a time during the hunting season. After some little parley the servants admitted the visitors, who at once proceeded to make themselves at home. The intruder was Mr Rokewood, a man of good family, and an acquaintance of the Earl of Totness. George Carew had won his spurs at Cadiz, with the Earl of Essex, and was well known to the bravest and the best in England, but it is very doubtful if his quondam friend Rokewood would have been admitted to Clopton had its owner been at home.

As Rokewood's application to be made free of Clopton was backed by John Grant of Northbrook, near Charlecote, and Mr Winter of Huddington, Robert Wilson, the Earl's bailiff, who knew nothing of the plot, was prevailed upon to admit the plotters. On the Sunday after Michaelmas day 1605, there was a great dinner given at Clopton, the Catholic gentry being sumptuously entertained there. One is tempted to speculate as to whether or not Shakespeare sat with his acquaintances and neighbours round the festive board at Clopton on that occasion. The conspirators soon afterwards appeared in London. Then came the famous 5th of November: Guy Fawkes was caught, and the conspirators again made their way into Warwickshire. Rokewood was the last to leave the town, and he was one of those who made a desperate stand at Holbeach at the end of the affair. The bailiff of Stratford was alarmed, and captured some of the conspirators in Snitterfield Bushes, and with them a bag containing "massing relics" from Clopton House. So ended this episode of the Gunpowder Plot, which will ever make Clopton one of the most famous of historic houses in the Midlands.

The exact position of Shakespeare with regard to the Essex rebellion will probably never be known, but it is significant that the Poet was undoubtedly under a cloud for a time. For instance, he was not appointed Laureate, an honour to which he may well have aspired, though others now unknown to fame were appointed.

The records are absolutely silent as to his name in the proceedings in the Gunpowder Plot, and we do not know which way his sympathies extended. He certainly was not active in the matter, a somewhat important fact when we consider that he was one of the leading men in Stratford. Holding, as he did, an appointment from the King, he would of course hold aloof from plots and conspirators, but he must have watched with keen interest the events which were happening in his immediate neigbourhood, and his sympathies may have been with the plotters though he took no part with them.

Lady Totness must have been known to him from his boyhood, and many a time must have seen him as he trod the paths leading to Clopton House. The house is considerably altered and modernised, but there are parts of it still standing old enough for Shakespeare to have looked upon. It was as familiar to him as the neighbouring house at Charlecote.

Bidford

CHAPTER XVI

THE SHAKESPEAREAN VILLAGES

"Piping Pebworth, dancing Marston,
Haunted Hillborough, hungry Grafton,
Dadgeing [1] Exhall, papist Wixford,
Beggarly Broom, and drunken Bidford."

IF all the traditions concerning William Shakespeare were collected they would fill the pages of a fair sized book. Most of these apocryphal stories, having some little foundation in fact that gives "to airy nothings a local habitation and a name," have at length become portions of the established faith of half the population of the Midlands; and *mirabile dictu* are taught in our schools, and repeated to American visitors by the street arabs of Stratford-on-Avon.

"Shall I tell you all about Shakespeare for a penny, Sir?" Should the stranger thus accosted desire to refresh his soul with learning; to take a deep draught from the Pierial Spring of the Bard's native place, he will be told in a strictly ecclesiastical monotone that

[1] A north-country form of "dodgeing," probably in its sense of slow, easy-going.

Shakespeare got drunk at Bidford! In justice to the youthful instructor of the travelled stranger, it must also be recorded that Portia's speech in the Venetian trial scene usually forms the per-oration of the young Stratford Gamaliel.

It is possible for one who has command of a good horse, or a bicycle, to visit the eight villages mentioned in the old rhyme in the course of a summer's day, though three counties must be entered. We cannot visit the places in the order in which they occur in the verse, but will depart from it as little as possible.

First, we may recount the legend as it has come down to our time. Nearly a century and a half after the Poet's death the story of his drinking bout first came into notice. A gentleman who visited Stratford in 1762, was told by the host of the White Lion Inn [1] that Shakespeare "loved a glass for the pleasure of society, and having heard much of the men of Bidford as deep drinkers, and merry fellows, went to that place to have a cup with them." On the way he asked a shepherd if the Bidford Drinkers were at home, and was told "they were absent, but that the Sippers were there, and would be sufficient for him." So indeed they were ;—he drank with them and was forced to take up his lodging for that night under a crab tree by the road-side. When he awoke he declared he would drink no more with—

> "Piping Pebworth, dancing Marston,
> Haunted Hillborough, hungry Grafton,
> Dadgeing Exhall, papist Wixford,
> Beggarly Broom, and drunken Bidford."

---

[1] The White Lion Inn appears to have been that in Henley Street. It was the best hotel in the town at the time of the Garrick Jubilee in 1769. There is a "White Lion" Hotel at Bidford now.

A crab tree, said to be the one under which the youth slept, became famous, and was called "Shakespeare's Canopy"; when cut down the wood thereof was fashioned into snuff-boxes, and other articles, for the curiosity collectors. There are genuine pieces of the tree belonging to the Trustees of Shakespeare's Birthplace, and at the Memorial Library.

The tradition is a very ancient one, repeated orally for many years before it appeared in print in 1762.

Mark how the legend grew. Malone obtained a tinkered version in 1790, and published it in 1821. The *Gentleman's Magazine* in 1794 published another variation, as did Ireland, in 1795, in his "Views on the Warwickshire Avon." Our friend, John Jordan, the poetic wheelwright, is answerable for the two latter variations of the story. Halliwell-Phillipps ("Outlines," vol. 2, page 327) states that "long after the time of Jordan, someone, without the least authority, asserted that the Sippers were discovered at the Falcon Inn, at Bidford." A room in a building once so called, though perhaps not a tavern at all in Shakespeare's time, has been indicated as the scene of the revelry. An old carved oak chair, now in Henley Street, is said to be the identical seat occupied by the Poet, and the inn sign, an eighteenth-century painting, is also to be seen at the Birthplace Museum.

All modern versions recount that upon awakening the Poet saw some men ploughing; asking why they were doing so on Sunday, he received the answer that it was Monday, not the Sabbath; thereby informing our hero that he had slept from Saturday night till Monday morning.

In 1857 Mr C. F. Green visited the district, made sketches at all the villages, and published a book on the legend.[1]   He mentions calling on a very old lady—one Mrs Ashwin of Bidford—who said that she knew the legend, and her informant could remember it "from the troublesome times of England, when the second Charles addressed his followers from the hostelrie of the Falcon previous to the disastrous battle of Worcester." This carries the tradition back to 1651. If the dates are examined it will be found that the story is not credible.

Mr Hurst of Bidford informed Mr Green in 1857 that the Falcon Inn was kept by one Norton in Shakespeare's time, and for a good number of years afterwards. In support of this statement he quoted the verses of Sir Aston Cokain, published in 1658, and addressed to Mr Clement Fisher, of Wincott.

> "Shakespeare your Wincot ale hath much renowned,
>   That fox'd a Beggar so (by chance was found
>   Sleeping) that there needed not many a word
>   To make him believe he was a lord.
>   But you affirm, and it seems most eaggar;
>   'Twill make a lord as drunk as any beggar.
>   Bid Norton brew such ale as Shakespeare fancies,
>   Did put Kit Sly into such lordly trances.
>   And let us meet there for a fit of gladness,
>   And drink ourselves merry in sober sadness." [2]

As for the rhyme of the villages it may be paralleled

[1] C. F. Green, "The Legend of Shakespeare's Crab Tree," 1857.
[2] There is some confusion in these verses. If Mr Sidney Lee is correct in supposing that this Clement Fisher lived at *Wilnecote*, near Tamworth, the poet, Aston Cokain, had mistaken that place for *Wincot*, near Quinton, adjoining Clifford Chambers. If Norton kept the Falcon Inn at Bidford, he would hardly have been living at *Wilnecote* on the Staffordshire border nearly half a century after Shakespeare's death. The probabilities are that Norton had no connection with Bidford except in the mind of some local gossip.

by one or two other local ditties, also credited to Shakespeare :—

"Silhill on the hill, Balsall in the hole,
Beggarly Barston and lousy Knowle."

another similar ditty runs as follows :—

"Sutton for mutton, Tamworth for beef,
Faseley a pretty girl, Brummagem thief."

another :—

"Dirty Gretton, dingy Greet,
Beggarly Winchcomb, Sudeley sweet,
Hartshorn and Wittington Bell,
Andoversford and Merry Frog Mill."

How these ditties originated we may never know, and indeed it does not very much matter that their origin is obscure. The Shakespeare legend accounting for one of them, it is now the fashion to discredit by assigning it to Jordan, the local poetaster, but if Mrs Ashwin's statement is in the main reliable the story and the verses are much older than Jordan's days. Considering the manners of the times there is nothing disgraceful in the part assigned by the legend to Shakespeare. It is exactly what any high-spirited youth might have done in his circumstances at that period.

DANCING MARSTON

It is now time we started on our journey. Crossing the river Avon by Clopton Bridge, we make for the Shipston road, and quickly arrive at the turn for Clifford Chambers and Chipping Campden. Here the road crosses the old disused tramway to Shipston-on-Stour, one of the earliest light railways in England, constructed by Stephenson. We then ascend a slight hill, and from the top obtain a fine view over the valley to Malvern, and presently descend to the stone bridge over the Stour, and continue almost straight on, up hill and down dale till Milcote station is passed. A turning to the right soon brings us to the first straggling houses of Long Marston, or Marston Sicca, as it is called in old documents, probably because there were few wells, or springs there.

Towards the southern end of the village, standing in an orchard on the north side of the church, and separated from it by a road, is one of those picturesque ecclesiastical buildings still to be found in this part of the country. It appears to have been a priest's house, but its history is somewhat obscure. The most interesting feature is a stone built gable with a Gothic window of good design.

In 1043 Marston was given by the Earl of Mercia to the Monks of Coventry, and it is said that one of the conditions then imposed was that a church should be built there. The place afterwards passed to the Monks of Winchcombe, and it is probably owing to their initiative that the present church was built. Part of the building dates from the fourteenth century, and there are later additions of some interest. The western tower, or belfry, of oak is a most peculiar feature; its age is rather difficult to discover, though it is said to have been made, and certainly underwent some reconstruction, in the seventeenth century, and a restoration about 1899.

To the south of the church stands a house, famous in history as one of the hiding places of Charles II. after the battle of Worcester in 1651. The King had found some hindrances in passing Stratford, but managed to cross the Avon by an old ford at a point a little below the mouth of the Stour, and seems to have gone directly to the house of Mr Tombs at Long

Marston. Charles being disguised as a serving man in attendance on Miss Lane, went into the kitchen, where the cook was preparing dinner. The fugitives appear to have been watched, and there were search parties scouring the country : one of these came into the kitchen while the King was there. His Majesty, being naturally alarmed, found some difficulty in winding up the meat-jack, and the cook, as the story goes, having her wits about her, seized the gravy spoon, and hitting " Jackson " across the back, bade him attend to his business. Charles pleaded that he was a poor servant of Mr Lane's in Staffordshire, and there they were not accustomed to have much roast meat.[1] This altercation allayed the soldiers' suspicions, and they departed, leaving the King to attend to the roast.

The house, which afforded an asylum to the fugitive King, is still owned by a descendant of the staunch old Royalist, Mr Tombs, and although the greater portion has been pulled down, or modernised, the kitchen, where his Sacred Majesty turned the jack, remains to this day, and is now used as the dining-room. The jack, a wonderful piece of mechanism of polished brass, reposes in a glass case upon the walls of the room, while over the window hangs a pike of the kind used by infantry during the civil wars, one of the few relics of the days of intestine warfare in the midland shires.[2]

Dancing Marston, once famous for its Morris Dancers, has not kept up its terpsichoric reputation, but some villages in the neighbourhood have carried on the tradi-

[1] The flight of Charles II. has formed the subject of an interesting book by Mr Allan Flea, wherein the story of the King's adventures is recounted.

[2] At Goodrest Farm, near Hales Owen, a house also associated with the flight of the King, a similar pike is preserved,

tion.   The old pastime of Morris Dancing has even now not quite died out, and there are still living many men, who in their youth joined a company of Morris Dancers hailing from Bidford, where a troupe is yet maintained.

Shakespeare mentions a game called "nine men's morris":—

> "The nine-men's morris is filled up with mud,
>   And the quaint mazes on the wanton green
> For lack of tread are undistinguishable."
>   "Midsummer-night's Dream," Act II. Scene ii.

But this game has no special connection with dancing: from the allusion in the play it appears to have been played by the country folk upon the village green.   It was also played upon a board with holes for movable pegs: and a species of the game was very popular with children in this district: at Wixford they appear to have indulged in the pastime while in church, and their scorings may still be seen on the window-sill of the Crew Chapel there.   Fortunately the "restorer" has not obliterated the marks made by the children.[1]

[1] *Nine Men's Morris*: the game was played during the fourteenth century, and was popular in the time of Queen Elizabeth.   It was played out of doors on a diagram marked on the ground, and also indoors on the tables of the village inns.   The following diagram represents the mazes on the green:—

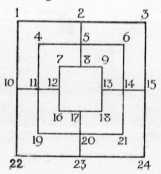

There is little more to attract a stranger in the village of Long Marston, though its scenery possesses a charm not easily described. The pleasant slope of Meon Hill, the luxuriant growth of trees, the quaint old cottages and homesteads, and the rural simplicity of the village constitute its chief attractions. It is a pretty country place, far removed from the turmoil of great cities : a place to dream in, or to spend a summer holiday when wearied with the constant rush of town life.

PIPING PEBWORTH

The road from Long Marston to Pebworth crosses a flat country to the foot of a little hill whereon the piping village stands. Pebworth, a small place with nothing particular to distinguish it, is in Gloucestershire, on the Worcestershire border.

The old stone church, dedicated to S. Peter, looks solitary and neglected. It is surrounded by tall trees, and the tower crowning a hill is a conspicuous object for some distance. In the grass-grown churchyard lies the stone effigy of a priest, probably of fourteenth century date. The old church still contains some interesting features.

Pebworth is so remote that it really needs some music to enliven the monotony of its existence. Alas ! its piping reputation is a thing of the past. The population appears to decrease, and we can quite imagine that in a few years the sleepy little place will have almost disappeared.

For the benefit of those whom it may interest it may be briefly stated that in the reign of Henry III. the manor of Pebworth was held by Roger de Quincey, Earl of Winchester : and that in the eighteenth century it passed into the family of Fortescue, and a portion which had belonged to the Abbey of Evesham, was owned by the family of Martin.

The hamlet of Broad Marston, or Marston Boys, formed the subject of a law-suit in the time of Henry III., Ernald de Boys being the plaintiff, and Anketin de Martin, and Agnes his wife, defendants.

The chief families commemorated by mural tablets in the church at Pebworth are those of Martin, Cooper, Howes, Eden, and Shekell : the last name is still represented in the village.

On the south side of the nave there is an aisle or chapel somewhat later in style than the other part of the church. In the will of Edmund Martin made in 1598, it was described as the " new aisle," and in the eastern end of the south wall there is a niche with a carved canopy, believed to be of post-Reformation date, and possibly made during the reign of Queen Mary. In the churchyard besides the effigy of the priest there are two lids of stone coffins of early date.

Drunken Bidford

A road from Pebworth leads westwards to the Littletons, and is crossed by the Roman Ichnield Street at about a mile from the village.   This Roman way runs northwards in almost a straight line to Bidford, where it crosses the Avon.   The old stone bridge was partly destroyed during the civil wars, but is still a picturesque object, notwithstanding its reparations.

The church on the further bank of the river, having been rebuilt, presents an uninteresting appearance, and were it not for its tower might be passed without notice.   This tower is ancient, the base slopes considerably, and the lower part resembles a fortress rather than a church tower.

We have now reached Warwickshire again, and are in the very heart of the legendary district. The fine old stone house, associated with the drinking bout, is coeval with Shakespeare, and is sufficiently interesting from an antiquarian point of view. One of the gables presents a curious example of timber work, and in all probability is older than the rest of the building. The many mullioned windows, and fine old chimneys, mark it as a place of importance in former days, and it once had a gallery projecting at the back, but this has now been destroyed.

Some men of Bidford still keep up their reputation for hard drinking. A few years ago the writer drove into Bidford on a pleasant autumn morning, when the "mop" was in full swing. It was pleasant to find that the good old custom of roasting an animal whole was then in progress, in front of the White Lion Hotel. That roast, with the attendant Bidfordians, was there and then photographed, by one of the party, and the picture is now included in the Photographic Survey of England at the British Museum. It may be said in passing that roast pig was found to be excellent fare, and much enjoyed by some of the hungry photographers. A little later in the day a party of jovial men of Bidford, sipping the fine October brew, was photographed.

The river here affords excellent boating, and Bidford is a good starting-point for an expedition to Evesham, or Tewkesbury.

Before leaving the village it will be best to go along the Stratford road for about three-quarters of a mile, to see the site of the celebrated crab tree, a scion of which grows by the road-side, near an iron gate. The old tree was cut down in 1824, but a drawing of it was made by Mr Green in 1823. It appears to have been

of unusual size, and of venerable antiquity,—at the time
of its demolition it was a weird and blasted trunk, fit
for the home of one of Macbeth's witches.

BEGGARLY BROOM

We still proceed northwards along the Ichnield Street,
crossing the railway line near Bidford Station, and take
the next turn to the left to Beggarly Broom, a poor
little village on the banks of the river Arrow. Its
tumbledown cottages with dilapidated thatch maintain
its beggarly reputation to this day. Few people linger
here, they usually return to the high-road again, and
soon reach Papist Wixford, which is less than a mile
distant.

PAPIST WIXFORD

For three centuries this village has maintained its
character as a seat of the old religion. Owing to the
influence of several powerful Catholic families, and a
succession of seminary priests, the doctrines of the
Reformation have failed to make much headway in
some villages of Warwickshire and Worcestershire.
At Alcester, Coughton, Chipping Campden, Broadway,
Wootton Wawen, and many other places the well cared
for Catholic churches denote a religious fervour conspicuously absent in other places.

The influence of the old Catholic family of
Throckmorton at Coughton Court has made itself felt
for generations past. In the time of Shakespeare the
Gunpowder Plot conspirators made their headquarters
in the houses of the Catholic families around Stratford.

These family mansions had hiding-places constructed
in the thickness of the walls, beneath the floors, or in

'Beggarly' Broom.

the spacious recesses of the chimneys, to enable priests, or recusants, to conceal themselves from pursuivants with search parties: unwelcome visitors who were wont to call when least expected or desired. Coughton Court has one of these " priests' holes " constructed in a turret of the great entrance. At Salford, a fine old mansion standing in the meadows beside the Avon, a cupboard in an upper room has a curiously contrived back swinging

'Papist'
Wixford

upon hinges, and thus forming the entrance to a "priests' hole." Across the river, at Cleeve, may be seen another hiding-place beneath the floor of one of the bed chambers.

In the reign of Elizabeth, when the penal laws against adherents to the Church of Rome made it a treasonable offence to practise their holy rites, these uncomfortable hiding-places were necessities to the Catholic community, and it was by similar means that religious observances were continued : the priests being able to secrete themselves whenever alarmed, and the congregation to disperse by various stairways or passages before the officers of the Crown could reach the chapel.

From a chapel in the roof at Compton Wynyates there are numerous staircases, and many old houses around Stratford have rooms in the roof, formerly used as chapels by the persecuted Catholics—in fact these persecutions, and the remembrances of them helped to fan the flame of religious ardour. Priests ready to risk life and liberty for religion's sake were never wanting, and as persecutions increased, faith in the proscribed religion advanced. The memory of those times still helps to strengthen faith among the simple-minded people of the Arden district.

The church at Wixford is small and picturesque : it stands beside a sunken road, supposed to be a military covered way of unknown antiquity, but perhaps connected with the Roman Ichnield Street. A mighty and venerable yew tree stretches its dark branches over a large part of the churchyard and shades the approach to the church, which is entered by a Norman doorway. There is a peculiar window here, cut out of a single stone. On the south side is a chantry chapel of the fifteenth century, containing a fine altar tomb to the founder and his wife. The tomb is covered by a large slab of Purbeck marble, in which is inserted a remarkably fine brass, representing Thomas de Crewe, and Julianna his wife. The former died about the year 1400. In the canopy and tabernacle work of the brass surrounding these figures, the arms of Crewe, and a very curious badge may well be noticed. The badge represents a human foot pierced, and in two instances is surrounded by what appears to be a crown of thorns. I have been unable to discover anything about this badge, which is repeated more than thirty times on the monument, but there is little doubt that it has a religious significance.

DADGEING EXHALL

A road to the north of Wixford leads to "Dadgeing" Exhall: why so called it is difficult to say, except possibly on account of the remote position of the village, making its people of slow and easy-going habits. It is a picturesque place with a fifteenth-century church, terribly "restored" in the nineteenth century. The name Exhall has a curious derivation, probably coming from the Anglo-Saxon "Eccleshalc," meaning the "Church-slope." Except the church there is not much to interest the antiquary in this village: it is little known, and has never been of much importance.

HUNGRY GRAFTON

From Exhall the road turns southward, and then to the north, before it reaches Temple Grafton, "Hungry Grafton" of the rhyme. Why so named is hard to determine, unless the poorness of the soil and its high and exposed position render it a hungry place, both for the farmer and his farm.

There are two Graftons hereabouts, Temple Grafton, or Grafton Superior, once a possession of the Knights Templar; and Grafton Inferior, also called Arden's Grafton, having been a possession of Simon de Arden of that brave old Arden stock to which Shakespeare's mother belonged.

Unfortunately the little church of Temple Grafton was destroyed in 1876. Grafton is one of the places where Shakespeare may have been married, but the evidence in its favour rests entirely upon the entry in the Episcopal Register at Worcester, under the date November 27th, 1582—a license for marriage

I

between " Wm. Shaxpere et Anna Whateley de Temple Grafton."

Haunted Hillborough

It is a far cry, some two miles along bye-roads from Grafton to "Haunted Hillborough," where the old Manor House, with its picturesque dove-cote, and interesting parlour, containing an ancient locker for bows and arrows, carries the mind back to the Tudor days, and is sufficiently quaint to warrant the legend of its being haunted. The poor ghost, however, has long been laid, and we may never know the strange history that led to the epithet being given to Hillborough. The Manor House lies but a short distance from the river.

We must now return into the Evesham Road, passing between the villages of Bidford and Welford. The eight villages have been visited, a roundabout journey of some thirty miles, and the labour involved has been amply compensated for by the quaintness and beauty of the places. In the course of the ride we have gone from the gravel beds of Stratford, and the rich alluvial plains beside the river, to the lias beds underlying Grafton, which give to these uplands their hungry character. It is interesting to notice the difference in the vegetation of these stony districts: for while in the valley near at hand all vegetation thrives and luxuriates, on the neighbouring slopes the trees seem to struggle for existence, and vegetation is sparse, the soil being too poor to suit the plants and trees that flourish near the river, and on the marls and gravel along its banks.

CHAPTER XVII

EVESHAM AND THE PLAYERS

AT the end of the sixteenth century it was no uncommon thing for a band of players under the patronage of a nobleman to go on tour, visiting the country towns in much the same way that travelling companies at the present day visit these places. The only difference being that now the companies travel by rail, and in those days the journeys were made by road. The company of which Shakespeare was a member was frequently on tour, as well as the smaller companies, such as that of Lord Chandos, to which Robert Armin belonged. Robert Armin's name occurs in the list of actors printed in the first folio edition of Shakespeare's plays, and he certainly belonged at one time to Shakespeare's company. In his curious book of anecdotes, entitled "A Nest of Ninnies," printed in London in 1608, Armin relates a story of one of the other actors, a poor half-witted fellow, Jack Miller by name, a native of Evesham. The story, though very slight, is especially interesting because it appears to have been known to Shakespeare, and the incident is referred to by him in "Troilus and Cressida":—

> "The fool slides o'er the ice that you should break."
>
> Act III. Scene iii.

And "hereby hangs a tale."

We will allow Robert Armin to tell his tale in his

own words, though we have somewhat modernised the spelling.

"In the town of Evesham, in Worcestershire, Jack Miller being there born, was much made of in every

Norman Gateway
Evesham

place. It happened that the Lord Shandoye's (Chandos) players came to town and played there; which Jack not a little loved, especially the clown, whom he would embrace with a joyful spirit, and call him Grumball, for so he called himself in gentlemen's houses, where he would imitate plays, doing all himself, king, gentleman, clown, and all : having spoke for one, he would suddenly go in, and again return for the other; and stammering as he did, make much mirth : to conclude, he was a right innocent, without any villany at all.

"When these players I speak of had done in the town, they went to Pershore, and Jack swore he would go all the world over with Grumball. It was then a great frost new begun, and the Avon was frozen over thinly; but here is the wonder, the gentleman that kept the Hart (an inn in the town), whose backside looked to the way that led to the river-side to Pershore, locked Jack up in a chamber next the Avon, where he might see the players pass by; and they of the town, loth to lose his company, desired to have it so; but he, I say, seeing them go by, creeps through the window, and said, 'I come to thee, Grumball.' The players stood all still to see further. He got down very dangerously, and makes no more ado, but ventures over the Avon, which is over the long bridge, as I guess, some forty yards over; yet he made nothing of it, but my heart ached when my ears heard the ice crack all the way. When he was come unto me I was amazed, and took up a brickbat (which lay there by) and threw it, which no sooner fell on the ice, but it burst. Was not this strange, that a fool of thirty years was borne on that ice which would not endure the fall of a brickbat? but every one rated him for the deed, telling him the danger. He considered his fault, and, knowing faults should be punished, he intreated Grumball, the clown, who he so dearly loved, to whip him, but with rose-mary, for that he thought would not smart. But the players in jest breecht him till the blood came, which he took laughing, for it was his manner ever to weep in kindness, and laugh in extremes. That this is true mine eyes were witnesses, being then by."

As a further illustration of the manners of the people in our country towns in the days of Elizabeth and James I., we may quote from a rare tract giving an account of a sensational murder which occurred in this very town of Evesham about the time of the visit of Lord Chandos' players. The tract is entitled:—

" A Brief Discourse of Two Most Cruell and Bloudie Murthers Committed Bothe in Worcestershire and Bothe Happening Unhappily in the Yeare 1583. The First Declaring how one Unnaturally Murdered his Neighbour and afterwards Buried him in his Sellar, etc.

.   .   .   .   .   .

"Imprinted at London by Roger Warde dwelling neare Holburne Conduit at the signe of the Talbot, 1583."

" A most cruell and bloody murder committed on New-Years eve last past, being the last day of December last past: being the last day of December 1583, in the town of Esam, in Worcestershire, by one Thomas Smith, a Town-dweller, upon his neighbour Robert Greenoll, who when he had cruelly murdered him made a grave in his Seller, and there buried him.

"In Esam, a handsome market-town in Worcestershire, well known, dwelled two young men, who by their usual trade were Mercers, as in ye country they call them so yt sell all kinds of wares: the one of them they called Robert Greenoll, a bachelor, and of such an honest conversation as he was not only well beloved in the Towne, where he dwelt, but also of those who had everie market day access thither for their needful necessaries, so yt was as well customed as any occupier in ye towne. The other was called Thomas Smith of indifferent welth likewise, and son to one of the most substantial men in ye towne, and joyned in marriage with a gentlewoman of very good parentage, so yt he likewise was well thought on of most and least. This Thomas Smith seeing Greenoll have so good utteraunce for his wares, and so well esteemed in such companie: if not upon this cause alone, though chiefly it bee accounted so, he began to envy the prosperous estate of him beeing his neighbour and friend, and the Devill so farre rulled the course of his envious intent as nothing wold suffise the desire thereof, but only making away of Greenoll by death, which though hee had no reason for, yet suche was the persuasion of the evill spirite with him. Manie platforms were laid, a thousand devises canvased over by this lewd man, which way he might work the death of his friendly neighbour: at last as the Devill wanteth no occasions to helpe man forward to his own destruction so he presented Smith with a fit opportunity, whereby he might execute ye sum of his bloody will, and as the repining at our neighbour's prosperity, is not onely monstrous, but a devilish nature, so this man compassed a monstrous and most devilish devise the verie conceite whereof is able to astonish the heart of a Jewe, or Mahomitans recreant, and thus it was as followeth.

"On new-yeares eve laste past, this Thomas Smith longinge and desiring the end of his unnaturall will, bearing the image of a friendlie countenaunce in the face but the very present shape of Judas' tretcherie in his heart, invited his neighbour Greenoll to his house where he promised to bestow a quart of wine and an apple, saying further, they woulde passe away the evening pleasantly in friendlie talke and drinking together, Greenoll beeing one desirous of eche man's friendship, and much the rather of his beeing his neighbour, and one of the same trade himself was: nothing mistrusting the villanous treason hyd under so smooth a show of neighberhood, gave him thanks and promising to come to him at night, and not to faile him. This pleased well the bloud-thirsting man, so that home hee went to determine the Instrument to do the deed withall, and then downe into his seller he goes to dispose a place wherein he might convey the bodie when he had slayne him: there he digged a grave.

    .   .   .   .   .   .

"It drew towards night, when as a play was cryed about the towne, whereto both old and young did hastely repair: and this Smith having a boye that served him in his shop, fearing leaste the boye should perceive anie thing, gave him money and bad him goe see the play: and bring him the whole report of the matter.

"This he did in the presence of Greenoll who was come according to his promise to keepe him companie, and the boye having fetched a quarte of wine and apples as his maister willed him, ran merily to see the play, leaving Greenoll and his maister by the fire pleasauntly talking.

"They twoo thus sitting alone did drinke to eche other verie familiarly, tyll at last Greenoll stouping to turne an apple in the fire, a fit time that Smith espied to accomplish his will; who taking an yron pestell wherewith hee used to beate his spice in the morters and which he had laid by him ready for the nonce, with this pestell (as Greenoll stouped to turne the apple) he gave him two such mightie blows on the head as hee fell down backward to the ground, yeelding forth a verie pittiful and lamentable groane," . . .

Smith hit him again several times, and then cut his throat.

The tract further relates that Smith stabbed his

victim with a knife and took the body to the cellar, where he buried it in a ready-prepared grave. "He smoothed it over so finely with a Trowell that plasterers use, so that it could be hardly discerned, and because he would worke the surer hee took Bayles of Flax which laye in his seller, and so shaked the shellings thereof over ye floore in all places, as no one could saye (but he that knew it) where the grave was."

.   .   .   .   .   .

It happened that at the town of Evesham all through Christmas time watch and ward was kept that no misorder or ill rule might be committed. One of the watchmen discovered that Greenoll's house had been entered, and wanted to examine Smith's premises, but Smith answered that he could not do this as his wife was away at K.N. (? King's Norton) and had taken the key with her. At last the crime was discovered, and Smith was tried at the assizes. He was condemned, but owing to the intercession of his wealthy friends, was hanged and buried, instead of being hanged in chains.

Now although we cannot positively state that the players who arrived in Evesham on New Year's Eve were the Lord Chandos' company, it is by no means improbable that they were. The time of year mentioned pretty well accords with "the great frost new begun" in Armin's tract, and from an independent source we have records of the great frost in Elizabeth's reign. The mention of the Lord Chandos' players perhaps requires some explanation. In 1571 (14 Elizabeth, Cap. 2) players were under the necessity of procuring a license from a Peer of the Realm, or some personage of high degree, otherwise they were liable to be judged as rogues and vagabonds. Consequently there were many companies under noble patronage travelling about the country, and although little is known of the Chandos troup, it is certain that Armin subsequently joined another well-known company. Both the Earl of Warwick and the Earl of Leicester were patrons of dramatic companies, and so it seems was Sir Thomas

Pershore Bridge

Lucy, for Puritan though he was, the Knight of Charlecote bestowed his patronage upon a band of play-actors, and it is of course possible that Shakespeare himself was, in his youth, one of Sir Thomas Lucy's company: but we must be careful to add that so far no proof of this has been found. The players who came to Stratford in 1580 were the Earl of Derby's, and the first payment recorded as made to players in Stratford was the sum of nine shillings paid to the Queen's players by John Shakespeare, the Poet's father.

Robert Armin and Jack Miller were the Poet's contem-

poraries.   It is probable that either from a perusal of " A
Nest of Ninnies," or by word of mouth from the author
of that amusing book, or one of his friends the actors,
Shakespeare was acquainted with Jack Miller's exploit on
the ice at Evesham ; but as the date of the tract is 1608,
and " Troilus and Cressida " was written about the year
1603, it seems most likely that Shakespeare derived the
story orally, unless, of course, the book was in manuscript five or six years before the date of its publication ;
but, in 1584, Shakespeare was living in the country,
fifteen miles away from the town of Evesham, and in
those days, just as at present, people were constantly
passing to and fro beween the two neighbouring towns
on the Avon's bank.   An event such as that here described
would very soon be known in Stratford, especially as the
players would probably pass from Stratford to Evesham
and then on to Pershore.

CHAPTER XVIII

PERSONAL relics of great men are always sought for by their admirers; when it is impossible to discover genuine relics, spurious ones in course of time are invested with a virtue to which they have no claim. Although there are many objects said to have belonged to Shakespeare, very few of these can be proved to have been his. The only things undoubtedly once in his possession are three MSS.—first, a deed of transfer of a property in Black-friars; second, a deed of mortgage of the same property, the former in the Guildhall Museum, London, the latter in the British Museum; third, his will with its three signatures. This will is preserved at the Probate Registry at Somerset House. London holds these three treasures with their five genuine signatures.

Other relics:—

1. A gold signet ring at the Birthplace Museum in Henley Street. The ring has an engraved beryl with the letters "W.S.," and a true-lover's-knot. It was found in a field at Stratford, and bought by the late Robert Bell Wheler, and presented by Miss Wheler to the Birthplace.

2. Shakespeare's sword. This is a short sword with a metal basket or shell. It was shown by Mrs Hornby in the early years of the nineteenth century, and said to be the weapon which he used when playing Hamlet.

It was sold at the sale at Christy's in 1896 for £5, 10s.[1]

3. Shakespeare's stirrups. These are of brass, and very curious; they also are at the Birthplace Museum.

4. His clock. Now in Aston Hall, Birmingham.

5. A tobacco box, with a burning-glass in the lid. This was taken by Mrs Hornby's son when he left home, and has since been lost sight of.

6. A Spanish cardbox, decorated with the arms of the King of Spain, and reported by Mrs Hornby to have been a present to Shakespeare. The box was sold at the sale at Christy's for three guineas.

7. Shakespeare's nutcrackers. These are of brass, quaint and curious objects formerly in the possession of the Burman family, who have been settled in Stratford from the fifteenth century. The nutcrackers were bequeathed to the Shakespeare Memorial by the late Dr Burman of Bishopton, and are exhibited in the Library.

8. Shakespeare's brooch. A small, heart-shaped, silver brooch with old paste adornments, and the name of Shakespeare engraved on the back. This was found in excavating at New Place, and is the property of Mr Rayborne of Birmingham.

9. Shakespeare's deed-box. A small, ancient coffer exhibited at the Birthplace.

10. Shakespeare's jug. A curious bulky jug of green glass, also in Henley Street.

11. Another jug. This is of white salt glaze with raised figures, at present exhibited in Henley Street.

12. A malacca walking cane. Formerly belonging to a member of the Hart family, and now at the Birthplace.

---

[1] At the Birthplace another sword, said to have been Shakespeare's, is shown in the Museum.

13. Shakespeare's desk.   An old school desk of mediæval pattern formerly stood near the north-west corner of the big schoolroom of Stratford-on-Avon Grammar School.   A tradition passed down from one generation to another of schoolboys, from time immemorial, has associated William Shakespeare's name with this piece of scholastic furniture.   Another tradition states that Shakespeare was for a time an usher, or under master, at the school; if correct, this may explain the association of the Poet's name with the desk, which many years ago was presented to the Trustees of the Birthplace, and is now treasured in the Museum.

14. Shakespeare's gloves.   These are now in the possession of Howard H. Furness, Esq., the well-known American Shakespearean scholar, whose labours in producing the new Variorum edition of Shakespeare's works deserve the fullest recognition from every student of English literature.   These gloves were given to David Garrick by the Corporation of Stratford-on-Avon at the Jubilee celebration in 1769.   That the gloves were believed to be genuine at the time they were presented to Garrick there can be no doubt, and also there is no doubt about their age.   Perhaps some day we may have the history of these curious gauntlets fully told, but at present it is necessary to accept the statement that they belonged to Shakespeare without actual proof being given.   Some genuine relics of this great man there must be; we would like to think that the gloves are among the number.

15. The chairs.   Four chairs are associated with Shakespeare's name.   The first was exhibited in the Birthplace until 1790, when it was sold by the last member of the Hart family resident in the Birthplace to the Princess Czartoryska, who carried it to Poland,

where it still remains as a greatly prized treasure. The second chair was removed from Bidford to Shakespeare's Birthplace, where it still remains. It is of oak, and has a well-carved back. According to tradition, it is the chair in which Shakespeare sat during his contest with the Bidford Sippers at the Falcon Inn at that place. The third chair is also of oak, and somewhat more curious than the two already mentioned. From a drawing preserved in the Shakespeare Memorial Library we are able to give the following details written at the side of the drawing by the late owner of the chair, which is now in the possession of Alfred Godwin, Esq., M.A., F.S.A.[1] The fourth chair is at present owned by Mr Manton of Birmingham, a descendant of one of the branches of the Shakespeare family formerly living near Wootton Wawen. Accord-

---

[1] COPY OF A RECORD ON THE BACK OF THE CHAIR.

" It is traditionally believed that Shakespeare sat in this Chair when he wrote most of his Plays.

" It came into the possession of Paul Whitehead, and of him Garrick wanted to borrow it for use at the ' Jubilee ' ; but he was indignantly refused the loan, and termed a ' Mountebank,' etc. At Whitehead's death it was bought by Mr B. Bradbury, and by him given to John Bacon (of Fryern House, Fryern Barnet), whose son presented the Chair to the Rev. T. J. Judkin, M.A., about the year 1834.

" It was afterwards presented by Mr Judkin's widow to her son-in-law, the Rev. Walter Field, Nov. 13th, 1871."

ADDITIONAL MEMORANDA BY J. DRAYTON WYATT.

After the death of the Rev. Walter Field, this Chair was sold by auction (with his Library) by Messrs Sotheby, Wilkinson & Hodge, at their Auction Rooms in London, March 1st, 1877, when it was purchased by George Godwin, Esq., F.R.S., F.S.A., &c., in whose possession it now (1884) is.

[The pattern on the back of the Chair is in *incised lines* only in a slightly sunk panel.]

ing to family tradition, it was given to an ancestor of the present owner by Gilbert Shakespeare, the Poet's brother.

16. A mulberry tree growing in New Place Garden until 1758, when it was cut down by the Rev. F. Gastrell, is said to have been planted by Shakespeare, probably in 1609. From this tree chairs, tables, and a great number of small articles, such as boxes and tobacco stoppers, were made by Mr Sharp and another resident in Stratford. One of the chairs was recently (1903) sold for £145. A descendant of the original tree is now growing in the garden.

CHAPTER XIX

PORTRAITS of Shakespeare are almost as numerous as the editions of his works, but it is not an exaggeration to state that of the hundreds of different likenesses of the Poet, all may be traced to some half-dozen genuine originals.

In "The Return from Parnassus," *Gullio*, one of the characters, remarks :—

"O sweet Mr Shakespeare! I'le have his picture in my study at the courte" (Act III. Scene i., page 58, edition 1886).

In the golden age of Elizabeth, as in the diamond period of Victoria, popular poets sat for their portraits to be painted at not infrequent intervals. The passage just quoted from a contemporary drama points both to the popularity of Shakespeare during his lifetime, and to the fact that the counterfeit presentment of the fashionable poet, playwright, and actor was a possession coveted by his admirers. In his day Shakespeare as an actor was as well known in London as Sir Henry Irving was in the reign of Victoria. Why, then, should we doubt that there are faithful likenesses of him still to be found?

The six most authentic portraits agree in representing him as a man of well-proportioned features : broad brow, high forehead, straight nose, large, expressive eyes, and

K

finely cut lips: the lower part of the face oval; in short as having a particularly well-developed head.

I. THE STRATFORD BUST

"Shake-speare, at length thy pious fellows give
The world thy workes: thy workes by which outlive
Thy Tombe, thy name must when that stone is rent
And Time dissolves thy *Stratford* Monument."

L. DIGGES.[1]

The *Monumental Bust* in Holy Trinity Church at Stratford-on-Avon stands first as an authentic portrait of Shakespeare. It is known to have been placed in the church soon after the Poet's death, and during the lifetime of his widow and daughters. It is referred to by Leonard Digges in the lines above mentioned, and is engraved in the first edition of Dugdale's "Antiquities of Warwickshire," 1656. Though conventional in treatment, and poor in execution, it possesses many points of resemblance to the other contemporary portraits: while its chief divergence may be remarked in the shortness of the nose, which is obviously due to an error, or misfortune on the part of the sculptor.

It is generally believed that the sculptor worked from a mask taken after death, because he has represented the mouth as half open with the jaw falling. This belief is strengthened upon close examination. The muscular development of the face appears to have been carefully rendered, and there are many indications that the work was actually done from a model taken from

[1] Lines prefixed to the First Folio of Shakespeare's Plays. 1623.

the face itself. The hair is treated in a conventional way.

The bust was painted to resemble nature, but, after several repaintings, alas! that resemblance has been entirely lost. A good photograph, however, gets rid of the crude colouring, and represents it in a more satisfactory manner. The facial line is perpendicular, and the forehead does not begin to recede until the top of the brow is reached; it then curves backwards in a regular and symmetrical dome. It is evident that as the Poet grew older he became bald from the brow to the crown of the head, a peculiarity that has led many later artists to picture him with an abnormally high forehead.

In 1748 the monument was repainted at the instance of an ancestor of Sarah Siddons, the expense of the work being defrayed out of the profits of a representation of " Othello " played by a company of strolling actors at Stratford-on-Avon. Fifty years afterwards Malone had it pickled and painted white. In the middle of the nineteenth century an artist named Collins cleaned the bust, and finding traces of the colouring as renewed in 1748, repainted it to suit his own fancy. Mr Collins is believed to be chiefly responsible for the brown colour of the eyes, as well as the crude colouring of the face.

Sir William Dugdale in his diary records that Gerard Johnson, a stone carver and monument maker of Dutch origin, made the bust and monument of Shakespeare. The Johnsons had business premises in Southwark, near Shakespeare's Theatre, and also made the monument of John a-Combe, in the sanctuary of Stratford-upon-Avon Church.

II. The Droeshout Engraving in the First Folio

" The figure that thou here seest put,
It was for gentle Shakespeare cut."

There can be no doubt as to the truth of this assertion. Any one who will compare the engraving in the folio with a photograph of the church bust must arrive at the conclusion that the sculptor and the engraver endeavoured to represent the same features, since the same characteristics are noticeable in both bust and engraving. The history of this likeness of Shakespeare is as follows:—

It was engraved by Martin Droeshout, a member of a Dutch family residing in London. At the time of Shakespeare's death Martin was but a youth, and he is known to have been about twenty-one years of age when the first folio was published; it is therefore highly improbable that he engraved directly from the life, indeed to do so would have been contrary to the usual practice of engravers. We must admit that the likeness is a copy from some earlier drawing or picture: probably that picture is extant.

The little company formed for the purpose of publishing Shakespeare's plays in collective form included some of his best friends, admirers, and fellows: it is therefore unlikely that they would have permitted an unauthenticated picture of the author to be prefixed to his works. Yet Ben Jonson, at least, appreciated the attempt of the young artist at its just value, and admitted that though the portrait was cut for gentle Shakespeare, the artist had striven to *outdo* the life. Though poor as a work of art, the portrait has at least the merit of being a likeness of the man it represents.   Crude, conventional, and harsh it may be, still it represents Shakespeare.

The engraving is known to us in two states.   First, the proof, formerly in the possession of Halliwell-Phillipps: the chief difference from all other copies being the omission of the shadow on the collar to the left of the face, that is to the spectator's right.   In all other known copies the shadow appears.   On the verso of the leaf immediately preceding the title-page of the first edition we have the verses signed "B. I.," universally accepted as Ben Jonson's.

> " This figure, that thou here seest put,
>   It was for gentle Shakespeare cut ;
>   Wherein the Graver had a strife
>   With nature to outdo the life :
>   O, could he but have drawn his wit
>   As well in brass, as he has hit
>   His face ; the print would then surpass
>   All, that was ever writ in brass.
>   But since he cannot, Reader, look
>   Not on his picture, but his book."

The same engraving was used in the second folio of 1632, and again in the third folio, 1664, though in this case the engraving does not appear on the title-page, but is placed above the verses on the preceding page.   It was used for the fourth and last time in the folio of 1685.

III. The Droeshout Original Portrait

Though the ancient portrait at the Shakespeare Memorial Gallery, Stratford-on-Avon, is now generally accepted to be the original of Martin Droeshout's engraving, we place it third on the list because, until lately, it was not so well known as the engraving. The history of the picture is briefly as follows :—

In the eighteenth century the portrait belonged to a member of the Hart family, and was exhibited in London. It next passed to another owner who sold it to Mr Clements of Sydenham, in whose possession it remained for nearly forty years, and by whom it was exhibited at the Alexandra Palace, where a fire occurred and the portrait narrowly escaped destruction. Being afterwards sent to Stratford-on-Avon, it remained at the Shakespeare Memorial until after the death of Mr Clements, when it was purchased from his family by Mrs Flower of Avonbank, and presented to the Shakespeare Memorial Association.

The portrait is painted upon a panel of elm wood, composed of two pieces, with transverse braces ; and the whole panel is covered with a coating of white, upon the top of which a light red pigment is spread. The face is solidly, but the rest of the picture rather thinly painted, and the detail is much finer than that of the engraving, though the resemblance between the two is obvious to the most casual observer.

A closer inspection leads to the conviction that this portrait is the original from which Martin Droeshout copied when making his engraving for the folio of 1623. The chief points to bear in mind are :—

1. That the picture is unmistakably an unrestored work dating from the early years of the seventeenth century.

2. That in the upper left-hand corner it bears the name " Willm. Shakespeare," in characters of early seventeenth-century date, and written in the same pigment as used for the lace and other adornments of the dress.

3. That below the name appears the date 1609.

4. That the head is quite life-size, while the body, being in perspective, is smaller in proportion.

5. That it is the only painting with contemporary evidence of being a portrait of Shakespeare.

Though darkened by age and of severe aspect, the face is represented as a faithful likeness, not flattering, but with most of its marked characteristics accentuated. The colour of the eyes is a dark grey, shaded with brown, corresponding with the Ely Palace portrait. The hair is arranged exactly as in the Droeshout engraving and the Ely Palace portrait, representing Shakespeare as bald from the forehead to the crown of the head. The moustache is upturned, and a small tuft of hair is visible upon the chin. The mouth is full and humorous in expression. When considered in comparison with the engraving, which it nearly resembles, Ben Jonson's lines, and the signature at the top of the portrait, we are led to the conclusion that this is a portrait of Shakespeare, painted from life. The evidence in its favour is conclusive, and it must therefore be regarded as the most interesting extant likeness of the Poet.

IV. ELY PALACE PORTRAIT

This ancient and remarkable portrait, undoubtedly a likeness of Shakespeare, probably contemporary, was given by Mr Henry Graves to the Trustees of Shakespeare's Birthplace. It so nearly resembles the Droeshout engraving that until the picture now in the Memorial Gallery was discovered, it was thought it might be the original of that famous print. Upon the background of the portrait appears the following inscription: " **AE.**

39 X 1603." This gives the age of the Poet in that year. The history of the picture as told by Mr Graves, who took considerable trouble to verify the several points, is as follows:—It belonged to a family long resident in Little Britain, a district of London, where Shakespeare is said to have visited them, and to have given his friends this portrait. At the death of the last member of the family the picture was sold, and passed into the hands of Thomas Turton, Bishop of Ely, from whom it derives its name. At the sale of the Bishop's furniture it was bought by Mr Henry Graves, who, recognising its supreme interest, gave it to the Trustees of Shakespeare's Birthplace at Stratford-on-Avon.

Like the Droeshout Original, the painting is on a panel. At some period of its history it was overcleaned, but not so badly as to destroy the likeness. Being smaller than the other ancient portraits of the Poet, the resemblance to the engraving is more marked.

V. Chandos Portrait

Of all the likenesses this has the longest pedigree, and has excited the keenest interest. It is perhaps the most unsatisfactory of all the old portraits of the Poet, representing him with a pursed-up mouth, a very full under lip, a decidedly Jewish cast of countenance, and wearing gold rings in his ears. It is stated to have been painted either by Richard Burbage, the actor, or John Taylor, and is said to have belonged first to Joseph Taylor, an actor and contemporary of Shakespeare, and to have afterwards passed into the hands of Sir William d'Avenant, then to Betterton's, next to Mrs Barry's. It is known to have been in the possession of Robert Keck, a barrister, and subsequently of Mr Nichol, whose daughter married James Bridges, third Duke of Chandos, from whom it took its name. At Stowe, in 1848, it was sold by the second Duke of Buckingham and Chandos to the Earl of Ellesmere, who gave it to the Nation.

The early portion of the pedigree being of doubtful authenticity, and the likeness itself possessing few points of resemblance to the undoubtedly genuine portraits of the Poet, it is considered to be an ideal likeness though not a life portrait, unless, indeed, Shakespeare is here represented in character. Yet it has been more often copied and engraved than any other portrait of Shakespeare, and being in the National Portrait Gallery, is the one most familiar to the British public.

VI. The Jansen Portrait

The Jansen portrait is best known from the print by Earlom, and another, both beautifully engraved, but flattering to the original. The picture is inscribed "AET. 46. 1610." It is at present the property of Lady Ramsden of Bulstrode Park, near Reading; and it formerly belonged to the famous Mr Jennens, who published an engraving of it as a frontispiece to an edition of Shakespeare which he commenced but never completed. The picture undoubtedly represents Shakespeare, and is worthy of more careful study than it has yet received. Little appears to be known about its early history, and the facts concerning its ownership after the death of Mr Jennens appear to be not definitely known, though there is little doubt that it is the picture that belonged to that eccentric student of Shakespeare. The Poet is represented with a pointed beard, and as a decidedly handsome man of courtly appearance. Numerous copies of the portrait have been made.

VII. THE STRATFORD PORTRAIT

In 1860 an artist named Collins visited Stratford, and finding an old portrait in a house in Church Street, at the corner of Scholars Lane, occupied by Mr Thomas Hunt, the Town Clerk, obtained permission to clean it. The old picture had belonged to the Cloptons, and, as no one thought much about it, or knew whose portrait it was, it had been used by the children of the family as a target. Mr Collins proceeded to restore it, and behold it became a portrait of Shakespeare! Photography reveals the fact that the full-bottomed wig of a gentleman of the eighteenth century is still beneath the paint which Mr Collins superimposed. The picture is clearly a copy of the bust in the church. Whether made by Mr Collins or at an earlier period, it is now difficult to say. At the time of the discovery its owner believed it to be an originial portrait of Shakespeare, and as such most generously gave it to the Trustees of Shakespeare's Birthplace. It is still preserved in the room at the back of the Birthroom, and for many years has attracted considerable attention.

MINIATURES

Besides these larger portraits of Shakespeare there are one or two ancient miniatures bearing his name, and evidently intended to represent him. It is not at all improbable that these are genuine likenesses, although there are other miniatures, also ancient, that certainly do not represent the Poet.

VIII. The Death Mask

In 1849 Dr Becker found at Mayenne, in Germany, a death mask representing a person with a finely proportioned head and features. Upon the death mask the year of Shakespeare's death, 1616, is inscribed; this led Dr Becker to believe that he had found the long-lost mask taken from Shakespeare's face, and used for the production of the monumental effigy in the church. The mask was brought to England, and to Stratford, causing great excitement in Shakespearean circles. Many of the measurements of the mask were found to correspond with those of the church bust, but the supporters of the theory apparently lost sight of the fact that the features and the contours of the face are unlike most of the other best authenticated portraits. The nose is aquiline, the chin slightly receding, and the forehead recedes immediately above the eyebrows. This last peculiarity condemns the mask at once: for while it is possible for the features to be slightly altered by the pressure necessary in taking a wax cast, it is obvious that no alteration is possible in the forehead. The church monument, the Droeshout engraving, the Droeshout original, the Ely Palace, and the Jansen portraits, all agree in this particular; that is, in making the forehead of the Poet wellnigh straight before it begins to dome towards the top of the head. The mask went back to Germany, and is probably there still; it was offered to the Trustees of the British Museum for £10,000, but no one seemed inclined to buy it at the owner's valuation.

IX. THE D'AVENANT BUST

A finely executed ideal portrait of the Poet, but not contemporary, adorns the hall at the entrance of the Garrick Club in London. It is of red terra-cotta, with a black surface. The bust was found during the demolition of the old Duke's Theatre in Lincoln's Inn Fields. Sir William d'Avenant, Shakespeare's godson, caused this theatre to be built in the reign of Charles II. After a chequered history it was at last closed, and subsequently used as a china warehouse by Spode & Copeland, the potters; finally being pulled down to make room for the Museum of the College of Surgeons. The bust became the property of Professor, afterwards Sir William Owen, who sold it for £300 to the Duke of Devonshire, by whom it was presented to the Garrick Club. The Duke had three copies made; one is now at the Crystal Palace, the whereabouts of the other is not known to the writer, though possibly it may be at Chatsworth, the third was probably given to Sir William Owen; at all events the Professor for many years had a copy standing in his garden at Richmond. At his death it was given by his son to the Shakespeare Memorial at Stratford-on-Avon. The so-called D'Avenant bust, though a fine work of art, is not a contemporary likeness. The features appear to have been copied from the Chandos portrait: the nose and the protruding mouth especially favour this idea. The dress, particularly the collar, is of the Cavalier period, and absolutely prove the late date of the bust.

CHAPTER XX

Two hundred years after the birth of Shakespeare, and about one hundred and fifty after his death, the desire arose in the hearts of the Poet's admirers to hold meetings in his honour in his native town. Considering the times, it is somewhat wonderful that a Poet should have been honoured with a national celebration within a comparatively short period after his death. The cult was of slow growth, but, like the oak and all other mighty things, this lagging indicates strength.

The people of Stratford, at least the more enlightened ones, were by no means blind to the merits of their great townsman whose praises were recorded in the ponderous pages of the Warwickshire antiquary, Sir William Dugdale. Their town hall had been rebuilt about the year 1768, and at that time the leading burgesses appear to have thought it incumbent upon them to do honour to David Garrick, the chief actor of the day. The freedom of the borough was accordingly presented to him in a very handsome manner, and for the adornment of the new hall, a request was made that he would give his portrait.

Garrick accepted the freedom, and graciously acquiesced with the wishes of the Corporation by presenting the town with his likeness, Gainsborough's masterpiece. This wonderful picture still adorns the town hall: as

does also another of Garrick's gifts, Roubillac's sta
of Shakespeare.

Garrick was no common genius, he above all oth
in the eighteenth century best interpreted Shakespe
and gladly embraced the opportunity to do someth
in the Poet's honour at the town of his nativity.
accordingly arranged a Jubilee, which took place in the
autumn of 1769.

A large wooden pavilion, built in the Bankcroft, a
piece of public land on the banks of the Avon, immediately adjoining the grounds of the present theatre,
formed the arena for the Jubilee, which lasted from
September 6th to the 8th. The programme was as
follows :—

On the first day, September 6th, the town was
awakened at five o'clock by the firing of cannon; and
soon after a band of masqueraders serenaded the
principal ladies.

> " Let beauty with the sun arise,
>   To Shakespeare homage pay " —

were the opening lines of one of the many songs written
for the occasion.

At eight o'clock the Corporation assembled, and a
public breakfast was partaken of at nine. Garrick, as
Steward of the Jubilee, had been presented with a
medal, specially struck, and a wand made from the
famous mulberry tree. At half-past ten a procession
was formed and proceeded to the church, where
the oratorio, "Judith," composed by Dr Arne, was
rendered by a choir led by the Drury Lane orchestra.
Leaving the church the procession reformed, led by
the steward, and followed by a large gathering of
gentry, who rode in coaches, chaises, etc. : it must

have been an imposing spectacle as it paraded the streets. A public ordinary was held at three, and illuminations and fireworks (brought by road from London) terminated the proceedings on the opening day.

Next morning the firing of cannon again aroused the populace, bells were rung, and serenading followed. Another public breakfast was held in the town hall, in like manner as on the previous day: and at eleven o'clock the company assembled in the pavilion to hear the "Dedication Ode" performed. This cantata, the words written by Garrick, and the musical portion composed by Dr Arne, went off without a hitch. Garrick, dressed in a brown suit with gold trimmings, recited the recitative parts himself. At the conclusion a comic element was introduced by a comedian named King, who, in reply to a challenge by Garrick, stood up and attacked Shakespeare for "domineering over our own passions, and making us laugh and cry as *he* thought proper." A public dinner at three, and songs at five o'clock cleared the way for the *pièce de résistance*, a grand masquerade in the newly built town hall, where a thousand people are said to have been present, many of the Poet's creations being represented by the masqueraders.

It was most unfortunate weather for the Jubilee: rain falling continuously on the second and third days prevented a procession of Shakespeare's characters taking place; many of the visitors therefore left the town. A horse-race for the "Jubilee Cup" was held on September 8th, on the pleasant course near Shottery, which is still used for a like purpose. That evening the rejoicings terminated with a ball at the town hall, where Mrs Garrick danced a minuet most admirably. At four o'clock next morning the distinguished assembly broke up, and the Jubilee, which will ever be memorable in the history of Stratford-on-Avon, was over.

Boswell and Dr Arne were among the distinguished guests at the Jubilee. The songs and music written for the occasion have now become classics. "The Warwickshire Lads and Lasses," written by Garrick, and set to music by Dr Arne, is familiar to most people; the tune is still a favourite in the county, and may be heard whenever the local volunteers assemble, or the Corporations of Warwickshire towns appear in state. The words, however, are not so well known, and will bear repeating.

WARWICKSHIRE—A SONG

By Mr Garrick

"Ye Warwickshire lads, and ye lasses,
    See what at our jubilee passes;
Come revel away, rejoice, and be glad,
For the lad of all lads, was a Warwickshire lad,
        Warwickshire lad,
        All be glad,
For the lad of all lads, was a Warwickshire lad.

"Be proud of the charms of your county,
    Where Nature has lavished her bounty,
Where much she has given, and some to be spared,
For the bard of all bards, was a Warwickshire bard,
        Warwickshire bard,
        Never paired,
For the bard of all bards, was a Warwickshire bard.

"Each shire has its different pleasures,
    Each shire has its different treasures;
But to rare Warwickshire, all must submit,
For the wit of all wits, was a Warwickshire wit,
        Warwickshire wit,
        How he writ!
For the wit of all wits, was a Warwickshire wit.

"Old Ben, Thomas Otway, John Dryden,
  And half a score more we take pride in,
Of famous Will Congreve, we boast too the skill,
But the Will of all Wills, was a Warwickshire Will,
        Warwickshire Will,
          Matchless still,
For the Will of all Wills, was a Warwickshire Will.

"Our Shakespeare compared to is no man,
  Nor Frenchman, nor Grecian, nor Roman ;
Their swans are all geese, to the Avon's sweet swan,
And the man of all men, was a Warwickshire man,
        Warwickshire man,
          Avon's swan,
And the man of all men, was a Warwickshire man.

"As ven'son is very inviting,
  To steal it our bard took delight in ;
To make his friends merry, he never was lag,
For the wag of all wags, was a Warwickshire wag,
        Warwickshire wag,
          Ever brag
For the wag of all wags, was a Warwickshire wag.

"There never was seen such a creature,
  Of all she was worth, he robbed Nature ;
He took all her smiles, and he took all her grief,
And the thief of all thieves, was a Warwickshire thief,
        Warwickshire thief,
          He's the chief,
For the thief of all thieves, was a Warwickshire thief."

The most novel feature of the Jubilee was the projected procession of actors and others representing the
chief characters in the plays. A halt was to have been
made at the Birthplace, and the whole street to appear
peopled with the forms of those the Poet's imagination
had conjured up. Falstaff and Miranda, Henry V. and
King Lear, Dame Quickley and the Merry Wives,

L

Rosalind and Celia, Macbeth and Julius Cæsar gathering around the house in which Shakespeare was born. Alas! the elements were unpropitious, and the procession was abandoned. But Garrick was a clever man, and quite aware that the procession he had arranged in the little Warwickshire town would be appreciated by a London audience. He introduced it to his patrons in town in quite a novel fashion. George Coleman, the dramatist, also wrote a humorous play, "Man and Wife," on the Jubilee, in which many of the worthies of the town were introduced, as well as the mistrustful yokels.

There was living at Leamington at that time an enterprising tradesman and antiquary, one James Bisset, who wrote and published a curious pamphlet, entitled "The Joys of the Jubilee," in which he describes, from personal observation, the proceedings at this festive time. This first Jubilee has been the forerunner of many similar celebrations, but has never been surpassed.

It happened that the pavilion was built upon land subject to flooding, and at that particular time there was a flood of unusual magnitude. The horses had to wade knee deep to reach the doors, and the company were obliged to walk over planks in order to enter the pavilion dryshod. This was regarded by local rustics as a judgment upon Garrick and his wicked doings; for the whole affair was viewed with distrust and suspicion by the lower classes. Probably this untoward event gave Garrick a bad impression of Stratford, making him believe it was a dirty place. Any one visiting it on the day after a flood would probably be of the same opinion, though mud left by the overflowing river very soon vanishes, and the town assumes its normal clean appearance.

The Celebration of 1827

Wars, and the unsettled state of the country, prevented any further demonstration in honour of Shakespeare between 1769 and 1827, yet the love of the Poet implanted in the breasts of his native townsmen, though not manifest by any outward sign, was only slumbering. In 1824 a Shakespeare Club was founded in Stratford, a club which still flourishes, and has continued its meetings with only one break to the present day; these meetings were first held at the Falcon Tavern, and now at the Red Horse Hotel: the Mayor for the time being presides. Numbering among its members the most influential men in the town and district, its deliberations carried weight, and after some discussion it was agreed to hold a triennial celebration, commencing on S. George's Day, April 23rd, Shakespeare's birthday.

This happy combination of the patron saint of England and the Poet, has proved of considerable importance, and is likely to develop into a National Festival.

The first day of the 1827 celebration (April 23rd) was signalised by a pageant such as Garrick had projected, but did not carry out at Stratford. The committee of the club, with the Mayor at their head, marched first; behind came a standard-bearer, carrying the Royal Standard, then a military band, then S. George bearing the ancient sword of the Corporation; S. George's banner, carried by his esquire, and the town banner came next in order; then followed a host of Shakespearean characters, and the Union Jack brought up the rear.

From the Guild Hall the procession passed along the

principal streets of the town to the Birthplace, where a halt was made. The Muses of Tragedy and Comedy descended from their cars, and placed a crown of laurel on a bust of Shakespeare; and an address was delivered by Mr Bond, an actor, who among other things said that he hoped the day was approaching when Stratford would become an arena for the development of histrionic talent. The procession then returned past the town hall to New Place, where the first stone of a theatre was laid in the garden of that historic mansion.[1]

After the laying of the stone a performance of the music for " Macbeth " was given in the open air; and at four o'clock a distinguished company sat down to dinner in the town hall. Next day a public breakfast at the White Lion Hotel in Henley Street was largely attended, and in the evening a masquerade ball took place in a temporary room erected in the Rother Market. On the third day a concert was given in the White Lion Hotel, and with this the proceedings terminated.

Mr Raymond's little theatre in Chapel Lane was by no means a success, the population of the town being too small to support a venture of this kind without outside help; and after the site of New Place became the property of the Shakespeare Birthplace Trustees, the plain little building was pulled down.

The Celebration of 1830

Two celebrations were held at Stratford during the reign of George IV.; and much to his credit that monarch consented to be patron of the second event.

---

[1] The original agreement between the members of the Shakespeare Club and Mr Raymond, the lessee of the new theatre, is still preserved in the Library of the Memorial Theatre.

The Shakespeare Club commenced preparations in the autumn of 1829, and secured a number of influential patrons. In those days the festivals were not favoured by the weather, dull and rainy days had been experienced before, and the season of 1830 was no exception to the rule. The morning of S. George's Day opened damp and gloomy. A royal salute was fired from Welcombe, and the little cannons in the Bankcroft echoed a reply. As usual the proceedings opened with a breakfast, and again a pavilion had been built, this time in the Rother Market, a large open place in the centre of the town above flood level. The fickle April weather, which at first threatened to spoil the show, suddenly cleared, and at two o'clock the sun shone forth upon the Shakespearean procession as it started to perambulate the town. The firing of cannon and the ringing of bells, the gay music of the brass bands, and the motley group of Shakespeare's characters produced a lasting impression upon the minds of those who were present.

Charles Kean, then about twenty years of age, personated S. George; and the other characters were represented chiefly by people living in the neighbourhood. The procession was an imposing one of considerable length. It is depicted upon an old painted screen now in the town hall, whereon ladies and gentlemen appear in the quaint costumes of the days of George IV.

A great dinner was prepared in the town hall, and commenced in the afternoon. Several speeches were made, and a loyal address to the King, who was prevented by illness from being present, was read and adopted. In the evening there was a dramatic performance, Kean taking part; and later on a masquerade.

On the second day there was a breakfast at the White
Lion Hotel, and after it, recitations and songs. In the
afternoon a miscellaneous concert was given, followed
in the evening by a theatrical performance, another
masquerade, and a fancy dress ball.

The third day, being Sunday, was a *dies non*, for the
Church had not recognised the genius of the Poet.
Monday, April 26th, opened favourably for the Jubilee,
and some 25,000 people assembled in Stratford to
witness the pageant parade the streets. The programme was much the same as on the previous days:
theatrical performances, and a *bal masque*. The pleasant
spring weather by this time overcame the showers, so
that the Jubilee had a brilliant wind up. One of the
great charms of these Shakespeare celebrations is that
they are held at the season of the year when delightful
weather generally succeeds the storms and cold of the
winter. People who have been shut up in towns for
some months find Warwickshire most delightful in the
spring, and there is no doubt that the period of the year
has a considerable influence upon the success of the
Stratford festivals.

THE TERCENTENARY CELEBRATION

If the two hundredth anniversary celebration was a
noticeable event, what must we think of the three
hundredth anniversary? The Jubilee which Garrick
inaugurated was not held until five years after the
proper time. In the nineteenth century Shakespearean
devotees were more exact in their observances of dates,
and the Tercentenary Celebration was carefully arranged
to take place in 1864, the three hundredth anniversary
of the Poet's birth. Before that time the Birthplace in

Henley Street had been purchased for the nation, but Stratford was still a small country town, somewhat difficult of access, and far removed from railways.

From 1830 to 1864 no festival was held in Stratford in honour of Shakespeare. The Shakespeare Club, however, still met, and in a quiet way observed the Poet's natal day. At a dinner on the 23rd April 1859, Mr Harries Tilbury, an actor, presided, and in his speech reminded the people of Stratford that the Scots did honour to their National Poet Burns by holding a centenary celebration : and expressed the hope that in England the tercentenary of Shakespeare's birth would be observed with triple energy and impressiveness. The hint then dropped was taken up by the committee of the Shakespeare Club. Dr Kingsley, the President, and Mr Granville, the Vicar, set the ball rolling in 1860 by interesting the Lord Lieutenant, Lord Leigh, in the matter. Apathy appeared to be dominant just then, and little more was done till 1861, when the club again held a meeting, and took some preliminary steps. A committee was formed, but little was accomplished.

In 1863 a large meeting, under the presidency of Lord Leigh, was held, to consider a recommendation of the committee : a concert, an oratorio, and theatrical performances were suggested, and met with approval. The chief idea was to raise a fund for a national monument to Shakespeare : this was popular, and £1000 was subscribed. Then arose a man whose energy brought the Tercentenary Celebration to a successful issue. The Mayor of Stratford at that time was Mr Edward Fordham Flower ; it was he who became the prime mover on the committee. His two sons, Mr Charles and Mr Edgar Flower, acted as his lieutenants ; Dr Kingsley as Honorary Secretary. As the scheme grew in magnitude, Dr Kingsley was compelled to retire, and a paid secretary was appointed. Many worthy burgesses, still living, worked on the committee. Ex-alderman Thompson, and Alderman Colbourne were appointed architects of the great building to be erected for the dramatic performances. Mr T. Mason, whose name is commemorated by the fine old house in Church Street—Mason Croft—offered a site in his paddock in Southern Lane; and plans for a duodecagon, capable of seating 5000 people, were prepared. Committees were formed in Birmingham and London, and the Mayor then visited many of the principal towns in England, endeavouring to secure the co-operation of their chief inhabitants to render the Shakespeare Jubilee a success.

The committee soon found that the scheme they proposed involved an enormous amount of labour, and would not satisfy everybody, and it required no little skill to pilot their bark through the rocks and shoals of jealousy and contrariness. That the committee should have done so without any serious occurrence, reflects the greatest credit upon them. The great pavilion, twelve sided in plan, 152 feet in diameter, 74 feet from the floor to the top of the lantern, soon arose. The scenery was chiefly painted by Mr O'Connor of the Haymarket, an artist who has left a record of this great pavilion, in a drawing preserved in the Memorial Picture Gallery. The spot whereon it stood is now marked by Lombardy poplars, one planted at each corner of the building.

On the 23rd April the Lord Lieutenant, the Earl of Carlisle, and the Archbishop of Dublin drove into the town in a carriage drawn by four grey horses, and were received at the town hall by the Mayor and Corporation.

A banquet was served in the pavilion, and when it was over the company walked to a field in the Warwick Road to witness a display of fireworks: so ended the first day's programme.   As the visitors returned to the town they were serenaded by the nightingale, usually in full song at this time of the year.   The following day, being Sunday, there were services at the parish church.   Archbishop Trench was the preacher.   This special service appears to have been the first of a long series, which still continues, for in 1864 the clergy awoke to the fact that Shakespeare was a great moral teacher.   The Archbishop, in a most eloquent sermon, said, " Of what supreme concern it is that those who do so much to form and fashion the national life, should be men reconciled with God's scheme of the universe, cheerfully working in their own appointed sphere, the work which has been assigned to them, accepting God's word because it is His, with all its strange riddles, and infinite perplexities, with all the burdens which it lays on each one of us. . . . Such a Poet, I am bold to affirm, we possess in Shakespeare."

On Monday a performance of Handel's " Messiah " was given in the pavilion, Sims Reeves being one of the singers, and in the evening there was a miscellaneous concert.   The morning of the fourth day was devoted to an excursion to Charlecote, and in the evening a performance of " Twelfth Night " was given in the pavilion. Why the dramatic performances were put off till the fourth day is not very clear: such an arrangement would certainly be unpopular now, when the demand for Shakespeare's plays in Stratford is loud and continuous, so much so that in a three weeks' programme it is only possible to present about three non-Shakespearean plays.

The Haymarket Company performed "Twelfth Night"

with Mr Chippendale as Malvolio, Miss Lindley as Olivia, and Mr Buxton as Sir Andrew Ague-Cheek.   After "Twelfth Night" a comedietta, "My Aunt's Advice," was given, and brought the evening to a close.

On Wednesday the "Comedy of Errors" was performed, and "Romeo and Juliet." On Thursday there was a concert, and in the evening "As You Like It" was performed.   A fancy-dress ball, a pageant, a concert, "Othello," "Much Ado About Nothing," and the "Merchant of Venice" brought the festival to a conclusion; it had lasted twelve days.

For a small town the celebration was an undertaking of such gigantic magnitude that its success speaks well for the committee of management, and for the enthusiasm of the literary people of the time.   It was of course a costly affair, and the receipts did not meet the expenditure; the deficiency, however, was met by the liberality of a few gentlemen, who had interested themselves in the festival.

1873-79

After 1864 celebrations were held every few years until the Memorial Theatre was built in 1877: as the history of this period has not been recorded, it may be interesting to put down a few facts about it.   It was by no means a dark epoch, though greater events overshadowed it.   In March 1873 a petition to the Mayor of Stratford, couched in the following words, was presented:—

"We, the undersigned, being of opinion that the anniversary of the birth of Shakespeare should always be observed in his native town, beg respectfully to request your worship to convene a town's-meeting for the purpose of considering the most fit and proper mode of celebrating the occasion on the 23rd April next."

The petition was signed by the following persons :—

HENRY KINGSLEY, M.D.	JOHN J. NASON, M.B.	THOS. HUMPHRISS.
FREDERIC KENDALL.	EDWARD GIBBS.	S. INNS.
JAS. COX, Jun.	ROBT. GIBBS.	JOHN MORGAN.
H. W. NEWTON.	HENRY DOWNING.	W. L. NORRIS.
C. F. LOGGIN.	CHAS. THOMAS.	EDWARD ADAMS.
J. J. JAGGER.	JOHN MOSS.	JOHN S. LEAVER.
R. M. BIRD.	FRED. WINTER.	

The Mayor, Mr William Stevenson, convened a meeting, and it was decided to hold a celebration. The experience of the Tercentenary made the Stratford people proceed with caution, and a one-day's festival was arranged. The morning of April the 23rd was ushered in by a merry peal on the bells of the parish church. At eleven o'clock the townsmen, headed by the Mayor, and accompanied by bands of music, formed a procession. At one o'clock Miss Glyn gave a reading of " Hamlet " at the Corn Exchange, and at half-past three a collation was served at the town hall, at which the Mayor presided, and Mr Charles Flower occupied the vice-chair. At eight o'clock there was a display of fireworks, followed by a ball at the town hall. All this programme was successfully carried through, at a cost of about £100, and a small balance was left in the hands of the Treasurer.

Next year an attempt made to carry out a similar programme did not succeed, apparently because no one would supply the dinner. Six years passed without any public celebration of the Poet's birthday, but a strenuous effort was made in 1879 to make up for the deficiencies of former years, and the opening of the Memorial Theatre proved a fitting occasion for public rejoicing that in the future celebrations would be held yearly in a theatre provided for that purpose.

The Annual Shakespearean Festivals

The first performance within the Memorial Theatre was given in 1879, and it was in many ways a memorable one, being the first of the annual celebrations, and the first to be held in the little theatre now famous throughout the world, and associated with the names of most of the great actors, English, American, and Continental, for the last quarter of the nineteenth century.

Barry Sullivan, Helen Faucit (Lady Martin), and Miss Wallis opened the theatre with a beautiful performance of "Much Ado About Nothing": Lady Martin as Beatrice was superb. This lady had for many years retired from the stage, but consented to return on this occasion only.

The inception of the Memorial was due to the late C. E. Flower, Esq. of Stratford, whose father took such a prominent part in the Tercentenary Celebration. Mr Flower commenced operations by forming a small association in the town: he then bestowed upon the association a large plot of ground adjoining the river, and extending from the Wash to the Bankcroft Gardens. A more unpromising site could scarcely be imagined: partly swamp, partly wharves and coal-yards, it was by no means beautiful. In fact, many people shook their heads, and prophesied that the scheme would not be a success. Mr Flower, having given the land, also gave £1000 towards the fund, and the other members of the association contributed from £100 upward. Subscriptions were also opened in America: Miss Kate Field was an energetic worker, Mr Edwin Booth became the first American governor, Miss Mary Anderson, Augustin Daly, Miss Ada Rehan, and Mr Jefferson followed their example.

The fund so obtained, however, was quite inadequate for the Memorial as projected: this included a Theatre, Picture Gallery, and Library, with the possible extension of a Dramatic School. Mr Flower then contributed upwards of £30,000 in order to complete the building, and form an endowment fund. The theatre at the present time is the only endowed theatre in England, and has been the means of raising the tone of the dramatic profession. The festivals are not conducted for the sake of profit, but solely with the idea of presenting to the public representations of Shakespeare's Dramas as perfect as possible.

By the end of the nineteenth century upwards of thirty of the plays had been performed upon the Memorial stage, a record beating even that of the Sadlers Wells' productions of Phelps. For the first time since the days of the old Globe, " Hamlet " was there presented in its entirety ; and the first year of the new century was inaugurated by a series of the English Historical Plays. Such a series had never before been attempted, and the achievement of Mr F. R. Benson, under whose superintendence they were given, was hailed with enthusiasm by the audiences assembled nightly to witness this most interesting revival.

The procession of kings and princes, from King John to Richard III., and the march of historical events, given in their right sequence, was a literary treat, long to be remembered by those who witnessed it. As the years go by it becomes more and more difficult to give new features to the festival, and it is much to be desired that the Stratford Celebrations should, in the future, not only include the acknowledged works of Shakespeare, but also some of the plays of his contemporaries, the bright galaxy of Elizabethan poets, whose works have been too long neglected by English actors. It has been argued that many of these plays are unsuitable for representation in these days; but this argument is scarcely applicable in the present instance, since the Stratford audiences are composed chiefly of ardent students, and lovers of the drama who understand too well the spirit of the sixteenth century to raise an objection, which though forcible in other places, does not apply to Stratford and the Memorial Theatre.

Queen Victoria's Diamond Jubilee Procession

The 24th June 1897 will long be remembered as the climax of the glorious reign of Queen Victoria. In London the most memorable pageant of the century paraded the streets, and attracted a vast concourse of people. But not in London alone did the nation rejoice at the completion of the sixtieth year of the reign of the best Queen of England. In every city, town, and village, throughout the length and breadth of the land, people with one accord assembled to celebrate the event. It was, however, reserved to one of the smallest boroughs to make the bravest show.

Perhaps next to the procession in the metropolis that of Stratford-on-Avon was the most interesting. It was arranged by Mr Henry Jalland, at that time the manager of Mr F. R. Benson's Dramatic Company: the dresses were lent by Mr Benson. Eleven cars, manned by the inhabitants of the town, paraded the streets : the subjects being, the Court of Queen Elizabeth, the Apotheosis of Shakespeare, and nine plays of Shakespeare, representing comedy, tragedy, history, pastoral and classic dramas. The procession was headed by the High Steward, Sir Arthur Hodgson, K.C.M.G., and the Mayor, Councillor William Hutchings. Each car was attended by a number of ladies and gentlemen on foot appropriately dressed. At the end of the procession some of the fairest Stratford maidens, dressed in white, and carrying baskets of flowers to strew upon the path, preceded a gigantic car bearing Lord Ronald Gower's bust of Shakespeare. The car was arranged in the form of a pyramid, and around the bust a number of priestesses, attired in white and gold, offered incense, while Fame held a chaplet of gilded bay leaves above the Poet's head.

The fluttering white garments, the glitter of golden adornments, the fragrance of incense and roses, all appealed to the senses, and fitly concluded a procession which has never been equalled in this country. It extended for nearly a mile, and the only regret of those who saw it was, that it lasted too short a time. Had the masquerading continued till the close of the day it would have been better, but no sooner had the procession perambulated the streets and returned to the Memorial Theatre, than the cars were dismantled, and the pageant dissolved. The participators made haste to divest themselves of their gorgeous raiments, and assume their ordinary attire, in order to see the other events that were taking place in the recreation ground and College paddock. In the afternoon a pretty ceremony of crowning the Rose Queen was arranged in the meadows, and a water procession, fireworks and illuminations ended the festivities in honour of the

Empress Queen. It was very fitting that the chief event of the day in Shakespeare's town, should have been a Shakespearean procession, including a representation of the court of Queen Elizabeth, the Poet thus linking the reigns of the two most famous queens of England.

Mill at Guy's Cliff

The Avon in Winter

CHAPTER XXI

THE SOFT FLOWING AVON

A RIVER passes in its course through many scenes: at first a tiny brook, babbling like a little child, it soon attains strength to do useful labour; and so passes on, performing many services, until at last it joins the mighty ocean, and is lost in an eternity of waters. Yet nothing is lost in this world: even the waters of the river when merged in the boundless seas assist in the economy of the world for the benefit of mankind and the lower creatures.

Rivers that rise among mountains descend noisily to the plain, but streams having a less exalted origin, meander pleasantly through the meadows from their source to the sea. The Warwickshire Avon is one of these. Flowing through a somewhat flat country,

M

where rocks are almost unknown, it is rightly accounted a silent river. Having its birth in Northamptonshire, hard by the battlefield of Naseby, where King Charles I. was finally defeated, it creeps on through grass and sedges for ten miles, dividing the counties of Leicester and Northampton, till Dove Bridge is reached, where the rivulet enters Warwickshire. At Rugby it is little more than a brook, and so approaches Stoneleigh Abbey, and Guy's Cliffe's interesting mansion and "Saxon mill."

Flowing by Leamington, past many pleasant gardens, and receiving the waters of the "high complectioned Leam," growing wider thereby before passing beneath the New Bridge at Warwick, it sweeps in a broader stream to the castle, whose towers and battlements are mirrored in the waters.

Passing through Warwick Park the river finds its way to Sherbourne and Barford, where a fine old bridge spans the stream.

Upon a brass tablet in Sherbourne Church a curious inscription records a benefaction to this bridge from John Smith, who died in 1624:—

. . . . . .

"I credit lykewise had, love and regarde
From most, but in eupetiall Rowley Ward
My scholler above others mee respected,
In all occasions hee never mee neglected.
By his advice, and care of my estate
I it enjoied, without svite or debate.
He pen'd my will, my lands hee settled svre
To piovs uses ever to endvre.
Towards Barford's bridge old rvynes first preparing,
And when in aftertimes they are ymparing."

The new church at Sherbourne, designed by Sir Gilbert Scott, is a fine specimen of modern ecclesiastical

Clopton Bridge from the "Swan's Nest"

architecture, adorned with rich marble, stained glass, and carved oak, the gift of the late Miss Ryland of Barford Hill. This lady, so well known for her practical philanthropy both in the country and at Birmingham, where she was a considerable landowner, not only built this magnificent church at Sherbourne, but among many benefactions, gave to the city of Birmingham two extensive parks.

Though little known Barford is in many ways an interesting village, with associations scarcely less attractive than those of Charlecote.

The church, rebuilt in 1844, has few features of interest except the tower, which is old, and bears upon its walls marks of cannonading received during the civil wars of the seventeenth century. It is said that when the Roundheads were marching towards Edgehill, the loyal people of Barford hoisted the royal standard on their church tower, and the Parliamentarians saluted it with cannon balls. A pretty story, and probably a true one.

The river now winds through meadows below a ridge of hills where Fulbrook Castle formerly stood. Though no trace of this ancient fortress remains to remind the traveller of the days of chivalry, it was once the seat of the son of Henry IV., John, Duke of Bedford, who built it in 1426.

The stream shortly passes a green sloping bank "Whereon the wild thyme grows, and the nodding violet blows," and so onward to Hampton Lucy, a village deriving its name from the lords of Charlecote, hard by.

This church is another fine specimen of Sir Gilbert Scott's art, but the tombs of the Lucys are not within its walls : these historic monuments may be found in the church at Charlecote, on the other side of the river. The inn at Hampton Lucy is managed by the clergyman of the parish, in the worthy desire to benefit his parishioners and the cause of temperance.   The experiment has been successful.

The Avon now enters Charlecote Park, passes the walls of the Lucys' mansion, and is joined by Wellesbourne Brook, called by Drayton "The Little Heile." It presently passes Alveston Ferry, Hatton or Halton Rock, and Tiddington.

Halton Rock is a name to conjure with in Stratford, denoting a pleasant place for a picnic, far from the madding crowd of summer holiday seekers, and beyond the famous rapids, scene of many adventures thrilling if not dangerous, often damping to the garments, though not the spirits, of Stratford folk on pleasure bent.

The winding stream flows gently on to Stratford, through level meadows fringed with purple loose-strife, meadow-sweet, yellow iris, and blue forget-me-not. Here many willows grow aslant the stream, forming bowers and shady retreats for tired oarsmen, until the Gothic arches of Sir Hugh Clopton's bridge appear in view.

Time was, and not so long ago, that boats of forty tons burden came up from Gloucester to deliver merchandise upon the wharves at Stratford.   Now all is changed, and where once the deeply laden barges lay along the river bank, pleasure steamers and small rowing boats are the only craft.

In the seventeenth century a noted engineering enthusiast, Andrew Yarrington, with the aid of the then head of the Clopton family, started a scheme for improving trade in the district by making the Avon navigable.   The "Swans' Nest," formerly "The Shoulder of Mutton," was built at that time for the accommodation of travellers, and is still one of the finest river-side inns upon the Avon.

Hard by are the old tramway bridge and the boat-house of the Stratford-on-Avon Boat Club. From this point to the railway embankment a public recreation ground skirts the river, and upon the western bank are the Bankcroft Pleasure Gardens and the grounds of the Shakespeare Memorial.

The stream widens before the town and then takes a broad sweep towards the beautiful gardens of Avonbank and the parish church of Stratford, shaded by a row of lofty elms upon the river's brink. The river seems loath to leave the Gothic fane where the ashes of Shakespeare lie entombed, and in point of fact the waters are kept in check by Lucy's mill.

Below the mill the Avon is at present allowed to wander as best it can over sandbanks, mud, and shallows, and into deep pools until it reaches Luddington. This portion of the Avon once afforded excellent boating, and might be restored to its former state as a navigable stream for pleasure boats were a couple of locks put in order.

When the East and West Junction Railway was formed the course of the river appears to have been somewhat altered, the stream having flowed more to the westward than at present, and the water was kept in check by another lock.

The Wyre Brake, haunt of nightingale, blackbird, and thrush, is one of the most charming places around Stratford: it is a thicket planted on the steep marl-bank with the river gliding dreamily at its foot.

The cliff beginning near the railway, extends almost to the mouth of the Stour, and is accessible by a public path running from the foot of "The Cross o' the Hill" to the top of the bank and onward. The path is narrow, overgrown with brambles, and shaded by branching trees; bluebells, violets, and cowslips grow upon its sides, and glimpses of the river, and vistas of the meadows beyond may ever and anon be seen

At Luddington

through the interlacing branches. Since William Black wrote his romance of "Judith Shakespeare," wherein he describes this walk and the meeting of Judith and the Wizard, the Wyre Brake has had an additional attraction for visitors to the town. The Wizard's stile, half-way through the Brake, is now a well-known trysting-place.

Here, in early spring, the first notes of summer birds may be heard, and the earliest wild-flowers gathered. The lark, rising from the meadows, greets spring with joyous note; the mocking cuckoo calls across the stream; and the chiff-chaff and reed-warbler, returning with the first warm days, join in the merry chorus.

The path ends in the meadows, and it is better for us to return to the East and West Junction Railway, since it is difficult to cross the Avon without trespassing. The old towing-path on the west side of the stream skirts the meadows to Luddington.

At a point a little below the mouth of the Stour, King Charles II. crossed the Avon after the battle of Worcester.

The Stour,

> "the brook of all the rest
> Which that most goodly vale of Red Horse loveth best,"

adds considerably to the waters of the Avon, and in stormy weather assists in flooding the meadows around Stratford.

From Luddington to Welford the river is fairly navigable for small boats, and at the latter place passes beneath an ancient bridge near the "Four Alls," an inn noted for its remarkable sign. Upon it are depicted the Parson, who prays for all; the Soldier, who fights for all; the King, who rules all; and the Farmer, who pays for all. These, according to a local legend, are all-in-all.

Of late years Welford has become the resort of pleasure seekers, and is one of the favourite river-side villages. It is a straggling place, exceedingly picturesque, with a fine old Norman church, repaired and partly rebuilt at subsequent periods. Scarcely a generation ago the upper portion of the tower was burnt and rebuilt. The ancient oaken lych-gate, on the south side of the churchyard, remains but little altered since the fifteenth century: it is one of the most beautiful lych-gates in this district, and forms a pleasing object in the delightful lane leading to the river.

Welford, it may be mentioned, is in Gloucestershire;

Binton, the neighbouring village, divided from it by the river, is in Warwickshire.

From Welford the river winds onward towards Bidford, where it passes beneath another ancient bridge; and having now received the waters of both Stour and Arrow, flows past Salford in a broader stream

WELFORD-ON-AVON

to Cleeve Prior, and so onward towards Evesham, passing Harvington, the Littletons, and Offenham. At Evesham it turns northward, skirting the hills at Norton.

About Norton, Fladbury, Cropthorne, and Wyre the scenery becomes very beautiful, the river winding considerably to Pershore in the south-west.

Pershore, like Evesham, is almost surrounded by the river, and owes much of its fertility to the waters, which thence flow onward to the foot of Bredon Hill, and after many windings at last join the Severn at Tewkesbury.

The Avon valley from Stratford to Tewkesbury has no rival; it is in truth the garden of England where fruit and flowers are most abundant. In spring the whole countryside is white with the blossom of fruit, and in autumn the heavy wains, laden with the orchards' produce, may be met in every lane. In its winding course through twenty-five miles of valley from Stratford

RUIN OF ARCHWAY, EVESHAM

to Tewkesbury, the Avon passes many fine old mansions, three great abbeys, and several famous battlefields.

The beauties of this river cannot be fully appreciated unless seen at all times of the year, from sunrise to sunset, and in ever-varying aspect. In winter, neglected by pleasure seekers, it is far from being deserted by the feathered denizens. Swans, widgeon, teal, and dabchick, here make their homes, the latter being frequently seen between the two bridges near the

Memorial gardens at Stratford. The moor-hen, one of the commonest objects, being always with us, is ever an attraction to a lover of nature. In early morning

The Abbey Gates
Tewkesbury

on a calm day the dim reflections of the hoar-frost laden trees, mirrored in the dull waters at Halton Rock or Wyre Brake, remind one of Wordsworth's description of Yarrow:—

> "The swan on still Saint Mary's lake
> Float double, swan and shadow."

At the spring-time of the year, every bush, every

yard of river bank teems with life: the water-rats [1] pop in and out of their holes or swim about from place to place in search of food; the summer migrating birds are first seen in the neighbourhood of the stream. The buds of a hundred varieties of wild-flowers begin to appear, and soon make summer glorious with their brilliant hues; while the meadows, enriched by the floods of winter, quickly assume fresh verdure.

An early riser in spring or summer will be well rewarded by interesting sights, not visible as the day advances. At daybreak many of the more timid animals and birds come to the river to drink, and may be seen by the wary oarsman as he pulls his boat quietly up the stream. In the shallows the water-ranunculus, with its mass of fairy-like blossoms, makes the passage difficult. In some sequestered spots the flowering-rush rears its delicate pink blooms among the green leaves; and here and there the flowering elder trees perfume the air, and the yellow globes of water lilies shine like gold upon the surface of the water.

The ever-changing seasons have each a peculiar charm; there are few more glorious sights than the varying tints of autumn leaves reflected in the clear brown water of the river during short periods of brilliant sunshine before winter storms break upon the valley. On such a day nature seems to repose, almost sleeping when S. Martin's summer rests in the lap of autumn, or later, when hoar-frost silvers the earth, and hangs like glittering jewels on the myriad leaves of sturdy oaks.

[1] The water-rat, so called, is not a true rat, but a harmless vegetarian—a water-vole—allied to the beaver.

The Avon's classic stream,

> " Embracing in its liquid clasp
> The verdure mantled mead
> Like a bright zone," [1]

Tewkesbury from the Severn

glides onward towards the Severn through pastoral scenes where

> " Many stately trees, and many cots
> And villages o'erspread the country round,
> And orchards, with their odoriferous breath
> That scent the air, and to the eye present
> One sheet of blossoms." [2]

In the past the Avon valley formed the arena of many a cruel fight ; now clashing arms and cries of contending

[1] John Cotton, " Song and Sentiment."
[2] Cottle.

factions no longer resound in the vale, but the constant river flows on, finishing its course as it began, near an ancient battlefield.

> " Now civil wounds are stopp'd, peace lives again :
> That she may long live here, God say amen ! "

CHAPTER XXII

PRINCELY WARWICK AND THE NEVILLES

No town in England can boast of a champion more famous than the redoubtable and legendary Guy, Earl of Warwick. Although diligent antiquaries have laboured to prove that Guy is a myth, and that his armour, porridge pot, and even the slippers of the Lady Phyllis are a mere assemblage of odds and ends, of no earlier date than the time of Edward III., and some as late as the reign of Henry VIII., we must confess that we prefer still to believe in the Guy of the romance.

These legends, instilled into us in early youth, are very beautiful. Why should our faith in Guy and his fair Phyllis, or in Lady Godiva and peeping Tom be shaken by the statements of these terrible people who delight in banishing romance, and upsetting all our most cherished traditions? For ourselves we will maintain our belief in the stories of our childhood, and leave the unhappy sceptics to dwell in their uninteresting atmosphere of unadorned doubt. Let us keep our garden of romance, with all its beautiful flowers and wild tangle of undergrowth: we would rather have it so than as a bare ploughed field.

The story of Guy, Earl of Warwick, may here be briefly related. According to the ancient pedigrees Guy was a son of Seward, Lord of Wallingford, and married Felicia, or Phyllis, the only daughter of Rohand, Earl

MILL STREET, WARWICK

N

of Warwick, who lived in the time of Alfred the Great
and Edward the Elder. Guy set out on a pilgrimage
to the Holy Land, and did not return until the reign
of King Æthelstan, A.D. 926, when he found the
Danes besieging Winchester. The Danish champion,
a giant called Colbrand, was prepared for single combat
against any of the Saxons. King Æthelstan could find
no one willing to undertake the combat till a poor
palmer, Earl Guy in disguise, came to the King and
besought that he might fight the Dane.

The combat commenced by Guy breaking his spear
on the giant's shield, and the giant cutting off the head
of the Earl's horse. Guy then fought on foot, and
beating the club out of his adversary's hand, cut off his
arm. Colbrand continued the combat until night, when
faint from loss of blood, he fell to the earth, but would
not yield, whereupon Guy cut off his head at one
tremendous blow. Having redeemed his country, and
established his credit as a warrior, the palmer made
himself known to the King, but under an oath of secrecy.
After having returned thanks in the cathedral at
Winchester, he retired to a hermitage beside the Avon,
and passed the closing years of his life in the cave
which still bears his name, and probably retains his
bones. He received his daily dole from the hands of his
devoted Countess, though he did not make himself
known to her until his death in the year 929.

Guy is said to have performed many other deeds of
valour, including the destruction of the great Dun Cow
which ravaged Dunchurch and Dunsmore.

There is truth as well as beauty in this legend,
although some unpoetic minds can perceive neither
truth nor beauty underlying allegorical stories, ancient
legends and folklore tales. The world would be poor

indeed were romance banished to make way for bare
historic facts whose import is not properly understood
by compilers of history, so called.

Guy, Earl of Warwick, is as real to us as Charlemagne
or Alfred the Great, and although his story first appears
in the fourteenth century, we should be sorry to regard
him as a myth, and lose his associations with the town
whose name he bore. We believe in Earl Guy, and do
not mean to give up faith because we cannot account
for all the details, or prove the story by documentary
evidence. Warwick without its Earl would be as
inconceivable as Stratford without the Immortal Bard.
It may be true that in days long past there lived a
famous champion bearing the name of Guy, who died
and was buried at Guy's Cliffe.

The events which form the groundwork of the story
of Earl Guy and his lady, the fair Phyllis, must have
been of fairly common occurrence during the Crusades:
and it is quite natural that the chronicler who lived
a generation later should both antedate his narra-
tion by a century or two, and embellish it with the
marvels of the crusading period: just as Dutch painters
in the sixteenth century represented Noah and his wife
wearing Elizabethan frills.

In this way a legend became a work of art, deriving
charm from the skilful management of its narrator. As
an artist develops a design from the simple form of a
wild flower, so the author of the romance develops his
story, giving to it the charm which art imparts.

The towers of Warwick and the grotto at Guy's
Cliffe are sufficient evidence of the reality of the knights
and ladies of old. Time has surrounded these ancient
fabrics with a halo of romance. When entering
Warwick the visitor passes beneath a gateway many

centuries old, and treads the very path which the old
Earls of Warwick trod in the days gone by. We
know that Queen Elizabeth, for instance, passed beneath that arch. We know that in earlier times the

WARWICK CASTLE FROM THE RIVER

King-maker was there; and that generations before
the present gates were constructed the warlike Saxon
lords followed the daughter of Alfred the Great, as
she passed in and out of her Midland stronghold,
founded some thousand years before the time of his
present Majesty King Edward VII. For at least a

thousand years this town of Warwick has been in existence: how much further its history goes back we need not here inquire. The natural advantages of its position caused this place to be selected for one of the chief fortresses of the Midlands: the fortress being the residence of the most powerful lords, a town naturally arose beneath its walls, and in course of time the town itself was enclosed within a fortification.

The fortunes of the Earls of Warwick waxed and waned with successive dynasties of princes, so that the history of the earls is an integral portion of the history of the country. The municipal history of the town possesses an interest of its own quite distinct from that of the castle and its lords.

The impressive grandeur and vast proportions of Warwick Castle are seen to best advantage from the bridge which spans the Avon to the south of the town. At the Norman Conquest the Saxon lords— the Ardens—were dispossessed of their estates, and the castle was granted to Henry de Newburgh, of the Norman family of Beaumont. Two of the new Earl's relatives held respectively the earldoms of Leicester and Worcester, consequently the greater part of the Midlands came under the sway of this powerful Norman house. It is said that the Norman baron married the heiress of Arden. The fourth Earl of Warwick, Newburgh, mated his daughter Alice to William Manduit. The fifth Earl had a daughter Margery, who married, first, William Marschal, and, second, John de Plessey. The sixth Earl died childless, and Margery's first husband held the title of Warwick for one year. The second husband held it until his death in 1265, when William Manduit, son of Alice, succeeded, but dying childless, his sister,

Isabel, who had married her kinsman, William Beauchamp of Elmley Castle, succeeded. Their three sons became ancestors of the Beauchamps of Worcestershire and Warwickshire.

The house of Beauchamp held the earldom until 1439, when Richard Beauchamp, the greatest of his name, died at Rouen. It was he who arranged the marriage between Henry V. and the Princess Katherine of France, and subsequently held the title of Regent of France. Richard had visited the Holy Land, and set up his arms in Jerusalem; was created Duke of Warwick, died at the early age of twenty-two years, and lies buried beneath a magnificent altar tomb in the centre of the Beauchamp Chapel, Warwick Church. His effigy in bronze lies on the top of the tomb, which is adorned with many bronze figures, and enamelled coats-of-arms. His sister, Anne, succeeded to his estates, and her husband, Richard Neville, the King-maker, became Earl of Warwick. Their daughter, Isabel, became the wife of the Duke of Clarence, whose son, the unfortunate Edward Plantagenet, was the last of that house.

These princely Nevilles were closely associated with Stratford-on-Avon. The arms of the Duke of Warwick, who was a member of the Guild of the Holy Cross, may still be seen on the walls of the Guild Hall at Stratford, though probably they can no longer be found upon the walls of Jerusalem. The Duke of Clarence owned a certain house in the High Street of Stratford-on-Avon, and must have ridden many times from the little market town to the feudal fortress at Warwick.

An ancient country town usually has a reputation for sleepiness: possibly its institutions may in a measure account for it. Certainly the capital of Warwickshire is a quiet little place, and is old enough to have earned repose. Its history extends back nearly to the Roman period, but there is some doubt as to its occupation by those energetic people. The earthworks

The Market Place
Warwick.

on Blacklow Hill may be of Roman origin, though altered considerably in the Tudor period, but not entirely obliterated : yet no records of the Roman occupation of this place have come down to us.

The name indicates that it was a stronghold of the Wiccii, a people who established themselves in the district of the Midlands broadly represented by the Diocese of Worcester. "The Faithful City" was a

Roman town, and also a stronghold of the Wiccian people.

The first historic event of importance noted by the old chroniclers is the settlement made by Alfred the Great, who bestowed Warwick upon his daughter Ethelfleda and her husband, the Viceroy of Mercia, as he is sometimes called. Tamworth and Warwick were both fortified at that time, and the hills, or mounds, which formed part of Ethelfleda's fortresses, still remain at both places. The redoubtable Guy is said to have held the castle in Saxon times, and it descended to Turchill de Arden, who strengthened it in the time of William the Conqueror. Probably the foundations of the castle date from this period of its history.

From the eleventh century to our own days the story of the castle is linked with the fortunes of some of the noblest names of English nobility. It is the home of romance; and its story when fully written will only be surpassed by the annals of another great fortress, the Tower of London.

The peculiar charm of Warwick Castle lies in it being still habitable, and used by descendants of the ancient earls whose names are household words in every English home, and whose deeds of prowess are known throughout the world.

From the time of Alfred to that of the Gunpowder Plotters is a period of seven hundred years; during that time the castle appears to have been almost continually occupied as a residence by the Earls of Warwick and their kinsmen. Many kings and princes during that period of seven hundred years visited it, and some of the chief events of English history were arranged within its walls. From the time of the Plotters to that of

King Edward VII. three more centuries have elapsed, and we find an Earl of Warwick still living within the ancient fortress. There is this difference, however: instead of armed retainers one may often see troops of children and poor old folk thronging the courtyard. The days of feudalism are past, and the owners of the castle move with the times. There being no longer any need of a King-maker and his bodyguard of armed men, the castle no longer resounds with the tramp of mailed feet: but when the country needs men to fight her battles in distant lands, the Earl and Countess of Warwick assemble Warwickshire yeomen, and the heir to the earldom, like his ancestors a thousand years ago, will leave his country to fight a foreign foe.

The methods are changed, and strangely so: the old religious fervour has given place to philanthropy, but the spirit of patriotism is as strong as ever, though the means of expressing it have altered with the centuries. Many dynasties of earls have passed since the time of Alfred the Great, still the castle remains one of the best examples of a feudal fortress of the Middle Ages. Its solid foundations date from those far-away days, but the towers and chambers have been rebuilt at various times. Guy's Tower and Cæsar's Tower are truly remarkable examples of fortification: the former was built by Thomas Beauchamp in the time of Richard II. It is a twelve-sided structure, five storeys high, standing upon high ground. The internal arrangements are extremely curious: the central chambers of each storey, running across the tower from north-east to south-west, have each two flanking chambers in the thickness of the walls. This tower, and also Cæsar's Tower, are in a wonderful state of preservation, but they need repair from time to time.

The gatehouse between the two towers is a veritable curiosity - box, full of small chambers, and curious passages, formed for the use of the garrison and for defensive purposes. In the basement of Cæsar's Tower there is a dreadful dungeon, into which we may well believe many important prisoners have been cast. The range of domestic buildings faces the river, and when viewed from the bridge are, perhaps, seen to best advantage; they are most picturesque, and quite as imposing as the garden front of Windsor Castle.

The massive walls rising from the river's brink present a formidable appearance, with irregular outline of parapet and tower. Luxuriant trees grow about the walls, mingling their shadows with the reflection on the water; the ruined and ivy-covered arches of a mediæval bridge complete the *tout ensemble* of impressive grandeur.

Two of the ancient gates of Warwick, the East Gate and the West Gate, remain standing, the authorities having very wisely kept the gateways intact while providing wide roadways beside them for increased traffic. In the market-place a few timber-framed houses present their ancient fronts to the street, and in the middle of the square a Georgian market-hall now in part serves the purpose of a local museum for the collection—an interesting one—of the Warwickshire Archæological Society and Field Club.

Warwick Priory has long ago been converted into a private residence; it is now a fine old mansion. Another stately ancient house, S. John's, stands at the lower end of the town opposite the street leading to the railway station. Upon the river banks, below the castle, there is a little district filled with beautiful old dwellings, each with a pleasant garden.

CHAPTER XXIII

S. MARY'S CHURCH, WARWICK

ONE characteristic of our larger parish churches is their stateliness: the Church of S. Mary, Warwick, possesses this trait in a great degree; it is interesting as an architectural monument, and especially for its historic associations; partly a Gothic structure, and also one of the best examples of an ecclesiastical building of Queen Anne's reign, and the burial-place of some of the noblest of Warwick's sons.

Standing upon a spot consecrated to religious uses before the Conquest, but subsequently desecrated, it appears to have been rebuilt in the reign of Henry I. by Roger de Newburgh, who in 1123 transferred the collegiate church of All Saints, within the castle precincts, to S. Mary's, in the town. During Stephen's reign the castle was besieged, and the town, including S. Mary's Church, consumed by fire. In the reign of Edward III. the ruined choir was rebuilt by Thomas Beauchamp; his son completed it in 1394.

Half a century later the Beauchamp Chapel was commenced: the founder, Richard Beauchamp, Earl of Warwick, began the work in 1443; the building occupied a period of twenty-one years (1464), but the consecration was delayed until 1475. The chancel appears to have been repaired about the same period.

This very beautiful Gothic church, enriched at the

expense of one of the most noble families in England, remained very much in its original condition till 1694, when a great fire consumed a portion of the town. The inhabitants removed their goods for safety to the church, and it is said that thereby the sacred building also was set on fire—the tower, nave, and transepts being completely wrecked.

The work of rebuilding was undertaken by Sir William Wilson of Sutton Coldfield, whose design, while imposing in outline, in detail presents an incongruous jumble of ornamentation. The general result, however, is good, and when viewed from a distance, the tower is indeed stately. At the end of the nineteenth century the church was again repaired. The chief portions which escaped the ravages of fire are the most interesting, including the Beauchamp Chapel, the Chancel, and the Chapter House, now a mortuary chapel of the Grevilles.

In the centre of the chancel, upon a high tomb, lie the recumbent effigies of the first Thomas Beauchamp, Earl of Warwick, and his Countess, Katherine, daughter of Robert Mortimer, Earl of March: both the Earl and his Countess died in 1369. The Earl is represented in complete armour, his feet resting upon a bear, his right hand clasping that of his wife, whose feet rest upon a lamb. Round the tomb are a number of figures believed to be connected with the house of Beauchamp; and below the figures are the arms, now almost obliterated.

There is a brass plate to the memory of Thomas Rous, the antiquary, and between the doors of the vestry, or chapter-house, may be seen the grave of the brother of Catherine Parr, William, Marquis of Northampton, died 1571, and was buried there by order of Queen Elizabeth, who bore the expenses of the funeral.

A Bit of Warwick

It is much to be regretted that no inscription has been placed upon the Marquis's tomb. The ancient chapter - house is on the north side of the chancel; around it are nine stone seats under canopies; in the centre of the room is the tomb of Fulke Greville, first Lord Brooke, who died in 1628, and whose epitaph, written by himself, runs as follows:—

"Fulke Greville, servant to Queene Elizabeth, counsellor to King James, and friend to Sir Philip Sydney. Trophaeum et Peccati."

Beneath the chancel there is an ancient crypt, partly Norman, and partly fourteenth century. One or two curious relics are here preserved, including the cucking or ducking stool, for the punishment of scolding women.

By far the most interesting and beautiful portion of the church is the Beauchamp Chapel, built at the end of the fifteenth century in the then prevailing style of perpendicular Gothic architecture. The entrance is from the south transept down a flight of steps. Within as well as without, the walls are carved, forming elegant tracery and canopied niches. On each side are stalls of oak carved with many quaint devices. At the east end is an eighteenth-century reredos carved by a local sculptor, and scarcely in keeping with the rest of the building. The mullions of the east window, the jambs, and the mouldings of the arch are enriched with canopied niches containing figures of saints coloured and gilt. The windows at Dorchester Abbey, in Oxfordshire, are enriched in this manner; there are few other examples of this style elsewhere in England. Behind the eastern wall is a sacristy or vestry, approached by a doorway on the north side of the altar, and now used as a library. The roof of the Beauchamp Chapel is magnificently groined and carved; on the north side some steps lead to a doorway opening into a small chamber with groined roof and fan tracery. This appears to have been a small chantry chapel, and from it a small flight of steps leads to another chamber with a window looking into the choir. In the chantry chapel are the remains of some sixteenth-century funeral ornaments, helmets, etc., not intended to be worn, but to be set up over the monuments in the church. The chief glory of the Beauchamp Chapel undoubtedly is the founder's tomb, one of the finest of the kind in this or any other country. The altar tomb on which the effigy rests is of Purbeck marble, elaborately carved, and enriched with figures in brass, gilt, and also a number of shields. The top of the tomb is covered by a brass hearse, portions of which are enamelled to represent various coats-of-arms. The hearse was originally covered by a rich pall of crimson velvet with gold fringe. The figure on the top of the tomb represents Richard Beauchamp in full armour, his head resting on his helmet, his feet upon a muzzled bear and a griffin. This effigy is of latten gilt, and is a remarkably fine casting. The accounts for the making of this monument have been preserved.

The next most interesting tomb is the great monument to Robert Dudley, Earl of Leicester, Queen Elizabeth's favourite. The Earl and his Countess are represented in the costume of the period; the Countess is upon the shelf, a little higher than that upon which the figure of her husband rests.

Robert Dudley died in 1588. On the opposite side of the chapel is a curious monument of the Earl's infant son, who died in 1584. The epitaph upon the tomb sets forth the honours and titles of the boy in quaint phraseology :—

"Here resteth the body of the noble Impe, Robert of Dudley, Bar' of Denbeigh, son of Robert, Earl of Leycester, nephew and heir unto Ambrose, Earl of Warwick, brethrene, bothe sones of the mighty prince John, late Duke of Northumberland, etc., etc."

Near the founder's monument is the tomb of Ambrose Dudley, "the good" Earl of Warwick, brother to the notoriously bad Earl of Leicester.

Near the entrance to the Beauchamp Chapel, on the wall of the south transept, is the fine brass of Thomas Beauchamp, Earl of Warwick, who died in 1401, and Margaret, his Countess, who died in 1406. This brass was rescued from the fire, and placed in its present

position : formerly it was fixed upon a high tomb at the
end of the south aisle.

Yet another brass must be mentioned, that of
Thomas Oken and Joan, his wife. Thomas Oken was
a native of Warwick, and a prosperous tradesman of
that town. He acquired considerable wealth, and left
it to endow various charities.

Quite recently a handsome tablet, with an emblazoned
coat-of-arms surmounting it, has been placed to the
memory of that genius of whom Warwick is justly
proud—Walter Savage Landor—author of "Imaginary
Conversations" and many other works. The Landor
house may be seen near the east gate, looking substantial
and enduring, and partaking very much of the character
of its former owner.

The Church of S. Mary at Warwick was collegiate,
and the endowment provided for the maintenance of a
dean and so many canons. In the reign of Henry VIII.
the income was valued at £247, 13s. 0½d., and in 1850
£4953, 0s. 10d. The college was granted by King
Henry VIII. to the burgesses of Warwick, and for many
years the old college was used as a school, and the residence of the schoolmaster until late in the nineteenth
century, when some of the charity funds having accumu-
lated, a new school with more ample accommodation was
built on the New Road from Warwick to Leamington.
The buildings of this King's School date from 1879. It
is called "the King's School," out of compliment to King
Henry VIII., who instead of bestowing the revenues of
the old college upon one of his favourites, graciously permitted the burgesses to retain this portion of their
possessions.

LEICESTER HOSPITAL, WARWICK

CHAPTER XXIV

LEICESTER HOSPITAL, WARWICK

It would be hard to find a more beautiful street scene than that in which the Leicester Hospital forms a foreground to a curious assemblage of quaintly timbered houses. The outline is so irregular, and the shadows cast by the projecting buildings so dark, that the scene seems almost to belong to a picture, and not to be a reality. The position on the edge of a hill heightens the effect, for one is always able to catch a glimpse of pleasant country, an expanse of sky, fields, and meadows beyond the town.

Like all other towns in mediæval times, Warwick had its trade guilds, which discharged many useful duties, and ought never to have been suppressed by that precocious boy, Edward VI., and his selfish counsellors.

Two of the guilds of Warwick, those of S. George and the Holy Trinity, had united, and about the reign of Henry VI. the fraternity built upon a plot of ground adjoining the town wall, near the west gate, a fine hall and other buildings. When the dissolution came the brethren of the guild very wisely bestowed their hall upon the burgesses of the town, who used it as their place of meeting, and set up a school in the chapel over the gate. This was continued until the Earl of Leicester, wishing to found a hospital for certain poor people, bethought him of the guild hall and intimated to the Mayor that he would like it.

On New Year's Day, 1571, the burgesses of Warwick dutifully presented to the Earl of Leicester a deed of gift conveying the old hall with its appurtenances to the Earl, who thereupon founded the hospital which bears his name. The foundation provided for a master and twelve men, who were, if possible, to have been soldiers, born in the counties of Warwick or Gloucester, or having dwelt there for five years : and should it happen that none should be found in the town requiring the assistance of the hospital, then the poor of Kenilworth, Stratford-upon-Avon, Wootton-under-Edge, or Erlingham were to be eligible. The hospital was amply endowed.

Robert Dudley and Ambrose, his brother, died leaving no legitimate issue, and their sister, wife of Sir Henry Sidney, was their heiress. Thus her descendant, Lord Lisle and Dudley of Penshurst, became patron of the hospital, which honour still continues in that family.

In 1813 it became necessary to readjust the income, and an act of Parliament for this purpose was obtained.

The old buildings of the hospital are constructed of timber, curiously carved with the badges of the Leicester and Warwick families, and at every available point an emblazoned coat-of-arms has been set up. Among these the pheon of the Sidneys is conspicuous. The entrance to the hospital is along a raised path whereon a row of pollard lime trees has been planted. There is a gateway, and then a little courtyard before the main quadrangle, and at the end a flight of broad steps leading to the chapel over the town gate.

The quadrangle is as picturesque as it can be, with cloistered corridor, a long flight of steps, and over-hanging buildings with carved barge-boards. There is a hall, the master's lodge, the old guild chamber, and the other apartments of the brethren. The banqueting-hall, where Fulke Greville entertained King James I., now serves a more useful, but lowly purpose; and it is a pity that this fine old room should not be restored to its original use. The kitchen, a quaint apartment, contains an oak cabinet once in Kenilworth Castle, some other curious furniture and armour, besides a chair, said to be Saxon, and certainly of antique workmanship. The master's lodge contains many beautiful apartments, but is not shown to the public. The small chapel over the gate is of some interest; and below it is a vaulted archway, formerly the only entrance into the town on this side.

Certainly Leicester Hospital is a curious and quaint place, ranking first among similar institutions in the country. Here many an old warrior has passed the evening of his life in comfort, being in the world, and yet out of it; living actually within the walls of an old fortified town, and yet being able to see across the fair vale of the Red Horse to the distant Cotswold Hills. Long may the institution flourish and receive within its gates those who in youth have done their part in the maintenance of the Empire, and after long years of service seek an asylum in which to spend their declining years in peace and comfort.

CHAPTER XXV

KENILWORTH

" *Leicester*. Imagine Killingworth Castle were your court,
   And that you lay for pleasure here a space,
   Not of compulsion or necessity."
      " Edward II.," Act V. Scene i.

IN the old coaching days two famous whips were discussing the momentous question of the finest coach roads in England. The one was in favour of the road from Coventry to Kenilworth,[1] and the other of the road from Kenilworth to Coventry.

In these days we would extend the journey and decide that the road from Stratford-upon-Avon to Coventry is far the most interesting and beautiful in the Midlands. The eight miles from Stratford to Warwick takes us through park-like meadows to the high ground of Sherbourne Hill, from which point there is a view of surpassing beauty. From Windmill Hill the prospect embraces the whole of the Avon valley to Broadway, and before descending to Long Bridge we get another view over the vale to Edge Hills. Next comes Warwick with its gates and towers. Passing through the main street of the county town, we turn to the left beyond the station, and soon arrive at the beautiful avenue

---

[1] *Kenilworth*, called also *Killingworth*, and in an old charter *Cinildewyrthe*, signifying the estate of Cynehild, a female name. The termination *worth* means an estate or manor usually well watered. Compare *Bengeworth*.

214

Kenilworth Castle

The Banqueting Hall

leading to Guy's Cliffe. A little beyond a path leads down to the old mill standing beside the Avon, and we here look across the water of the mill-pool at the mansion above the hermitage of the famous Guy.

To the left of the road is Blacklow Hill, scene of the tragedy which bereft Piers Gaveston of life in the reign of Edward II. A cross with an inscription beneath it records this event, which happened in the year 1312.

> " *Arundel.* The Earl of Warwick seized him on his way;
> For being delivered unto Pembroke's men,
> Their lord rode home thinking his prisoner safe;
> But ere he came, Warwick in ambush lay,
> And bare him to his death; and in a trench
> Strake off his head, and marched unto the camp."
> Marlowe's "Edward II.," Act III. Scene ii.

Past Blacklow Hill the road still runs northwards through the picturesque village of Leek Wootton until Kenilworth is reached. It winds through the town and branches east and west towards Coventry and Birmingham. The road to Coventry for a considerable distance is fringed on either side by a wide lawn bounded by rows of lofty trees. From this avenue a glimpse is obtained of the famous spires of Coventry.

A short distance from the town of Kenilworth, standing in a fine timbered deer-park, watered by the classic Avon, is Stoneleigh Abbey, formerly a monastery, now the ancestral home of Lord Leigh. It is one of the most palatial houses in the county, full of art treasures, and interesting from its association with famous people.

Kenilworth is the home of romance, and the legendary story ranks only second in importance to its history. King Arthur's name is associated with the place, which is also said to have been one of the manors of the mythical

Kenelm, King of Mercia, whose tragic death is related in a later chapter dealing with Winchcombe. This origin of the name may be nothing more than an etymological guess made by Sir William Dugdale, but there is little doubt that there was a fortified settlement here in pre-Norman days, though the veritable history does not begin until the reign of Henry I., in whose time the manor was granted to Geoffrey de Clinton, royal chamberlain. It was he who built the square Norman keep, the most substantial portion of the castle, which has withstood the ravages of time and warfare, and still remains the most perfect part of the ruined fortress. Yet Kenilworth was more than a fortress, it was also a palace, much frequented by English nobles and sovereigns down to the time of Queen Elizabeth.[1]

Its beautiful situation and salubrious air rendered it a very fit residence for princes in search of pleasure or retirement. Formerly defended by a great lake, now drained, and by high walls and bastions, it was a place

---

[1] The castle hath the name of Killingworth, but of truth, grounded upon faithful story, Kenilworth. It stands in Warwickshire, seventy-four miles north-west from London, and as it were in the centre of England: four miles somewhat south from Coventry, a proper city ; and a like distance from Warwick, a fair county town on the north. Of air sweet and wholesome, raised on an easily mounted hill, it is set evenly coasted with the front strait to the east, and hath the tenants had town about it, that pleasantly shift from dale to hill sundry where, with sweet springs bursting forth ; and is so plentifully well sorted on every side into arable, mead, pasture, wood, water, and good air, as it appears to have need of nothing that may pertain to living or pleasure. To advantage, it hath, hard on the west, still nourished with many lively springs, a goodly pool of rare beauty, breadth, length, depth, and store of all kinds of fresh-water fish, delicate, great, and fat ; and also of wild fowl beside.*

---

* Laneham's Letter.

KENILWORTH BANQUETING-HALL

of great strength, able to withstand a six months' siege, which actually happened in the reign of Henry III. John of Gaunt built the noble banqueting-hall: Robert Dudley, Earl of Leicester, added the magnificent suite of apartments bearing his name, as well as the gatehouse, the only part of the castle now inhabited.

Edward II. was imprisoned here, and Queen Elizabeth witnessed those princely pleasures which formed the subject of Laneham's famous letter, and provided material for Sir Walter Scott's beautiful romance.

The Norman builder of the castle founded a priory hard by: the gatehouse and certain foundations and fragments built into the present church are the only remnants of this religious institution.

A comparison may well be drawn between the castles of Warwick and Kenilworth. While the former is still inhabited by the earl who bears its name, the latter, having been a royal palace, shared the fortunes of its various owners, until the time of the great rebellion, when Cromwell's commissioners came down upon it, drained the lake, and sold all that was convertible into money. Doubtless they would have let out the castle as a stone quarry had any one been willing to buy the stones, and it is fortunate for us that we are still able to gaze upon the old walls of the noble chamber wherein John of Gaunt, and many another English prince was wont to banquet.

Charles II. granted the castle to Lord Hyde, whose descendant, the Earl of Clarendon, is the present owner, by whose liberality the public are allowed to inspect the ruins.

England is not too richly endowed with ancient castellated palaces, and one cannot help feeling that everything should be done to preserve Kenilworth from decay. One would fain see the breaches in the old walls repaired, and where practicable, the chambers protected by a roof and windows. That the palace should ever be again occupied is scarcely to be expected, yet as time goes on it is possible that it may be so. Its central position in the Midlands, and its wonderful associations must ever make it a place of importance. Merlin and King Arthur, King John, Simon de Montfort, King Edward II., old John of Gaunt, "time honoured Lancaster" and his son, Henry Bolingbroke, Queen Elizabeth and her favourite, the Earl of Leicester, Henry Prince of Wales, son of James I., lodged within its walls, and have left a legacy of tradition and romance which must endear the name of Kenilworth to generations yet to come.

The present entrance to the castle is by a gate leading from Clintons Green; to the left Leicester's gatehouse is to be seen, and to the right the deep ditch before the walls to the north of the castle. Immediately within the wall of the outer ward and to the north of Cæsar's Tower, as the Norman keep is called, were the gardens of the castle, a grassy slope leading upwards to the ruin. As we stand looking into the inner ward we see the massive tower of the first Norman baron, its walls, some thirteen feet thick, and a little farther the noble ruins of the great hall with handsome traceried windows of the perpendicular period. To the left is the gaunt skeleton of the Tudor palace built to receive Queen Elizabeth, and beyond are the walls and ruined bastions of the outer defence of the castle.

Although as a ruin Kenilworth is melancholy and somewhat disappointing, it is well to preserve it as much as possible from further decay. As one of the Presidents of America wisely said of another historic place, " It is a good thing to preserve such buildings as historic monuments which keep alive our sense of continuity with the nation's past."

KENILWORTH CHURCH DOORWAY

CHAPTER XXVI

GIBBERING GHOSTS, HOBGOBLINS AND WITCHES

"Ghosts, wandering here and there."
"Midsummer Night's Dream," III. ii.

EVERY district has its own dialect, folklore, and ghost stories, differing more or less in detail, but having many points in common. Ghosts and witches still hold their own as articles of faith in villages around Stratford, where the country folk, though averring they are not frightened at "ghostes," will not go to the haunted spots alone after dark.

Many ancient mansions are regularly haunted by "grey ladies," priests, and gentlemen in garments of antique cut. In some houses these visitants are treated with all respect, and their appearance taken as a sign that the disturbed spirits require prayers to be said for their repose.

There are ghosts of the orthodox type, many of them headless, "night hounds," "night calves," and "stags," the "night coach," and the "hooter" or "Belhowja," all paralleled in other districts, but locally supposed to be peculiar to the vale of the Red Horse.

At a place along the Shipston road, between Stratford and Alderminster, a ghostly calf comes through the hedge with great noise of breaking sticks: but when the hedge is examined no trace of anything unusual can be found. The ghost of Shottery brook still frightens the children on winter nights; though who she is, and why she should haunt the water is unknown. The Wellesbourne ghost also haunts a stream, and has an unfortunate habit of walking without her head. What has become of that usually useful appendage history does not relate. At Leicester Hospital, Warwick, another headless ghost used to be seen, but now it is supposed to be at rest. In connection with this spectre, it is said that it has not appeared since the chapel over the west gate was repaired. During the reparation some stones were removed from the spandrel of one of the arches, and in a cavity of the wall a skeleton in rusty armour was found. The skeleton had no head. The remains were interred, and the spectre no longer walks abroad.

At Chadshunt there was a ghostly coach and four, which was driven furiously to the front door and then vanished away in the darkness. The night coach within living memory has been seen at Wellesbourne, along the road from Charlecote: the driver is headless. At Hidcote Boise, a hamlet of Mickleton, the night coach has also appeared, in fact, according to the credulous, it was a fairly common phenomenon in the district.

We are told that in a deep combe or valley, called Mickleton, or Weeping Hollow, the Mickleton Hooter was at one time often heard. A pathway along the bottom of the hollow is a reputed Roman road, now little frequented: the steep and rocky sides of this glen are covered with trees and bushes; it is a solitary and romantic spot. Belhowja here had his home, and made night hideous by his howlings, yellings and screechings. He was never heard in the daytime.

Mr Scarlett Potter, in an interesting and scholarly article published in *Time* of August 1884, relates that at the close of the eighteenth century a person bearing the name of Staunton came to reside in the manor house of Hidcote Bartrim. He appears to have been devoted to scientific pursuits: these, and his solitary life, procured for him the reputation of a necromancer, but fortunately for him, he was said to be only a "white wizard." "It was currently believed," says Mr Scarlett Potter, "by the peasantry of the neighbouring villages, that all the time-honoured phantoms of these hills—the 'Night Hounds,' the 'Night Coach,' and the 'Mickleton Hooter'—yielded to his exorcisms, and were laid to rest." With respect to the Hooter it may be remarked that in deep valleys it is by no means unusual for subterranean rumblings to be heard. Another version of the Hooter makes an owl responsible for the sound. One night, so the story runs, a man of Mickleton found himself benighted in Weeping Hollow and lost his way. Whereupon, in his extremity, he began to shout, "Man lost, Man lost"; the bird of wisdom from his perch on high replied, "Who-oo-o-o"; the man replied, "John Brown of Mickleton"! ! ! !

In the district beyond Dovedale in Derbyshire, near that mysterious river, the Manifold, strange sounds have occasionally been heard in the valleys. The country folk have told of sudden reports, accompanied by crashing stones and blue red flames, and of a somewhat similar nature to the Mickleton Hooter. Modern science has effectually laid the Derbyshire marvel, having proved that it occurs only when there is a tempestuous high wind. The wind blowing upon one face of the rock, filling and over-filling its clefts, or caves, forcing its way into the many openings and fissures in the cliff, compresses the air inside to a degree that escapes occur with such force as to hurl stones and dust across the valley. Thus is the mystery exploded, and possibly the sounds in the Mickleton valley may have been produced in a manner somewhat similar.[1]

Of the Keytes of Hidcote Bartrim and Ebrington some romantic stories are told. Sir William Keyte at one time resided at the old house of Avonbank, adjoining the churchyard of Stratford-on-Avon. It is said that being much involved in debt he nevertheless commenced to build a country mansion, and when it was finished, invited his friends, neighbours and creditors to a house warming. While the party was proceeding Sir William set fire to the mansion and was burnt to death. His remains were interred in a vault beneath Ebrington Church: no monument or inscription marks the spot. A huge kite, carved in stone, and holding the family armorial bearings in his claw, still adorns the roof of the orangery in the garden of Avonbank.

At Loxley there was a witch who could turn herself into a hare; she appears to have troubled the people in the village, and one night some men went out to shoot her, whereupon she immediately turned into a hare. The men fired, but the hare escaped, though apparently wounded. Next day, when some of the villagers called upon the old woman, they found she would not sit down, and they therefore drew the conclusion that their theory of the metamorphosis was correct. This story was firmly believed in within living memory.

The latest ghost is quite up-to-date, and rides a ghostly bicycle. This is not at all remarkable when we consider that mediæval ghosts appear in ghostly

[1] See *The Denstonian*, April 1899.

armour: surely a twentieth century spirit would naturally possess a ghostly bicycle.

Doubtless this list of prodigies and wonders might be much extended, and doubtless, also, the Psychical Research Society would explain away these seeming marvels; though to people obliged to trudge along lonely lanes in the twilight, or the darkness, the hobgoblins and ghosts are very fearful realities.

Although the tales are in themselves usually absurd, and the invention of timid minds, they may have some foundation in fact, obscured it may be by incrustation of romance gathering around a story repeated from mouth to mouth by people of the utmost veracity. Far be it from me to scoff at the supernatural—"there are more things in heaven and earth, Horatio, than are dreamed of in our philosophy."

Ghosts are erratic, proverbially so: the ghost of Hamlet's father sometimes appears upon the platform, and sometimes beneath the surface of the ground like an old mole. There are in the plays of Shakespeare enough ghosts to satisfy the most enthusiastic member of the Psychical Research Society: and we may be sure that if there are still ghosts in Warwickshire, there were many more in the days of the great Dramatist.

The absurd stories here related are examples of the folklore of the district, and are given merely to illustrate the common superstitions.

CHAPTER XXVII

COMPTON WYNYATES

THERE is a story told about Compton Wynyates which if not actually true, has yet some foundation in fact, since, undoubtedly, it is a difficult place to find; though when found the labour of the seeker is amply repaid. It is said that Oliver Cromwell sent a troop of Roundheads to take Compton Wynyates, but after marching round it for a week the troopers returned to their general saying they could not find the house.

The way from Stratford lies across Clopton Bridge straight along the Banbury road to Ettington, and gradually ascends. When about a mile out of the town it is worth while to turn and look back over the sloping fields towards Stratford. The little town seems to be nestling under the low hills to the north-west, and the church spire, and the tower of the Shakespeare Memorial rise above the red-tiled roofs. We are now in the open country and soon pass on the left the tangled thickets of Alveston Pastures, where the moss grows luxuriantly on the banks, and the violet brings its fragrance to the air. A little further Goldicote is reached. This is the country seat of C. H. Joliffe, Esq. Here the country swain can "tune his merry note unto the sweet bird's throat." It is a rare place for wild birds, well known to Stratford boys, and the scene of many a bird-nesting foray.

A lane to the left by Park Leys leads to a hill-top commanding one of the finest views to be found in Warwickshire. The Vale of the Red Horse stretches far in the distance, and many a ridge and hill-top can here be discerned. The lane continues into Loxley village, a place associated with Robin Hood and his merry men. A fine chain of earthworks crowns the hill, and the ridge and furrow of ancient cultivation may be seen on either hand. The towers of Warwick Castle stand out among the trees to the north, the blue ridge of Malvern bounds the prospect to the south-west, while southward Breedon and the Cotswolds rise above the plain. To the east the long line of Edge Hill bounds the horizon. Kineton and Radway lie between this vantage point and Edge Hill, the field whereon the armies of King and Parliament met on October 23rd, 1642. We must now retrace our steps to the main road, which turns to the right to cross the deep cutting of the East and West Railway, and then proceeds in a switchback fashion to the village of Ettington. Had we continued on the road to the right we should soon have found ourselves descending to the valley of the Stour, and have joined the Shipston road at a point immediately opposite the fine old church of Alderminster.

Ettington is a delightfully situated village on high ground, noted chiefly for its colony of those estimable people calling themselves the Society of Friends. There is an old Friends' Meeting-house in the village, and an extremely hideous church. The glory of Ettington is its ancient park and mansion of the Shirleys, who have been settled here from time immemorial. But

Compton Wynyates

Lower Ettington and Ettington park will be found mentioned elsewhere in these pages. Our road goes onward between green hedgerows and coppices, past the village of Pillerton Priors, till a point eight and a half miles from Stratford is reached. Here the road enters the fields, and more than one gate has to be opened to admit the passage of a carriage, or even of a cycle.

The village of Oxhill is one of the quaintest and most picturesque places one could wish to see, and the road turns and twists about its cottages and homesteads as though loath to part from a spot so favoured. All vegetation is luxuriant, the fields have a park-like look which betokens the neighbourhood of some lordly owner. A little further, and we are in the domain of Compton Wynyates, though we cannot yet see the house. To the left of the road may be noticed broad fish ponds, and to the right the curious church belonging to the mansion. It was an ancient place when the Roundhead soldiers wrecked it, and cast the monuments of the Comptons into the moat, where they lay amid slime at the bottom of the water until England's civil broils had worn themselves out. The Comptons were firm adherents to King Charles, and they and their house suffered for their loyalty. The history of Compton Wynyates has been told over and over again; it is indeed a romance throughout. The place was given to William Compton, a favourite of King Henry VIII. The much-married Tudor was capable of great affection, which he lavished upon William Compton, granting him an augmentation from the royal arms that he and his descendants might ever remember a king's favour. He granted him the custody of the park of Fulbrook, between Stratford

and Warwick, and the castle there, built by John,
Duke of Bedford, brother of King Henry V. Compton
accompanied his royal friend to the Field of the Cloth
of Gold.   About 1509 Sir William pulled down the
Castle of Fulbrook, and used some of the materials
to build his new house at Compton Wynyates. The
house which he built remains but little altered since
the days of Bluff King Hal; it is a poem in brick and
stone mellowed by the hand of time, and, like some
old monarch of the forest, has grown hoary with age.
The great-grandson of the builder fell in love with
Elizabeth Spencer, the only child and heiress of one
of the merchant princes of London. The merchant
was opposed to the wooing, desiring that his daughter
should mate with someone of his own choosing, and
not with a gay young noble of the court of Queen
Elizabeth.   However, "love laughs at locksmiths,"
and Lord Compton cheated the thrifty Lord Mayor
of his daughter. Being in league with the baker's
boy who supplied the household of the alderman with
bread, the nobleman changed clothes with the baker,
and shouldering the huge bread basket took it into
Canonbury House one morning. The loaves being
delivered, the merchant's daughter got into the basket,
and the lover hoisting his load upon his shoulder,
proceeded to carry it out of the house, but at the
door he met the alderman, who complimented him upon
being at work so early, and gave him sixpence as an
encouragement for early rising. The lovers were
married, the alderman repudiated them, and nothing
would persuade him to forgive his daughter. Lord
Compton, however, had a powerful friend in Queen
Elizabeth, who dearly loved an intrigue. Sending
for the Lord Mayor, she asked him to stand sponsor

with her at the baptism of a child, and he, being
flattered by the attention of the Queen, consented,
and added that as he had disinherited his daughter,
the Queen's god-child should be his heir. The heir
was his own grandson! How the Queen must have
laughed! The memories of these old Comptons linger
about the mansion, their spirits appear to haunt its
chambers, every room has its tradition: here a king
slept; there some of the Royalist garrison were
murdered; in this secret oratory the adherents of
the old faith practised their rites and ceremonies in
the troublous times when men were persecuted for
their religious opinions. Unlike many ancient baronial
mansions, Compton Wynyates is still inhabited: it is
to this day the home of the Marquis of Northampton,
who cares for it as a father for his child, and is
proud of owning the most beautiful Tudor mansion
in all England. The writer well remembers the first
time he visited the old mansion, on a glorious day in
early autumn. It was like looking at a picture, and
its beauty was so perfect that it was hard to realise
it, the reality, was not a dream.

Having come from Stratford by way of Ettington we
may return through Brailes, passing down a steep hill,
where the little village of Winderton looks down upon
the valley. Brailes is famous for a noble church,
called the " Cathedral of the Feldon "; like Campden it
has a lofty embattled tower. Within the last few years
the hand of the restorer has been at work within the
church; it is now swept and garnished, and looks
painfully neat and new. From Brailes one may pass
through Cherington, and through the beautiful park
of Weston House, formerly the home of the Sheldons,
and now the seat of Lord Camperdown, and so join

the main London road some four miles from Shipston.
A shorter way would be to approach Shipston by the
Banbury Road through Barcheston.   At Shipston we
need not tarry: we are ten miles from Stratford on a
famous coach road, and should reach our destination
without any difficulty.

CHAPTER XXVIII

THE CAMPDEN WONDER

ABOUT eleven miles from Stratford, upon high ground on the borders of the Cotswolds, stands the picturesque market town of Chipping Campden, formerly headquarters of woolstapling, and famous for its trade in that commodity. The beautiful church, quaint market-hall, and numerous well-preserved ancient houses bear witness to the prosperity of the place in former times. It is now a quiet little town, and has lately become the home of that useful band of workers known as the Arts and Crafts Association. Those who take delight in visiting quaint, old-world towns cannot fail to be pleased with Chipping Campden.

There is a local legend, that owing to a curious case, which occurred here, the laws of England were altered so that now no one shall be executed for murder unless the body of the person said to have been murdered can be produced, but this is fiction.

The account of this case may be found in a somewhat rare pamphlet published in 1806, probably reprinted from an older tract, the narrator being Sir Thomas Overbury of Burton in Gloucestershire.

It appears that one Thursday in August 1660, William Harrison, steward to Lady Campden of Chipping Campden, walked from Campden to Charingworth, a place about two miles away, in order to collect

237

some rents, and, as he had not returned by eight o'clock at night, his wife, being alarmed, sent their manservant, John Perry, to seek his master. Neither Mr Harrison nor John Perry returned that night, so in the morning Edward, the steward's son, set out to make inquiries. He met Perry coming home. They then went together to Ebrington and to Paxford without finding any trace of the missing man; but as they were returning towards Campden they had news that a poor woman had found a hat, band and comb in the highway between Ebrington and Campden. The hat and comb were hacked and cut, and the band bloody; there was no doubt that they had belonged to Mr Harrison, and although search was made in the neighbourhood, no trace of the missing man could be found.

Suspicion now fell upon Perry, who had not returned home when sent to look for his master. The man was unable to give a good account of himself when examined before the Justices of the Peace, but after a good deal of cross-examination, he said he knew his master was murdered, though he was not guilty of the crime. Being urged to confess what he knew about it, he at last said that his mother and his brother Richard had murdered his master, telling a most circumstantial tale of the whole affair.

Joan and Richard Perry were then apprehended, further search made in the fish ponds, and even in the ruins of Campden House, which had been burnt during the civil wars. Joan and Richard denied the charge, but John still affirmed that he had spoken nothing but the truth. The search for the body continued without result.

A curious piece of circumstantial evidence was now brought forward. As the prisoners were returning

At Chipping
Campden
The Market Place

from the house of the Justice of the Peace where they had been examined, "Richard Perry following a good distance behind his brother John, pulling a clout out of his pocket, dropped a ball of inkle, which one of the guard taking up, he desired him to restore, saying it was only his wife's hair-lace; but the party opening of it, and finding a slipknot at the end, went and showed it unto John, who was then a good distance before, and knew nothing of the dropping and taking up of this inkle: he, being showed it, and asked whether he knew it, shook his head, and said, Yea to his sorrow, for that was the string his brother strangled his master with. This was sworn at the evidence at their trial."

It appears that some time before a robbery had been committed at Mr Harrison's house, and Perry being questioned about this affair, said that it was his brother who had commited the robbery.

At the next assizes, which were held in September, John, Joan and Richard Perry had two indictments found against them: one for breaking into William Harrison's house and robbing him of £140 in the year 1659, the other of robbing and murdering the said William Harrison in the year 1660. The judge would not try them on the last indictment because the body was not found: they were tried upon the first indictment for robbery, and pleaded not guilty, till somebody prompting them, they afterwards pleaded guilty, begging the benefit of his Majesty's pardon and act of oblivion, which was given them. After the trial they again denied that they were guilty of the robbery or knew who did it.

At the next assizes the three were tried for murder, and pleaded not guilty. John's confession was proved by several witnesses, but the other two still maintained that they were innocent.   Finally they were all found guilty.

We have now a very curious account of the execution, the details of which are sufficiently divergent from those of an execution at the present day, to show how far civilisation has advanced in two hundred and fifty years.

The prisoners were brought to Broadway Hill, in sight of Campden, and upon this conspicuous elevation a gibbet had been erected, so that the execution might not only be a public one, but the remains of the poor wretches might long remain an object-lesson for evil-doers in the neighbourhood.   The mother was first executed, because she was a reputed witch, and was said to have so bewitched her sons that they could confess nothing while she lived.   Richard suffered next, and while upon the ladder he stated that he was entirely innocent of the fact for which he was about to die.   He besought his brother in great earnestness, for the satisfaction of the whole world and his own conscience, to declare what he knew.   John thereupon told the people that he was not obliged to confess to them ; yet immediately before his death he said he knew nothing of his master's murder, nor what had become of him, but that they might hereafter possibly hear.   And so the curtain closes over the first act of the drama : the poor mangled bodies of the mother and her two sons swinging on the gibbet upon Broadway Hill.

The next chapter opens with an account of a remarkable kidnapping, which in those days was not so impossible as in our own times.   The account is contained in a letter written by William Harrison, who was supposed to have been murdered, to his neighbour, the distinguished lawyer, Sir Thomas Overbury.

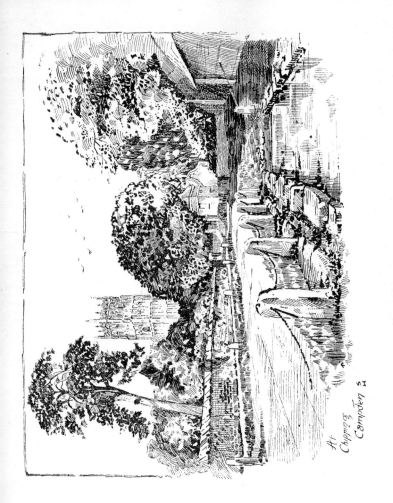

At
Chipping
Campden.

Mr Harrison states that as he was returning home with Lady Campden's rents, a sum of £23, he was attacked by a horseman in a narrow passage in Ebrington furzes.   Defending himself with his cane against the sword of the horseman, he was finally overcome by another who wounded him in the thigh.   A third horseman presently appeared.   They did not then take his money, but mounted him behind.   His arms were placed about the waist of a horseman, and his wrists were fastened with a spring lock.   They then threw a great cloak over him and galloped away.   On the Sunday afternoon following, Mr Harrison was carried to Deal.   Here he was sold for £7 to a man who took him on board a ship.   After being on board for about six weeks he was transferred to a Turkish vessel and placed in a dark hole; there he remained for some time before being landed, and sold as a slave to a grave physician who had been in England and could speak English.   After sixteen months the physician fell sick, and calling his slave, told him that in case of his death he must shift for himself.   Harrison had been given a silver gilt bowl by his master; this he used as a bribe to obtain a passage in a Portuguese ship bound for Lisbon, and from that port, by the kindness of a stranger, he was enabled to procure a passage to England.[1]   Thus ends one of the most remarkable stories, if true, of kidnapping recorded in the annals of the district.

---

[1] The story was dramatised in 1902, and acted in Stratford-on-Avon by a clever troop of travelling actors (Mrs Sinclair's Company) with great success.

CHAPTER XXIX

THE LEGEND OF WINCHCOMBE

At Winchcombe may yet be seen a small stone coffin said to be that of Kenelm, king and martyr. In vain do we search the pedigrees of the Saxon kings for the name of Kenelm: yet for many ages his legend has been known, and the memory of the boy-king revered. Whether he was an actual person, or merely existed in the imagination of a monkish chronicler, matters little. The legend, indeed, bore fruit, so much so that several churches in honour of the boy were founded, and a great monastery arose over his supposed tomb.

Kenelm, so the legend runs, was King of Mercia at a period when the capital of the district was at Winchcombe. Perhaps it would be nearer the truth to say that he was a sub-regulus, or chieftain, in Mercia. At the time of his father's death Kenelm was but a boy, and the guardianship of his affairs naturally fell to his sister, Quendrede, a princess much older than he.

Quendrede was ambitious and in love; she desired the kingdom for herself and her lover, and little Kenelm was kept out of the way. On the bleak ridge of Clent, in Worcestershire, stood a royal hunting lodge, and there the little king was sent to pass the time as best he could, far from the capital of his land. One day the lover of the wicked princess slew the king while hunting, and buried him in a lonely spot among the hills, placing a great stone over his body.

The scene now shifts to Rome. On a certain day, when the Pope was saying mass before the High Altar of S. Peter's, a white dove flew into the church, carrying in its beak a scroll of parchment, which the bird let fall upon the Holy Table. The Pope took up the scroll and read the words upon it :—

> " In Clent, in Cowbage, Kenelmc Kyngborn,
>   Lyeth under a thorn, his hede of shorn."

The Pope caused inquiries to be made as to the meaning of these words, and finding that Kenelm was a king of Britain, sent messengers to that country to unravel the mystery. In due time the messengers arrived and found their way to Clent. Now it happened that an old woman of Clent used to turn her cows to pasture on the hills. The cattle wandered away, feeding where they listed, but one white cow always betook herself to a spot near a great stone and there remained. Strange to relate, though the cow showed no inclination for food, she became fatter and sleeker than the other members of the herd. This miracle being reported to the Pope's messengers, they soon found out Cowbatch and the stone, and rolling it away they found the remains of the murdered king, and beside him the sword with which he had been slain. From under the stone a spring of fresh water gushed forth : the spring and stone are there to this day, as the present writer can testify.

Two parties of monks were sent to claim the body of the king : one came from Gloucester, and the other from Winchcombe, the two great towns of that part of Britain in those days. Taking up the remains with all respect, the churchmen started on their homeward journey. On the way, however, a dispute arose between the two bands of monks as to the possession of the body, but towards evening one of the number, "a right wise man," probably the Abbot of Winchcombe, proposed a solution of the difficulty. He said, "Let us all rest during the night, and those that wake first in the morning shall take possession of the body." When the morning broke, the men of Gloucester arose, but the monks of Winchcombe had forestalled them, had taken up the body, and were already well on their way home. The Gloucester monks thought they had been outwitted, and started in pursuit: the day was very hot, and as the Winchcombe monks toiled up the hill with their burden, weary and thirsty, they perceived that their pursuers were gaining. Then the Abbot thrust his staff into the earth, immediately a spring of water gushed forth; whereat the holy men were much rejoiced, and quenching their thirst, again set out and reached the city.

The wicked Princess Quendrede hearing the bells pealing, asked the meaning of the joyous sound, and was told that the remains of her royal brother were being brought into the town. Seizing a service book she proceeded towards a window of the palace, and as the procession passed, commenced reading the prayers backwards. Immediately both her eyes tumbled out of their sockets, and fell upon the book.

The martyred king was buried beside his father in the church at Winchcombe, and his tomb became an object of pilgrimage until, at the Reformation, the monastery was destroyed. Some few years ago the tombs were opened, and in the small stone coffin the skeleton of a boy, and the remains of an iron sword, were found. The two coffins are now placed within the church, and an inscription setting forth the main incidents of the story is set over them, the late owners of Sudeley Castle, Mr and Mrs Dent, having been instrumental in this act of reverence.

The chapel of S. Kenelm still stands beside the spring on Clent Hill: it was counted a holy shrine and a place of pilgrimage.

The town of Winchcombe, referred to in the legend as a seat of royalty, and a place of considerable importance, has declined from its former grandeur: it is now a little sleepy country town, whose chief and only glory is the fine parish church, notable for the stone coffins supposed to be those of its Saxon princes, and for a remarkable series of grotesque heads carved in stone around the church. These carvings have given rise to a proverb, and, indeed, it will be difficult to find an uglier set of gargoyles than those of Winchcombe. The monastery and all its extensive buildings, except the church, have disappeared, but there remains an ancient hostel, dating from pre-reformation days, and worthy to be noticed by the tourist.

A little to the south of the town stands Sudeley Castle; its late owners, Mr and Mrs Dent, caused it to be carefully repaired, so that it yet remains one of the most interesting examples of a fortified dwelling-house in this part of the country. In the latter years of the reign of Henry VIII. Sudeley afforded an asylum to his last Queen, Catherine Parr, who died within its walls, and was buried in a vault beneath the chancel of the church. Mr and Mrs Dent ordered a stately monument, with a recumbent effigy of the queen, to be placed over the royal vault. In the windows are numerous figures representing former owners of the castle from its foundation. During the Cromwellian wars Sudeley suffered considerably, and yet bears traces of the spoilers' hands. The castle is not a show place, though it contains a wonderful collection of antiquities, and the rooms occupied by Queen Catherine are preserved. The park and gardens are especially beautiful.

The road from Stratford to Sudeley lies through Broadway, from which place it is distant some eight miles; it is about the same distance from Winchcombe to Cheltenham, the Cheltenham road passing over Cleve Hills, whose summit commands beautiful views as far as Malvern.

A number of bungalows and pleasant villas have been built along this road. The district around Sudeley and Winchcombe is beautiful: its attractions were sufficient to induce the Roman settlers in Britain to build their villas along its hillsides. The remains of some of these Roman dwellings have been discovered, and the foundations of one have been carefully preserved, and covered over by Mrs Dent. The Romans of old could appreciate beautiful and healthful situations quite as well as the modern Englishman, and their country houses were arranged in a way far superior to many buildings of modern times. Perhaps one can best appreciate the antiquity of civilisation in England by a careful study of the remains of Roman dwellings erected nearly two thousand years ago by the Italian legions who colonised this island.

CHAPTER XXX

LOXLEY AND ROBIN HOOD

THE name of Loxley is not peculiar to Warwickshire, it is found also in Nottinghamshire and Staffordshire: all three places are said to have been the home of Robin Hood.

Naturally Warwickshire people maintain that the picturesque village situated four miles from Stratford is the place from which the outlaw took his name—"Robin Hood of Loxley." A fairly good case has been made for Warwickshire by the late Mr Tom Burgess, and his able editor, Mr Joseph Hill. Certainly this village is romantic enough in appearance to recommend it to lovers of beauty without any aid of legendary lore of the outlaw of Sherwood.

The church and village are built upon the western slope of a low range of hills, well wooded and somewhat precipitous. In early times, probably before the Roman invasion, these hills had attracted the warlike people then inhabiting the portion of Britain on the south bank of the Avon. A long line of intrenchments marks the positions fortified by these people. Though the earthworks are in places difficult to trace owing to the woods and thickets covering the hillside, the ramparts and ditches may be clearly seen in several places, especially where the sloping ground has prevented the operations of agriculture. There is no record of any find of implements or arms in the neighbourhood, and probably no search has been made, though the earthworks are well known.

The church lies on the north side of the high-road from Loxley to Wellesbourne, and its venerable and exceedingly picturesque appearance, embowered in trees and surrounded by a grass-grown churchyard, dotted with moss-covered stones, well accords with the traditions of old outlaws of the days of chivalry. The masonry of the walls in some places, especially part of the north wall of the chancel, which exhibits the characteristics of herring-bone work, appears to be ancient, possibly pre-Norman, but during the eighteenth century the church was partly rebuilt in a bastard style of architecture. It now consists of a tower at the south-west angle of the church, though apparently formerly joined at the east side by a south aisle, now destroyed: a nave, chancel, and small vestry on the south. The base of the tower, of rude ancient masonry, possibly was altered in the thirteenth century; on the first storey is a good lancet window of early English character, but the highest part is modern. Some stone coffins, moved from their original positions, have been placed against the walls of the chancel: a chalice found in one of these coffins is now lost. Upon the exterior of the south wall of the vestry may be noticed a number of well-carved tablets commemorating members of the Southam family, long settled at Loxley.

As in many places in the district marks and deep scratches upon the wall, in this instance upon the tower, may be noticed, where, according to the local tradition, the archers of Loxley in former days sharpened their arrows when shooting at the butts.

A road through the fields leads from this village

to Ettington, and ascends above Goldicote to a considerable elevation, from which one of the most extensive views over the Vale of the Red Horse is obtained.

The road joins the highway to Banbury near the railway bridge over the deep cutting at Goldicote, whence it descends to Alderminster and meets the Shipston road opposite Alderminster Church. Though rather a rough road for cyclists, this way from Loxley to Alderminster is one of the most pleasant in the district, commanding extensive views over the vale. It is within a short distance of Stratford-on-Avon, but is little frequented, and therefore unspoiled by modern improvement.

Henley-in-Arden

CHAPTER XXXI

HENLEY-IN-ARDEN

SIDE by side stand two townships in the Forest of Arden, the elder consisting of a few houses and a church, dominated by a hill covered with remains of trenches and mounds of a once formidable castle. Such is Beaudesert.

The other township, though of later date, has become more important than its elder sister. Its church, guild house, and market cross denote the neighbourhood of well-to-do traders; and its numerous houses, closely built along both sides of the highway, remind us that the old road once carried most of the traffic from one centre of population to another—from Birmingham and the north towards London. There is a general likeness between long-street Atherstone, Henley-in-

Arden, and other road-side towns. At Henley the street is broad, showing that the houses were built before encroachments were made upon the King's highway. All along the road from Birmingham to Stratford we may mark strips of land, encroachments upon the highway, enclosed by the neighbouring landowners. That this should be allowed is an injustice on the part of private individuals towards the public generally; but the encroachment has gone on, and is still going on in many districts without a word of protest from the local authorities.

Henley being essentially a traders' settlement, dominated by a feudal castle, was a safe place for merchants to congregate. These early inhabitants obtained grants of markets and fairs, and people from near and far came to transact business here.

The castle of the De Montforts upon the hill at Beaudesert played an important part in the settlement of the district; and its first owner, Thurstan, builder of the church at Beaudesert, obtained a grant of the site of the present town of Henley from the Earl of Stafford. The payment imposed by the Earl upon the Lord of Beaudesert was somewhat curious, being a pair of scarlet hose, or three shillings in lieu thereof.

In early times a market was held in the churchyard at Beaudesert on Sundays after mass, but in 1222 Henley had grown sufficiently to have a market of its own, and also a yearly fair; and by this time Sunday marketing was not in fashion. The charter for a market and fair, obtained from the King by Peter de Montfort, fourth Lord of Beaudesert, marks an epoch in the history of Henley. This great noble, Peter de Montfort, had been a ward of William de Canlelupe of Aston Cantlow, and, growing up, became a man of mark, so much so that his name figures in a ballad of the time.   He was a friend and contemporary, as well as a kinsman of Simon de Montfort, whose name will ever be linked with the story of England's struggle for freedom and constitutional government.   Peter de Montfort was a valiant soldier, and under Henry III. held the office of Warden of the Welsh Marches and the custody of the counties of Stafford and Salop.   On one occasion he was chosen as an ambassador to the French Court.   He was one of the twenty-four gentlemen appointed to govern the kingdom, and he led his Warwickshire followers at the battle of Lewes.   Fighting for his kinsman, Simon, he fell at the battle of Evesham in 1265.   Henley was shortly afterwards burnt, probably in the troubles which ensued from that conflict.

In 1284 a second Peter de Montfort, son of the former, obtained pardon and fresh grants of his possessions at Henley.   He had been taken prisoner at the battle of Evesham.

The lords of Henley continued to reside at their Beaudesert Castle for some time longer, until two brothers, John and Peter, obtained possession of the estates.   John was the elder, and took part in the execution of Piers Gaveston on Blacklow Hill.   Afterwards, having marched with the English army into Scotland, he was slain at the battle of Stirling.   Peter, the younger brother, was at that time a cleric, but had taken to wife one Laura de Astley de Ullenhall, by whom he had a son, John, who married the heiress of the Clintons of Coleshill, and became founder of the family of the De Montforts of that district.

About the year 1348 Guy de Montfort, the last direct descendant of the house, married a daughter of the

Earl of Warwick, and thus the castle and manor, and other lands of the De Montforts, passed to the Beauchamps, and was in course of time granted away to Sir Baldwin Freville and Sir Thomas Boteler. The Boteler portion continued in the same family until the days of Queen Elizabeth, who granted it to Ambrose Dudley, Earl of Warwick, at whose death it reverted to the Crown. The other portion after a time came to Francis Smith of Wootton Wawen, whose descendants still own it.[1]

It need not be a matter of surprise that the castle of Beaudesert has disappeared, for it did not suit the Earls of Warwick to have strongholds in the neighbourhood of their own castle. Kenilworth, of course, was an exception, but we find that the earls were jealous of the castle at Fulbrook, and that also has disappeared, as did the castle of Aston Cantlow, and, in later times, that at Milcote.

There was no reason, however, for depopulating the little town of Henley, and, moreover, it brought a considerable revenue to its lord, so it has continued to our day, and has retained many of its antique customs and liberties. The advent of the railway and the marvellous growth of Birmingham are beginning to make alterations in this sleepy little place. For a long time the coaches passing on their way between Birmingham and Stratford, north and south, caused a certain stir and bustle in the street. When the coaches were discontinued the town became quieter than ever, until bicycles began to appear, and the high-roads became once more busy with traffic. We may expect Henley to grow with the increase of motor vehicles, but it will still retain some of its old

[1] See *Transactions of the Birmingham and Midland Institute*, a paper by J. Crouch, Vol. 21, and John Hannett, "The Forest of Arden."

timber-framed houses, old-world appearance, and interesting reminiscences of former days.

The first chapel, built in the reign of Edward III. at the charge of the inhabitants of the town, was rebuilt in the fifteenth century upon the old site.   The church now consists of a nave, north aisle, and a tower at the north-west corner.   The porch is at the west end, facing the street, and is ornamented with battlements of rather unusual form.   The nave has a high pitched roof, extending at the same height from end to end, so that externally there is no division for the chancel. The vestry is on the north-east side, and may have been a chapel of a chantry founded in the reign of Edward III.

The chancel suffered restoration in 1857, and at that time appears to have been fairly cleared out, but it had been considerably altered at a earlier period.

John Hannett in his "Forest of Arden" records that in removing the flat ceiling over the nave, the canopy of the rood loft, gilt and coloured, was found in a position corresponding to the base of the screen below.   The pillars joining the loft and the base are cut away. There is only one ancient monument remaining, a slab with a cross engraved upon it, and the name of Richard Stoke, who appears to have been a priest of the church or chantry.

A few remnants of the old pewter service formerly in the church, and a survival of the old guild, are still preserved here.   Before leaving Henley a brief notice must not be omitted of the local worthy, now, alas! numbered with the great majority.   John Hannett was for many years a much respected resident of the town.

Mr Hannett is well known to English bibliographers as the author of the first systematic account of the art of bookbinding, and locally by his interesting little volume of notes upon the Forest of Arden.

CHAPTER XXXII

ALCESTER

THE paucity of Roman remains in this part of England has led to the exaltation of Alcester as a Roman town, yet there is little to prove that it was a place of much importance. A careful examination of the neighbourhood might reveal the existence of certain military works such as are found around most stations where the legions of Italy camped during the Roman occupation of Britain. That Alcester was ever of much magnitude we doubt; on the other hand there are indications of its having been a military station upon one of the Roman roads. The low-lying ground upon which the present town is built appears to have been liable to floods, and if there was a camp here, it is probable that little of it remained at the time S. Egwin, the Saxon Bishop of Worcester, is fabled to have cursed the smiths of Alcester, who overpowered his preaching by the clang of their hammers.

The identity of Alcester with Alauna of the itineraries is somewhat doubtful, though possibly there were two places of the name. The fact that is not doubtful is that the Roman Ichnield Street passed through this portion of the Forest of Arden. From Honeybourne and Beoley, Alcester is about equidistant; at both Honeybourne and Beoley remains of a Roman camp may be traced. We know that stations on the road were ten

Roman miles, or about nine English ones, apart, consequently Alcester is exactly the spot where a camp should occur. Very few remains of the Roman period have been found here, beyond a few coins, and a statue built into a wall of the vicarage garden. On the hills in the neighbourhood there are some earthworks that might repay investigation, and it is not at all improbable that the remains of a summer camp might be identified.

In the town several fine specimens of timber-built houses yet remain, as well as an old hall of somewhat quaint design, and a spacious parish church.

The town hall is of two storeys, the upper portion being supported upon an arcade of cylindrical pillars and semicircular arches. The spaces between the columns have now been filled in, so that the lower storey is no longer open to the street. In this respect it resembles the town hall of Stratford, and a further resemblance may be noted, the town prison was in one corner of the ground floor.

The church, unfortunately, with the exception of the tower entirely rebuilt, still retains a fine monument to Fulke Greville and his wife, and one or two other interesting things. Over the monument is a helmet put up by the heralds at the time of the funeral. The sword, banner, and gauntlets completing the funeral ornaments have disappeared. On the south wall of the tower is a curious triptych worth noticing; this is dated 1683. The doors when open display upon the inner sides a painting representing a number of tradesmen with the emblems of their trades. On the centre of the panel is an inscription as follows:—

"Behold within this table are the names with the memorable acts of those who have most liberally extended their bounty to help tradesmen and relieve poor and aged people dwelling within the town and parish of Alcester."

At the east end of the north aisle is a screen of carved oak which is said to have come from Warwick Castle. At the east end of the south aisle is Chantrey's monument to the second Marquis of Hertford, who died in 1822; and under the tower another marble figure of Sir Hamilton Seymour. This is the work of Count Gleichen. Some years ago the head of a pastoral staff of carved ivory was found in the rectory garden. This was bought by the British Museum in 1903 for £100.

The town as at present constituted probably owes much to the influence of the members of the Benedictine Abbey, founded in 1140 by Ralph Pincerna. This Abbey stood on the "Island," so called because the River Arrow and a moat surrounded it. The monastery continued to flourish until the Dissolution, when Henry VIII. granted it to William Sewster and John, his son.

The manor, divided at one time into two moieties, one that of Fitz Hubert, the other of William de Boteraux, was united in 1330-31 by Sir John Beauchamp, and so finally passed into the hands of the Grevilles, Earls of Warwick. The history of the manor appears to be interesting, and yet remains to be written. A fair was granted by King Edward I. to Walter de Beauchamp—an important advantage to the town.

Leaving Alcester by a road at the north-west the little village of Arrow is soon reached. Here there is nothing noteworthy beyond the very picturesque cottages, and the little church, the burial-place of the Marquises of Hertford. Arrow was anciently the seat of the Burdetts, who during the Wars of the Roses espoused the side of the house of York. A romantic story connected with this family is told in "Historic Warwick-shire." At the west end of the village is the entrance to Ragley Park, the seat of the Marquis of Hertford: a finely situated mansion built in the classic style of architecture fashionable in the eighteenth century.

In the days when George IV. was King, Ragley was more than once favoured by the presence of the "Finest Gentleman in Europe," who found a congenial friend in the owner of the estate. It is related that the King one day remarked that a hill, conspicuous from a drive leading from the hall, would be a fine site for a castle. The Marquis ordered a castle to be built, and the next time Royal George drove that way the towers and battlements of a sham castle met his gaze and flattered his vanity.

Although the town of Alcester has little to interest a tourist, it is a convenient centre from which to pay visits to many of the picturesque villages in the neigh-bourhood. Coughton Court, the ancient seat of the Throckmortons, lies about a mile north of the town. Coughton, in days gone by, was a large fortified manor house, defended by a moat, now filled, and having a very handsome embattled tower at the entrance at the west side. A portion of the building surrounding the quadrangle was pulled down years ago, but the three remaining sides are strikingly picturesque. Some buildings on the north are apparently anterior in date to the main edifice, and include a hall, kitchen, and other rooms still in a fair state of preservation. At the time of the Gunpowder Plot Coughton became the rendez-vous of some of the chief conspirators, and the ladies who were concerned in the plot came here for safety. Father Garnet also was here. An old cross by the road-side is popularly supposed to mark the entrance to the Forest of Arden.

CHAPTER XXXIII

THE road from Stratford-on-Avon to Shipston-on-Stour descends at about five miles from Stratford to the river which gives the latter town its name. To the left are the level meads of Ettington Park, bounded by a range of low hills, and beyond the park the little village of Halford, with its bridge over the Stour, where the passage is said to have been contested in a sharp skirmish between the Cavaliers and Roundheads in the civil wars of the time of Charles I. The by-road turns off to the left, crosses the bridge and ascends the hill on the way towards Upper Ettington. There are several fine old inns in this neighbourhood. One, a stone-built house of some antiquity, stands back from the main road, another is on the hill above Halford Bridge. We are here on a portion of the old Fosse way, which crossed the Stour at this point, and appears to have originated the name of the village. The inn at Halford is a noted hostelry, possessing one of the finest old bowling greens in the county. The manor was in the possession of the Earls of Warwick after the Norman conquest, it subsequently descended to the Giffords and Cantelupes. Dugdale mentions a very peculiar rent paid in the time of Edward I. by John de Breggewrithe for three acres of land here——by homage, and the service of finding for thirty-six poor people on Christmas day a loaf of bread each, a herring and a flagon of beer.

The church at Halford is dedicated to S. Mary. It retains traces of Norman workmanship, including the chancel arch, and north doorway with curiously carved tympanum. On the south side of the chancel arch is a very curious cruciform hagioscope.

From Halford the road skirts the eastern side of the beautiful park at Ettington, the ancient possession of the Shirleys.

Ettington has often been cited as an instance of a manor which has continued in one family from the time of the Saxons to our own day. It has lately become the custom to decry stories of Saxon proprietorship, and to date the beginnings of the families of our ancient landed gentry from the Norman period at earliest. In the past antiquaries have been prone to favour the legends of Saxon ancestors; in the present day there are genealogists who are altogether too sceptical, and require proof where no proof can possibly be given. Probably the truth lies midway between the credulity of the old school, and the scepticism of the modern.

In the case of the Shirleys we have two facts to deal with. In the Doomsday Book of Warwickshire it is recorded "Sasuualo holds of Henry (de Feriers) seventeen hides in Etendone," and that a priest, a soldier, twenty-five bordarii, and two thanes or freeholders were included in the manor. It is only fair to conclude from these facts that the town was well established before the Norman Conquest. The presence of a priest denotes a church, and the thanes a respectable Saxon population. Saswalo can scarcely have been a Saxon, yet he may have married a Saxon lady though he held his lands at that time under a Norman baron. He was the direct ancestor of the present owner of the estate.

Saswalo had a son, Henry, and another son, Fulcher. The latter's son, Sewallis, first assumed the name of Shirley from a manor of that name in Derbyshire, and after an agreement with his brother Henry to purchase his birthright, became possessed of the manor of Ettington. He was succeeded by his son Henry in the reign of King John. Henry was succeeded by Sir Sewallis de Eatingdon, and the latter's son and heir, Sir James, appears to have resumed the name of Shirley, and to have married the daughter of Simon de Walton, Bishop of Norwich in the reign of Henry III. About this time there arose a curious family disagreement; Sir James, being forcibly deprived of his estate by Ralph, his son, petitioned King Edward I. for a restitution, but dying before the matter could be settled, Ralph continued to possess his father's estates. He was the first knight of the shire returned for the county of Warwick in 1294, and dying in 1327 was buried beside his wife, Margaret Waldershef, under an altar tomb in the south transept of Ettington Church. The mutilated effigies of the knight and his lady may still be seen there.

The manor descended in a direct line till it came to Sir Hugh, who fell in battle at Shrewsbury wearing the armour of Henry IV. This knight is mentioned by Shakespeare :—

" *Prince Henry*. Hold up thy head, vile Scot, or thou art like
Never to hold it up again ! the spirits
Of valiant Shirley, Stafford, Blunt, are in my arms ;
It is the Prince of Wales that threatens thee ;
Who never promiseth but he means to pay."

The widow of Sir Hugh's son, in the reign of Henry VI., leased the manor to Thomas Porter, whose only daughter, Agnes, marrying John Underhill, led to the settlement of the Underhill family in the parish. It was one of these Underhills who sold New Place in Stratford-on-Avon to William Shakespeare.

The elder branch of the Shirley family obtained the Earldom of Ferrers, establishing their home in a different part of the country, while the younger branch maintained their ancient inheritance at Ettington. To this point the reader may be referred to a most interesting volume, " Lower Ettington, its Manor House and Church," privately printed in 1869, by a late owner of the estate.

We may here notice a very curious family connection, linking Shakespeare with the Shirleys, the Earl of Essex, and Lord Ferrers of Chartley. In brief, one of the Ardens of Park Hall by a marriage with Sir Edward Devereux became the ancestor of the present Viscount Hereford. The Devereux family were descended on the female side from William, Lord Ferrers of Chartley. Sir Henry Shirley in the seventeenth century married Dorothy, younger of two sisters, and co-heiress of Robert Devereux, Earl of Essex, and consequently co-heiress of the ancient baronies of Ferrers of Chartley, Bouchier, and Louvaine. In consequence of this match, and as a reward for distinguished loyalty on the part of the Shirley family, King Charles II., in 1677, determined the abeyance of the barony of Ferrers of Chartley in favour of Sir Robert Shirley. In another place mention has been made of Catherine, who was daughter of Edward Arden of Park Hall, William Shakespeare's kinsman, wife of Sir Edward Devereux. Though very slight, the connection is worthy of notice in passing.

The first Earl Ferrers of the Shirley family married Elizabeth, daughter and heiress of Laurence Washington of Garsdon, Wilts, grandson of that Robert Washington of Northampton, from whom George Washington is descended. This marriage of a Shirley with a Washington is only one instance out of many of the honourable alliances made by members of George Washington's family.

A stone's-throw from the manor house stand the remains of the picturesque ruined church, now private property. The venerable ivy-covered tower, the arcading adjoining it on the north side, the chancel steps, a piscina in one of the pillars, the south transept and fragments of walls on the south side, are sufficient to indicate its former splendour. There are few traces of the old Norman building which was pulled down and entirely rebuilt in the reign of Henry III. At one time an important building, measuring 126 feet from east to west, and 75 feet across the transepts from north to south, it was unroofed in 1798, when a new parish church being built on another site in the village of Upper Ettington, some of the old furniture and the bells were removed to the present church. At that time a great part of the old edifice was razed; the south transept, which, being the burial-place of the family, was the only part retaining a roof. This transept and the tower were repaired in 1825 by Evelyn John Shirley, Esq. It is stated in the history of Ettington that the windows were filled with ancient painted glass, part of which originally formed the great Jesse window in the chapel of William of Wykeham's college at Winchester. A chapel of S. Nicholas founded at Ettington in the reign of King John has disappeared, as well as many of the ancient monuments but the mutilated effigies of Ralph Shirley and Margaret, his wife, who died in the reign of Edward II., 1327, and was a person of great consequence at that period, serving under Edward I. as a valiant knight, and subsequently under his son, Edward II. The south transept now contains all the monuments to the Shirley family; the best of these is a magnificent tomb, erected by the Hon. George Shirley in 1776, to the memory of his father, the first Earl Ferrers. Upon it are three figures, the central one representing George Shirley, and those on either side his father and mother in their coronation robes.

Some few years since an alteration took place in the mode of spelling the name of this village, which gave rise to some amusing verses written by a visitor to the place, and printed in the second edition of Mr Shirley's history of the manor.

> " Hitherto I've been ready, while still in the dark,
>   To break bread when invited to Eatington Park :
>   Henceforth I shall hold myself ready instead
>   To partake, more enlighten'd of Ettington bread."

It should be noted that Lower Ettington, being the private residence of the Shirleys, is not a show place, though at this point it may not be out of place to refer to the Underhill family in connection with Ettington and Shakespeare, since it so chanced that the Poet bought his Great House at Stratford-on-Avon from one of the family, and had his title thereto ratified by another. We shall see what kind of people these Underhills were with whom Shakespeare had dealings, and how the affairs of the town were linked with theirs. They were people of learning, distinction, and wealth.

William Underhill, who owned the Great House at Stratford, was the second son of Edward Underhill of Ettington, by Margaret, his wife, a member of the ancient family of Middlemore of Edgbaston. Their memorial

brass is still preserved on the south wall of the tower of
the old church at Ettington. Edward's elder son,
Thomas, afterwards occupied Ettington. William was
born about 1523, and being bred to the law became a
member of the Inner Temple and married Ursala, one
of the daughters of John Congreve of Stretton in the
county of Stafford. In 1551 he acquired property at
Barton-on-the-Heath, a place mentioned by Shakespeare
in the "Taming of the Shrew." About this time William
Clopton, owner of New Place, was travelling in Italy,
and one William Bott, acting as his agent, obtained
possession of the house. Bott appears to have had no
very good reputation, and William Underhill was several
times employed by people in the neighbourhood to help
them against him. In 1567 Underhill bought New
Place from Bott, and in the next year he purchased the
manors of Idlicott and Loxley from Ludowick Greville
and others. He was thus a very considerable landowner in the county, and used his influence for the
benefit of his neighbours. We find that the Stratford-
on-Avon Council in 1568 paid "for a dinner for Mr
Underhill at the Swan 17/4," probably in recognition
of services rendered. He died on March 31st, 1570, and
was buried at Ettington under a marble monument
whereon were the arms of Underhill impaling Congreve.
William, his only son, was born in 1554, and was a
minor at the time of his father's death. Christopher
Hatton, his kinsman, obtained a grant of his wardship
in 1571.

We now come to an event of some interest and
importance, followed by a tragedy by which Shakespeare
himself was affected. In 1597 William Underhill the
second sold New Place to William Shakespeare. On
the 6th of July in that year Underhill made his will and

died next day.   He had two sons, Fulk, the elder, who died a minor, and at the last moment confessed that he had poisoned his father.   Fulk's brother, Hercules, succeeded to the estates, and in 1602 completed the transfer of New Place to Shakespeare.   In an able paper by Mr William Underhill of Hove, in Sussex, it is surmised that by the sudden death of the father, the original vendor, the conveyance of New Place was incomplete, and that a supplemental deed was necessary to establish a valid title.   Most of the above particulars of the Underhill family will be found in full in the paper before mentioned, and also much interesting information concerning the transfer, in Halliwell-Phillipps' "History of New Place."

CHAPTER XXXIV

THE central position of Stratford-on-Avon made it a somewhat important place during the Civil Wars of Stuart days. The battlefield of Edgehill lies but a few miles eastwards from the town; Coventry, headquarters of the Puritans, and Birmingham, similarly affected, were not far distant: Worcester and Oxford, noted for their adherence to the Royal cause, both looked upon Stratford as a point of connection. Any movements of troops from the north, towards Oxford or London, caused the River Avon to become a strategical position of importance; and the bridges crossing the stream at Warwick, Stratford, Bidford, and Evesham were points of vantage to be seized upon by one or other of the contending parties. Lord Brooke, "Fanatic Brooke," owner of Warwick Castle, being a Puritan and one of the most zealous adherents to the Parliament in the Midlands, found Stratford somewhat of a thorn in his flesh. He therefore determined to take it, and as it was a place with no means of defence except the river, he had very little trouble in accomplishing his object.

The story of the battle at Stratford is quaintly told in a little quarto news-tract of the time :—

271

"A TRVE RELATION

of the death of the Lord Brooks, who was slaine by
a bullet discharged against him as he stood in a
window against the Minster at Lichfield;
With the description of a bloody conspiracy prevented
by God's providence, from destroying the Councell
of warre at Stratford-on-Avon, wherein is a true
relation of these particulars following:—

    1. Of the marching of the Lord Brooks his army.
    2. The Parliament forces that went to Stratford.

The Lord Brooks.	Captaine Gardner and his
Colonell Purifoys.	Regiment.
Captaine Bridges.	A Regiment of Dragooners.
Captaine Hunt.	A Regiment of Foot.

    3. The Cavaliers Commanders.

Colonel Wagstaffe.	Captaine Triske.
L. Robert.	L. Sallington, &c.
Ser. Ma. Russel.	

    4. The manner of the fight at Stratford.
    5. The manner of the contriving of the Plot.
    6. The blowing up of the Town Hall, and the
       hurt it did.
    7. The Lord Brooks his valour before his death.
    8. The relation of his death.
    9. Advertisement to the City of London.

LONDON,

Printed for Thos. Bates, and to be sold at his shop
in the old Baily, Anno Dom. 1643."

Towards the end of February 1642-43, Lord Brooke
was marching about the country, taking up positions
of importance, and making preparations against the

Cavaliers. News came to him that a detachment of 300 men from the King's army had been sent to Stratford, and on Friday, the 24th of February, his Lordship, being then at Warwick, sent twenty "dragooners" to give the people of Stratford a night alarm. "By reason of the fear thereof they were kept waking all the night." At eight o'clock on Saturday, the 25th, Lord Brooke with his main force drew near the town: this force consisted of Colonel Purfoys' regiment, Captain Bridges, troops under Captain Gardner, and Captain Hunt, a regiment of dragooners, and one of foot. It is said that the country came in that abundance, protesting to live and die in defence of Lord Brooke and Parliament; that there was no need for any of them to march with this part of the army to Stratford. From the account given in the pamphlet it seems that the attacking force came from Warwick by the lower road, and consequently had to cross the river before they could enter the town.

A party of dragooners were first sent across, and drawn up in the form of a half moon, somewhere near the end of Bridge Street, and the Cavaliers, hearing that the enemy was approaching, sallied out and drew up their forces. Then Lord Brooke "let fly a drake against them, which ran through the midst of them and put them to great fright." The men of Warwick advanced, and the garrison retired into the town fighting: they were pursued, and fled in disorder, leaving their commander, Captain Triske, dangerously hurt. Triske, in another account, is "Twist a Dutchman."

The Cavaliers had stored a quantity of ammunition in the town hall, and as Lord Brooke marched towards that building with the intention of holding a council

s

of war there, the ammunition exploded and the town hall was wrecked. The Parliamentarians assumed that the enemy had intended to blow up their leaders, but there are some doubts as to the correctness of this assumption: the explosion may have been accidental.

The wrecking of the town hall caused "a most lamentable and pitifull cry in the towne." One of the townsmen was killed, and four more burnt and bruised. This town hall was built in 1633: it remained for some time in a shattered state, and was afterwards repaired and strengthened with iron bars till 1767, when the greater part was taken down, and the present building erected, and dedicated by David Garrick at the Jubilee in 1769.

A column of the old town hall is still preserved in New Place garden, a solitary monument to the part played by Stratford during the wars of King and Parliament.

The Roundheads broke down a portion of the bridge, effectually stopping the road to Oxford, and it was not till 1651 that the bridge was properly repaired: an order of the Sessions was then made for the work to be done at the expense of the county.

Small and unimportant as was this battle of Stratford when viewed in relation to the great battle on Edgehill, it is yet a memorable event in the annals of the town.

The events which followed the battle of Stratford form one of the most romantic episodes in local history. Queen Henrietta Maria at that time took an active part in the campaign, and, had the conduct of the war remained in her hands, the final result might have been very different.   In order to help Charles, the Queen had gone to the continent with certain treasures, which she pawned to obtain arms and ammunition.   In the spring of 1643 the Queen landed in Yorkshire, and the adherents of the Royal cause in the north of England at once flocked to her standard.

Sir William Dugdale has given an account of the remarkable march made by the Queen and her army from Yorkshire to Oxford, showing that wherever the Queen appeared she was entirely victorious, and that the spirit of chivalry stimulated her officers to perform valiant deeds.   The Queen rode at the head of her army, managed her affairs with spirit, and, to inspire confidence, acted in every way as a general would have done.   While on the march she took her meals in the open air, and upon coming to a village or town, called upon it to surrender, and made her headquarters at the chief house at each place.   It was on the 11th of July 1643 that her Majesty arrived at Stratford-on-Avon. The previous night had been spent at King's Norton, one of the Queen's own manors, where the house occupied by her still stands.   The room in which she slept, with the oratory adjoining it, may be visited. A few years ago the truth of the tradition was strangely authenticated by a letter written by Henrietta Maria, being found behind the mantelpiece in the room associated with her name.   This letter was recently in the possession of a former tenant of the house, one of the Lee family.

Prince Rupert came out of Oxford to meet the Queen, and stationed himself at Stratford-on-Avon, but he seems to have been in communication with her at King's Norton.   The King with a large body of troops followed Rupert as far as Kineton, where he expected to meet his Consort.　This was the position of affairs when Henrietta Maria marched into Stratford at the head of an army of 3000 foot, 1500 horse, a train of artillery, and 150 waggons laden with ammunition.　The advent of such an army into the little town must have caused considerable excitement in the place.　Prince Rupert was already quartered there, according to tradition, at the Red Horse Hotel in Bridge Street.　It is a significant fact that the Queen was entertained on that day, and the two following days, at New Place by Shakespeare's daughter, Mrs Hall.　The significance of this is twofold; first, it proves that New Place was one of the best houses in the town; secondly, that Shakespeare's descendants were well affected to the Royal cause: their house being chosen in preference to the College, then owned by the Coombes, who were not above suspicion of having leanings to the side of the Parliament.　The further progress of Henrietta Maria and her army was quite triumphant.　The meeting of the King and Queen on the plains of Kineton put heart into the Royalists' cause, and a medal was struck to commemorate the event.　For a short time after Lord Brooke's descent upon the town, Stratford-on-Avon was held for the Parliament, but the advent of the Puritans was anything but gratifying to the family at New Place, and their Royalist friends and neighbours.　The Parliamentarians, however, were soon ejected.

CHAPTER XXXV

CAVALIERS AND ROUNDHEADS

THE BATTLE OF EDGE HILL

AT Edge Hill King Charles I. lost an opportunity: the
tide in his affairs was not taken at the flood, and to the
end of his days the unfortunate monarch was bound
in shallows and in miseries. For two days before the
battle the King's army and that of the Earl of Essex
had been marching in parallel lines, scarcely twenty
miles apart, yet neither knew where the other might be
found, until Prince Rupert's scouts came in sight of the
enemy's watch-fires near Kineton. The King immediately moved his army to Edge Hills, and Essex saw that
his onward march was stopped. Here was the King's
opportunity: the position was impregnable, but food was
scarce, and Charles formed a false opinion of his people.
Englishmen, he argued, would not fight against their
King in person. The King should have remained at
the top of the hill, and have kept a tight rein upon
the impetuous Rupert. He did neither: the one chance
an error in judgment led him to throw away, and
his generalship was not strong enough to restrain
Prince Rupert, who commanded the right wing. The
King's standard was set up above Radway, upon a spot
now marked by Radway Tower. Rupert attacked the
enemy's left wing, charged down the hill, and up the
slopes on the other side of Radway brook. This

impetuous onslaught routed the Parliamentarians. Having achieved this, the Prince should next have attacked the enemy's centre by a flanking movement, but he did nothing of the kind. On the enemy's right Wilmot attacked, but was unable to cross the hedges and ditches. This check gave Essex the advantage, and he immediately attacked the centre of the Royal army: the King's standard was taken, but quickly recovered by Captain Smith of the Skilts, Sir Edmund Verney, the standard-bearer, being killed. Rupert returned to the field too late, and the King had to retire from Essex, who had followed up the advantage gained at the beginning of his attack. Up to this point neither army was entirely victorious, and the Royalists might even then have won a decisive victory. But night was closing over the battlefield, and the soldiers were weary with marching and fighting. The two armies drew off, and both sides claimed the victory. This battle was fought on an October afternoon in the year 1642. The bells of Radway Church were ringing for evening service when the King descended to the valley; this fact is sufficient to show that the best use had not been made of the morning hours. The wooded slopes of Edge Hills no longer resound with the battle cry; the peaceful country, remote from towns, and as yet untouched by railways, appears to-day no likely place for the mustering of armies, and the struggle of contending factions: yet who shall say how soon the hill sides may again be covered by the tents of an encamping host? Old battlefields have often been the scene of other conflicts, perhaps in consequence of their strategic value.

After studying contemporary tracts it is not difficult to come to a conclusion as to the result of the battle.

Allowing for party feeling, both the Royalists' and the Roundheads' accounts agree in the main.   Rupert's attack on Essex's left wing is admitted to have been entirely successful, but instead of at once rallying his troops and again returning to the attack, he allowed his men to pillage, and did not return until too late in the day.   The fight must have been a most stubborn one ; according to one account the King's losses amounted to 3000 men, while the Parliament lost 300 : on the other hand the King claims to have killed five times as many as were lost on his own side.   The exact numbers of the slain can never be known, but we may be sure that in a fierce pitched battle, like that of Edge Hill, the casualties were very great.   The most curious account is that given by a minister who had followed the army of the Earl of Essex ; this man had discreetly retired to a hill at a little distance, and viewed the battle through his spy-glass.   As shades of evening fell, fearing to be left in the open fields, he made the best of his way to Warwick : " Not knowing what the issue of things might be, in the darksome evening, while it was yet light, I rid to Warwick among hundreds of drawn swords, and yet was saved from the least touch of a bloodthirsty hand."

The account published by the authority of the King at Oxford, while it has a distinctly favourable colouring to the Cavaliers, is the same in general outline as that published by the Parliament, both admitting that the battle was not decisive.   The King clearly lost his opportunity : he could easily have outnumbered Essex, whose reinforcements did not arrive until the day after the battle.

There is a tradition, likely enough to be true, that some of the fugitives from the fight took refuge at Stratford, and that many of them died there.

CHAPTER XXXVI

A VISIT TO GLOUCESTERSHIRE

A PLEASANT ride from Stratford will bring one into the heart of the Cotswold Hills in Gloucestershire. Possibly in the time of Elizabeth it may have taken a man two days to ride so far, though a good horse would manage the journey easily in one. At any rate it is clear that the author of " Richard II." and " Henry IV." was well acquainted with the Cotswold country.

A branch of the Shakespeare family had settled at Dursley, in the neighbourhood where dwelt " Clement Perks, of the Hill," and " William Visor, of Wincot." Over and over again in this Midland country we have evidence of Shakespeare's knowledge of topographical details : take, for instance, that wonderfully vivid passage in " Richard II.," where Bolingbroke and his friends arrive in " the wilds of Gloucestershire," and make inquiries about the neighbourhood. They were near Dursley and within sight of Berkeley Castle.

" *Northumberland.* How far is it to Berkley, and what stir
             Keeps good old York there with his men of war ?
    Percy. There stands the Castle by yon tuft of trees."

To this day the castle may well be described in the same words, and, as a matter of fact, has been so described more than once by people who knew not the play.

The Cotswold men and the Cotswold sports receive

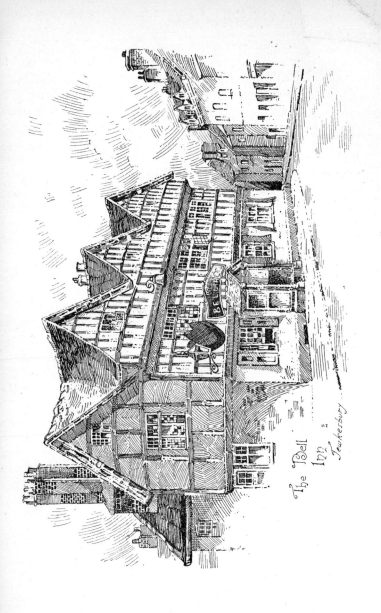

The Bell Inn
Tewkesbury

attention at Shakespeare's hands, and the references, incidental indeed, are yet significant. The Cotswold sports, formerly held near Broadway Tower, twelve miles from Stratford, though now no longer held, have left their memory behind them. All sorts of games were practised by the country lads assembled there

At Broadway.

to vie with one another in friendly contests of strength and skill. The spot chosen as the arena for these sports was the grassy summit of the hill above Broadway, near the great road from Evesham towards London, within sight of Stratford. The four-shire stone is in this neighbourhood, and the Wolds extend for many miles south-west towards Bath and Bristol, but at Broadway they really begin; they bound this part of the Avon valley, and their outline is a conspicuous object southwards from the town of Stratford-on-Avon.

The picturesque village with its irregularly built street of quaint old stone houses is now famous. In this beautiful neighbourhood artists have found a suitable home, so there is a little colony of artistic people living at Broadway. "Middle Hill," formerly the seat of Sir Thomas Phillipps, the bibliophile, and now of Edgar Flower, Esq., stands on an eminence above the village overlooking the fair vale of Evesham.

Elsewhere it has been shown that Shakespeare was familiar with Evesham, that an Evesham man was a member of his company in London, and that he knew at least one good story in connection with the ancient monastic town. Indeed it requires no stretch of the imagination to suppose that the ruined abbeys of the Avon valley suggested to his mind one of the most beautiful sonnets (73). Evesham Abbey, perhaps, answers best to this description: of all our great churches of the vale it has suffered most at the hands of the spoilers. Now a single arch and tower are all that remain above ground of the once stately church, but in the days of Elizabeth much more was standing of that "bare ruined choir."

> "That time of year thou may'st in me behold
> When yellow leaves, or none, or few do hang
> Upon the boughs which shake against the cold,
> Bare ruined choirs, where late the sweet birds sang."

The imagery is, of course, direct from nature, and the grove in winter is likened to the ruined choirs; the birds are the choristers who once chanted sweetly in all monastic churches, and these—the ruins with past glories and associations—serve as an emblem of the man whose prime is past. Alas! our prime is over all too soon—

> "Consumed with that which it was nourished by."

This, however, is a digression, for are we not in Gloucestershire Wilds, with Justice Shallow, Master Silence, and Honest Davey?

We hear of "Goodman Puff of Barson," of Barton-on-the-Heath, of Berkeley, and of Cirencester in Gloucestershire. There are also references to more local matter in the fruits of the district. Justice Shallow regales Sir John Falstaff on pippins of his "own graffing," on "leather coats"; apples and warden pears fit for pies are mentioned in the "Winter's Tale." It always seems to me that Justice Shallow's country house was somewhere near Broadway, on the borders of Worcestershire and Gloucestershire, where each farm-house has its own orchard, where we breathe the sweet air of the hills, and life seems lighter and more enjoyable than in the lowlands with its river mists.

Tewkesbury mustard [1] being mentioned by Shake-speare suggests an intimate acquaintance with that town; more so, perhaps, than the scenes in "Henry VI.," which are of necessity placed upon "the plains near Tewkesbury," because the final battle of that period was fought upon the meadows watered by the Severn and the Avon.

Tewkesbury is in Gloucestershire, near enough to the Worcestershire border to be associated with that county also; and as it lies but a morning's ride from Stratford, we may believe that Shakespeare knew the place, with its fine monastic buildings, and mighty Norman church, the burial-place of many of the

---

[1] Five kinds of mustard grow wild in this district. The Common (Sinapis nigra); the Wild, or Cherlock (S. arvensis); the Hedge (Sisymbrium officinale); Mithridate, or Pennycress (Thlaspi Arvense); Tower (Turritis glabra). Bright yellow flowers of the mustard have often been noticed upon the banks of the Severn near Tewkesbury, and it is highly probable that the plant was cultivated here and manufactured into the mustard of commerce.

characters immortalised in his historical plays.   Situated amid rich meadows near the confluence of two rivers,

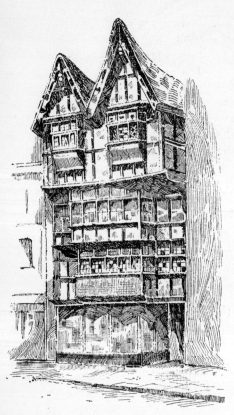

the massive tower of the abbey church forms a conspicuous and beautiful object in the landscape : upon closer inspection the church loses none of its beauty. It is one of the finest of the class in England, reminding one of those great fanes raised by the Normans in their own land ; indeed, it is more continental in plan and arrangment than many of the other abbey churches in the county. The clustering chapels around the choir, the magnificent chantries and tombs, the great windows filled with ancient coloured glass, the bulky cylindrical columns, all inspire the beholder with wonder at their strength or beauty, while the associations of the place carry the mind back to the days of William Rufus, and down to those of the Wars of the Roses.

A Quaint House at Tewkesbury

The approach to the abbey on the north leads through

The Warwick
    Chantry in
Tewkesbury Abbey

Sidney Heath

the churchyard to a rather plain and massive porch, but before entering it is best to go to the west end and see the great arch which is the most peculiar feature of the

Tomb of Hugh le Despencer

abbey. At the west end of the nave two small and very characteristic Norman towers, or turrets, with restored pinnacles, rise above the roof, and are joined almost at the top by a semicircular arch beneath which is

T

a great window, and a doorway of later date. The jambs
with mouldings and pilasters of this arch rise 64 feet
towards the roof, the space between them being 34 feet
wide.   This must be one of the finest arches in England,
a remarkable example of the Norman builders' art,
dating from about the year 1120. The church is of
noble proportions, being nearly 300 feet long, with transepts, from north to south, 124 feet : these figures give
some idea of the great size of the church.   The richness
of the decorated work in the choir, and the massive proportions of the nave by contrast add considerably to
the beauty and impressiveness of the building.

The great Earls of Gloucester, Fitz Hamon, Robert
Fitz-Roy, and the De Clares, were the first great
benefactors, then came the Despencers and Beauchamps : it is the connection with these three families
that makes the history of Tewkesbury so interesting.   Besides a series of monuments to the old
abbots the abbey contains many memorials to the
illustrious dead, who were formerly lords of this part
of England.

Around the sanctuary, and between the great piers
which support the arches, are arranged a number of fine
canopied tombs and chantries, whose sides of lace-like
tracery support graceful canopies of tabernacle-work.
A broad aisle separates the choir from a number of
clustering chapels, now shorn of their altars, but retaining many of their old monuments which served
the purpose of screens to the chapels.

The chapel of S. Margaret has one of the finest of
these tombs to the memory of Sir Guy de Brian, Lord
of Welwyn, who married the widow of Hugh, Lord
Despencer. Sir Guy bore the English standard at the
Battle of Cressy (1346). A little more to the east, at

the entrance of S. Edmund's Chapel, is a beautiful screen of wrought stone in lace-like geometrical tracery, the cenotaph of Abbot Wakeman, the last Abbot of

Tomb of John Wakeman   Tewkesbury Abbey

Tewkesbury. It was evidently intended that a figure of the Abbot, in his habit as he lived, should have been placed on the tomb, but events happened to prevent this being put into execution. As a warning against pride the Abbot caused a repulsive figure, representing himself in death, a *memento mori*, to be placed upon the tomb: worms and toads are around the emaciated limbs of the effigy.

Hard by is the tomb of "false, perjured, fleeting Clarence," and his Duchess, who lay in a vault having an entrance at the back of the high altar: their bones are said to be mouldering there to this day. Here, also, lies hapless Prince Edward, who lost his young life beneath the shadow of the old grey tower. The Prince is said to have been buried in the centre of the chancel near the tower; an inscription on a modern brass plate records his death. There is no certain record of the exact place of his murder; some accounts stating that he was killed on the field of battle, others that the tragedy took place in a room of a house in the main street of Tewkesbury. Shakespeare probably followed some well-known tradition, but we must remember that in placing the death of the young prince upon the field of battle he may have been simply generalising: for the purposes of the drama it does not matter whether the Prince was murdered in a house or on a field, and it is more convenient for stage purposes that it should take place upon the battlefield.

In the clerestory window of the chancel much fine old glass is still to be seen, representing figures of former lords of Tewkesbury, and much pomp of heraldry is there. The colours are rich and varied, a great contrast to the crude colouring of modern stained-glass windows.

The abbey compares very favourably with that of Westminster, the great Norman columns impart to it an appearance of solidity and grandeur which is wanting in the more famous abbey beside the Thames. Fortunately the church is particularly well preserved and being

High Street

Tewkesbury

somewhat off the beaten track, has escaped, to some extent, the ravages of the Reformation and civil wars.

There is not much left of the domestic buildings of the abbey, but a large and stately gatehouse still stands to the south-west of the church: and across the way the old half-timbered hostelry, The Bell, remains. This may have been a guest-house, or a hostel for strangers and pilgrims.

In recent times the authoress of " John Halifax, Gentleman," Mrs Craik, made her home within its ancient walls, and a monument to that lady has been placed in the church. There is a pleasant garden open to the public beside the river, and in the town should be noticed several mediæval houses with characteristic broad mullioned windows, extending across almost the whole width of the façade. In one or two instances fine tracery of carved oak in the heads of the windows have been preserved.

Tewkesbury is a good centre for visiting Cheltenham, Gloucester, Deerhurst, Malvern and Worcester, though perhaps Malvern may be preferred for its elevated position.

THE TOWER OF HAMPTON-IN-ARDEN CHURCH

CHAPTER XXXVII

A RAMBLE IN THE FOREST OF ARDEN

IF there is nothing grand in Warwickshire scenery, there is at least much that is pleasing. The rich undulating landscape, with green hedge-rows, comfortable farm-houses nestling in the hollows, and old towers of village churches peeping from among elm trees, little streams purling through valleys, overshadowed

by willows and fringed with tall rushes : this Warwickshire country is indeed a land of fertile fields, green
pastures, and contentment.   A ramble in such a land,
either awheel or afoot, will well repay one who delights
in country sights and sounds.

> " Under the greenwood tree
>   Who loves to lie with me,
>   And tune his merry note
>   Unto the sweet bird's throat,
> Come hither, come hither, come hither :
>   Here shall he see
>   No enemy
> But winter and rough weather."

Starting from Stratford along the Birmingham road,
past Wilmcote and Bearley, and the entrance to Edstone Hall, the fine old coach road at Wootton Wawen[1]
crosses a bridge whereon may be seen a record of the
distance from London—one hundred miles.

To the left are the remains of fish-ponds belonging
to one of the most ancient monasteries in the county.
In the Saxon period a monastery was founded here,
and a charter relating to it is extant.   (A copy is in
the Shakespeare Memorial Library at Stratford-on-Avon.)
It appears to have been destroyed before the Norman
Conquest, though the Priory Church remains to this day.
Robert de Stafford refounded the monastery, giving
it to the monks of Conchis in Normandy.   After many
changes it was granted to the Carthusians at Coventry
in the time of Richard II., but restored to Conchis by
Henry IV., and at length given by Henry VI. to the
recently founded King's College, Cambridge.

[1] Wootton Wawen ; the name is supposed to be derived from
" Wagen," or " Wawen," a Saxon who owned this town in the woods,
and, according to Dugdale, " was a man of great quality in his time."

On the right stands the mansion, Wootton Wawen Hall, built by Lord Carrington in the seventeenth century. The descent of the manor from the time of the Norman Conquest is of some interest. It was given to Robert Tonei, otherwise Stafford, and was held by his descendant until the reign of Henry VIII., when it fell to the Crown on the attainder of the Duke of Buckingham.

> " Much
> He spoke, and learnedly, for life ; but all
> Was either pitied in him, or forgotten."

Buckingham was beheaded, and his manors seized by the Crown officials.

The next grant was to Thomas Grey, Marquis of Dorset, whose son, Henry, being attainted by Queen Mary, it was given to Sir John Grey, from whom it was purchased by Dame Agnes Symthe, and her son, Sir Francis Smythe. A grandson of the latter received from James I. a charter of free warren here, and his son, Charles, was knighted and afterwards created Lord Carrington by Charles I. The manor descended to his kinsman, Francis Carrington, whose daughter married Peter Halford, and their daughter married Sir Edward Smythe, Bart. of Acton Burnell, in Shropshire : in whose family the manor still continues.

Besides this principal manor there was another in Wootton, belonging to the family of Harewell, whose ancient monuments may be seen in the church.

Wootton Wawen Church, one of the best preserved Saxon buildings in Warwickshire, and full of interest, will well repay a visit. The lower portion of the central tower, a portion of the nave, and the chancel are of Saxon date : the chancel arch being less than 5 feet wide. On the south there is a fine chantry chapel,

The windows of the church in Dugdale's time contained the arms of Catesby, formerly a powerful family in the district, Beauchamp, Wootton Priory, King's College, Henry VI., Harewell, Stafford, and the Abbey of Conchis. In the chantry chapel there are some fine monuments, including an altar tomb of Sir John Harewell, 1428, and a brass to John Harewell, Esq., his wife and family, and a canopied tomb of Francis Smith, Esq. There is also a small collection of chained books on theological subjects. The walls of the church were anciently covered with mural paintings; traces of these remain.

William Somervile, author of " The Chase," is buried here, and in the churchyard may be noticed a tombstone to his huntsman, John Hoitt. The inscription on the stone, though now almost illegible, has fortunately been preserved upon a new tablet placed over the doorway inside the church. The lines are by the Rev. John Gaches, a former vicar of Wootton Wawen, Fellow of King's College, Cambridge, and a friend of the famous Dr. Parr, rector of the neighbouring church at Hatton; they are as follows:—

> " Here Hoitt, all his sports and labours past,
> Joins his loved master, Somervile, at last:
> Together went they echoing fields to try,
> Together now in silent dust they lie.
> Servant and Lord, when once we yield our breath,
> Huntsman and poet are alike in death.
> Life's motley drama calls for powers and men
> Of different casts to fill each changeful scene ;
> But all the merit that we justly prize,
> Not in the part, but in the acting lies :
> And as the lyre, so may the Huntsman's horn
> Fame's trumpet rival, and his name adorn."

Passing from Wootton we reach Henley-in-Arden

in two miles. The town is built along the road, and contains a fine church, a market cross, and a number of ancient houses. In the latter half of the nineteenth century, an industrious antiquary, John Hannett, lived at Henley-in-Arden: it was here that he wrote his book, "Bibliopegia," one of the earliest treatises upon the outward form of literature, but he is perhaps best known by his extremely interesting work, "The Forest of Arden," published in 1863. Hannett passed the greater part of his long and useful life in a picturesque cottage next to the "Three Tuns" Inn, on the east side of the street, where he died in 1893 in the ninetieth year of his age.

The fine site of Peter de Montfort's castle, and the well-preserved Norman church of Beaudesert are worth visiting; they lie but a short distance to the east of the town. A stiff climb brings us to the summit of "Castle Mound." What a history is here contained! Once the stronghold of a powerful baron, now a grass-grown mound, possibly fortified by the Romans long before the Norman soldier built his castle on the hill.

It is hazardous to jump to conclusions, but there are now so many streams in the neighbourhood of Henley-in-Arden that it seems quite possible that the lowlands about the town were at one time covered with water, and that the site of Henley was a mere of some considerable extent. A range of hills runs from the north-west to the south-east of Henley, dominating the lowlands to the west. The works at Beaudesert, whether Norman or earlier, face those of Camp Hill on the north, which prove that this district was the home of warlike people in early times. Within a few miles' radius of Henley, chiefly to the east, there are several earthworks, including that great one now known as Harborough Banks, a Roman camp where Roman remains have been found. The vallum incloses an area of about twenty-six acres.

The extensive remains of "Camp Hill," situated close to Liveridge Hill, and about two miles to the north of Henley, are said by Hannett to be connected by an ancient road with Harborough, and to be a Roman outpost. If the road from Birmingham to Stratford is a Roman road, this earthwork may mark the site of one of the military stations, and we should expect to find the next station somewhere to the north of Stratford, possibly about Bishopton Hill, though there are no clear indications of earthworks hereabouts.

In local traditions it is curious to note how history is perverted. A Roman earthwork is usually assigned to Oliver Cromwell, who is credited with placing his cannon behind the ramparts on Camp Hill, a fortification probably unused in warfare for more than a thousand years. Oliver Cromwell, indeed, is the one general ever uppermost in the mind of the tiller of the land.

Continuing along the Birmingham road, and ascending Liveridge Hill, a turn to the right, *via* Lapworth, will bring us to Knowle Station along tortuous lanes.[1]

Lapworth, with its extremely interesting church, still containing the arms of the Catesbys and De Montforts, is worthy of a visit. The manor of Lapworth belonged in Henry III.'s time to Henry Pipard, who had two daughters. One was the wife of Sir Robert de

---

[1] The most direct route to Knowle Station is a turn some miles further on, at Hockley Heath, past the Nag's Head Inn. The byways are difficult to follow.

Harcourt, the other of Sir Thomas de Bishopesden. The portion which came to the Harcourts was granted by them to the Brandestons. In the reign of Edward III. the manor passed to Richard de Montfort, illegitimate son of Peter, lord of Beaudesert. Richard's son had a daughter, Margaret, wife of John de Catesby, of Ashley S. Leger. John de Catesby's eldest son, William, married Philippa, daughter of Sir William Bishopesden, so the two portions of the manor were reunited, and belonged to the Catesbys, who sometimes occupied Bushwood House in the parish of Lapworth. Bushwood was a moated manor house, and adjoining it was a great lake upon which Robert Catesby, the Gunpowder Plot conspirator, is said to have hatched the conspiracy while sitting in an open boat.

It is about five miles from Lapworth to Knowle, a village with a fine old church, and once the home of a celebrated guild, whose roll of membership contains the names of many of Shakespeare's ancestors. The guild, founded by Walter Cook, a canon of Lincoln in Richard II.'s time, was suppressed with other guilds at the Reformation. The names of the Shakespeares who are mentioned in the registers will be found on page 3 in the first chapter.

About two miles from Knowle lies Temple Balsall, so named because it was given by Roger de Mowbray, in the reign of Stephen, to the Knights Templars. The Templars built a church and house for their brethren at Balsall, a preceptory subordinate to that of the Temple in London. The order was suppressed by Edward II., but shortly afterwards that king gave their lands to the Knights Hospitallers, otherwise the Knights of S. John of Jerusalem.

At the Dissolution it was given to Queen Catherine Parr; and subsequently Queen Elizabeth gave it to the Earl of Leicester, whose descendant, Lady Catherine Leveson, bequeathed the estate to found a hospital for four poor widows.

The hospital, adjoining the south side of the church, is built round three sides of a quadrangle, and is now a picturesque and quiet harbour of refuge for those who have met with misfortune. The church and old refectory of the Knights are still standing. The former was "restored" by Sir Gilbert Scott in 1849: still it is a very fine specimen of a Templars' church. There being no division between the nave and chancel gives the church the appearance of a

Porch and Gates of
Solihull Church :

noble hall, but the floor is raised in stages towards the east end though the roof is of the same height and span throughout.

Three miles to the north of Balsall lies the extensive village of Solihull, where there is a large cruciform church somewhat similar to that of Stratford-on-Avon. The style of the chancel is early decorated, of a beautiful and peculiar type, dating from the end of the thirteenth century. The cuspings of the side windows are singular and very elegant. The east window is a fine example of reticulated, or interlaced tracery. On the north side of the chancel is a building of two storeys: the upper storey having two windows opening into the chancel, was a chapel dedicated to S. Alphege. The lower chapel may have been a sacristy, but retains its old stone altar.

Among the monuments in the church may be noticed a brass to William Hawes and Ursala, his wife, builder of Hillfield Hall, 1610, and under the tower arch another brass to Willyam Hyll, gentleman, and Agnes and Isabel, his wives. There is also a brass plate bearing the following inscription, evidently copied from the one on Shakespeare's tomb at Stratford-on-Avon:—

"This stone is not placed here to perpetuate the memory of the Person interred beneath it, but to preserve her Ashes sacred from Violation ; Therefore

"' Good Friend, for Jesu's sake forbear
To dig the dust inclosed here.' 1746."

A chapel in the north side was used as a pew by the Greswolde family for several generations.

Opposite the church stands an old inn, famous for its bowling-green, surrounded by arbours of cut yew. The mansion of the Greswoldes, Malvern Hall, lies to the east of the church, but the original hall of Solihull is near the station. It is an interesting specimen of a small manor house built in the fourteenth century, consisting of a hall with open timbered roof, and a two-storeyed building at one end. The hall has been divided into two storeys in exactly the same way as Robert Arden's house at Wilmcote.

The village of Berkswell, with its Norman church, lies about four miles to the east of Solihull. Beneath the chancel is a crypt, of very early date: a somewhat unusual feature in Warwickshire churches, and of

Berkswell Church

special interest. The porch, with a room over it, is exceedingly picturesque. The name of the place is clearly derived from a well, near the vicarage, which to this day supplies an abundance of pure water.

We are still in Arden, and within three miles of Hampton-in-Arden, famous for its black and white houses, built of the forest oak, and prettily situated about five miles from Coventry.

U

Turning southwards, a six miles' ride will bring us to the gate of Kenilworth Castle. From Kenilworth we may return to Stratford through Leek Wootton and Warwick, or vary the excursion by going round through Stoneleigh and Leamington.

GUILD HALL AND ALMSHOUSES IN 1901

CHAPTER XXXVIII

GUILD OF THE HOLY CROSS

GUILDS, societies constituted for religious, benevolent, and trade purposes, were amongst the most useful institutions of the Middle Ages. The number of guilds in Warwickshire was considerable, the brotherhoods being found in cities and towns like Coventry, Warwick, Stratford-on-Avon, and Birmingham; in the country places, such as Knowle and Aston Cantlow. Stratford, in early times, had several guilds, all at length merged into one—" The Guild of the Holy Cross."

In the middle of the thirteenth century, probably about 1269 (Wheler in error gives the date 1296), Robert de Stratford obtained permission from Godfrey Giffard, Bishop of Worcester, to found a hospital, and erect a chapel for the brethren and sisters of the Guild of the Holy Cross. In the fifth of Edward III., 1332, the Guild was enriched; and in the seventh of Richard II., Richard Fille gave certain messuages and land without license, whereupon the gift was forfeited to the Crown. Again, in the time of Henry IV., about the year 1403, Letters Patent were granted to Thomas Aldebury, clerk, Nicholas Sauser, jun., and Thomas Compton, sen., for permission to keep the possessions of the earlier Guild, and also to start a new fraternity to the honour of the Holy Cross and S. John the Baptist.

The Guild property at that time was extensive, consisting of twenty messuages, three shops, half a yard land, and a moiety of two burgages. The possessions were situated in Stratford-on-Avon, Wilmcote, and Rhyne-Clifford. The brethren had power to elect eight aldermen, a master, and two proctors. There were also two priests to celebrate divine service in the chapel. By the survey of Henry VIII. it appears that there were four priests belonging to the Guild, and a schoolmaster. There was a house for the priests, with five chambers and a garden, probably occupying the site of the old vicarage and pedagogue's house. By ancient custom the fraternity met once a year, to settle accounts with their tenants, and to partake of a feast.

Wheler states "that Henry IV. was accounted the founder of the Guild: and that one of the priests (teacher in the grammar school) celebrated divine service in the chapel, for the convenience of infirm people, who could not attend at the church, which was at a considerable distance from some parts of the town." In confirmation of this statement it is interesting to note that the arms of Henry IV. are painted upon the wall at the upper end of the Guild Hall, upon one side of the picture of the Crucifixion; while on the other side is a shield bearing the arms of the Earl of Warwick of those days. That is to say Beauchamp, quartering Despencer.

The present Corporation of Stratford are the successors of the Guild of the Holy Cross, and though the name Guild is no longer applied to the governing body, it retains and manages many of the possessions of the ancient fraternity as well as performing many of its duties.

The Register of the Guild, a manuscript of considerable importance, is preserved among other Corporation records at Shakespeare's Birthplace, in Henley Street; also the accounts of the Guild, extending over a long period. These records prove that the patrons of the

GUILD CHAPEL AND GRAMMAR SCHOOL

fraternity were both numerous and of exalted position; kings and nobles being among the number,[1] while the brethren and sisters represent most of the respectable families in the district. The names of members enrolled year by year, though to the uninitiated apparently of small importance, in reality are of great use to antiquaries and genealogists, who are here enabled to find names of ancestors of families, some still living in the neighbourhood, others settled in distant parts of the world. These lists were commenced many years before parish registers were thought of.

The accounts are full of interesting and minute details of the manners of a bygone age, as well as of many curious customs and usages. They prove, for instance, that the townsfolk of Stratford, at a very early period, provided for the instruction of their children: and also that they were quite as fond of feasting then as now, and that they entertained one another, and the strangers that were within their gates, in right liberal fashion. They also provided almshouses for the poor and needy, relieved the distressed, erected public buildings, and paid sums to artists to decorate the walls of their chapel and their hall. They were very solicitous that religious services should be maintained, and that masses should be said for the repose of the souls of their ancestors and friends. They directed that the bell should be tolled in case of death, and provided wax lights for funerals. Besides these minor services, they undertook many works of public utility, and, in short, their records prove them to have been a pious and God-fearing set of people, doing their best to put in practice the divine

[1] In 1477 the ill-starred George, Duke of Clarence, the Lady Isabel, his wife, and their two children, enrolled their names as members of the Guild.

precept of brotherly love, and co-operating for the general benefit. It is not unlikely that what has been again may be, and that some future government may see well to re-establish guilds upon something like the ancient lines, for there can be no doubt that the suppression of the fraternities was in many instances an act of injustice towards the people, though of course it was obvious that the management of guilds in some cases was not always what it might have been.

The dedication of the Guild Chapel has been stated to be to the Holy Trinity, though it was the chapel of the Guild of the Holy Cross: yet it is repeatedly referred to as the chapel of the Trinity, and may possibly have had that dedication. This might lead, and probably has led, to some little confusion because the parish church bears the same dedication. The wall-paintings in the interior of the chapel set forth the story, or legend, of the invention of the Cross, as well as the martyrdom of Thomas à Becket, the legend of S. George and the dragon, and certain symbolical pictures: but, as far as the present writer is aware, the emblem of the Trinity was not represented. Over the chancel arch a great wall-painting of the Doom, and between the windows the figures of certain saints completed the decoration of the nave. Since this portion of the church was built in the time of Henry VII., the paintings cannot be earlier than the reign of that monarch.

The Guild accounts appear to open in 1353, when Robert Pont and John Pateshurst were proctors of the Guild. In 1394-5 we find some curious payments, such as " 12d. for the window of the church; 9d. for a man hired to make a 'gotter' of straw; 6d. for washing the vestments; 1d. for carrying 'unius clausae' to the Church, &c." Some expenses of the great feasts are given. In Henry IV.'s time, for instance, the following

is the account of beer bought for the feast :—
"4 sesterns of good beer bought from Lucy Brasyer,
6s. ; the price of a gallon, 1½d. ; 1 sestern of 'penyale,'
12d. ; 10 gallons of 'smalleale,' 5d. ; 2 sesterns of good
beer bought from Agnes Iremonger, 3s., the price of
a gallon, 1½d. ; 14 gallons of good beer bought from
Margery Ilmygdon, 21d., the price of a gallon, 1½d. ;
13 gallons of 'smallale,' 6d. ; 20 gallons of good beer
bought from Agnes Mayel, 2s. 6d., the price of a
gallon, 1½d. ; 10 gallons of 'smallale' bought from
Alice James, 15d. ; 6 gallons of 'smallale,' 2d."

Expenses of the feasts increased as years went on,
and we find in Henry VI.'s time enormous quantities
of provisions were consumed on these occasions. 270
geese were purchased at 2½d. per head, 72 pullets,
60 at 1½d., and 12 at 1d. For feeding these birds
3 quarters of malt, 1 quarter of oats, and 3 bushels
of barley are bought for the geese, while 4d. was
spent in corn for the pullets, and 2s. for riding into
the country for four days to collect all this poultry.
32 gallons of milk, and 1350 eggs were used. Sixpence was paid for 2½ ozs. of sugar, and 9d. for dates.
Wages were paid to cooks, brewers, and butlers, and
12d. to two women for washing the dishes for three
days. Fourpence to another woman for washing dishes
for two days. The doorkeeper had 3d. ; 4d. was paid
for carrying beer to the hall. The washing of the
linen, or "napry," formed an expensive item for the
year, 4s. being paid. Besides the poultry already
mentioned, 10 calves and 3 sheep were killed for the
feast at the expense of 2s.

Various sums of money were spent on the entertainment of people who came to the town. For instance,
in 1452-3, 13d. was paid for bread and beer, 17d. for
wine, 14d. for hens, 6d. for capons, 12d. for wine, given to

Old
COURT
Sheep St
Stratford

the Lady of Oversley, and to the servants of Richard, Earl of Warwick, coming with William Harewell, Esq. In 1450 we find the Guild described as the Guild of the Holy Cross, the Blessed Mary the Virgin, and S. John the Baptist. This description is also given at the commencement of the sixteenth century.

Various payments were made to the schoolmaster; to the artists who painted the walls of the chapel, and for painting the images therein. Sums of money were expended upon paint, and glass for the chapel; for tiles for its roof at various times. In short, the study of the old Guild accounts presents a wonderful picture of the life of the burgesses of Stratford in the Middle Ages. They appear to have lived well, to have been comfortably clothed, and decently buried, and sufficiently educated out of the revenues of the fraternity.

MANOR HOUSE, SULGRAVE

CHAPTER XXXIX

HOME OF THE WASHINGTONS

THE family which gave freedom and the first President
to the United States of America was long settled within
a day's ride of Stratford-on-Avon; and although the
associations of the old Washington stock are much
stronger in Northamptonshire than in Warwickshire, it
cannot be out of place in a book dealing with the heart
of England to devote a chapter to the old homes of this
vigorous race.

A walk across the park from Lord Spencer's house at
Althorp, in Northamptonshire, leads to Brington, with
its interesting church, containing the stately monuments
of the Spencers, and an ancient brass to the memory of
members of the Washington family. The armorial
bearings of the Washingtons, a device now incorporated

in the flag of the United States, were familiar in the
midland shires centuries before a scion of the house
carried the arms with him to his home in New England.
Whether or not George Washington gave his own arms
to the United States is a moot point, and it may be that
the fact of the Stars and Stripes occurring in both devices
is only one of those coincidences met with every day and
all the world over, but it is more likely that they were
suggested by the silver shield with red bars and stars:
—" Argent, two bars gules, in chief three mullets of the
last," in heraldic language, the old armorial bearings of
the ancestors of George Washington.

Our pilgrimage in the present instance is directed
towards Sulgrave, a village in Northamptonshire, about
three miles from Moreton Pinkney Station on the East
and West Junction Railway, some twenty-six miles to
the east of Stratford-on-Avon.

Sulgrave is a remote village in the heart of an agricultural country.   It contains an interesting church, and
the remains of an old manor house.   An estate here
appears to have belonged to one of the religious houses
in Northampton, the monastery of S. Andrew, which
being dissolved by Henry VIII., had no further need of
its possessions.   Laurence Washington, a wealthy
citizen of Northampton, and at one time Mayor of the
borough, obtained a grant of Sulgrave, and removed
there when he had built a house for himself and family.
A portion of this manor house remains, but it has de-
generated into an ordinary farm-house.   The interest
attached to it as the home of the Washingtons rightly
elevates it in the eyes of all good American citizens, and
endows it with an interest almost as great as the home
of the Warwickshire Poet at Stratford-on-Avon.   The
old doorway of this Tudor mansion is ornamented with

the arms of Queen Elizabeth and the initials "E.R." under the gable and above the sun-dial. The porch has in the spandrels of its arch the arms of the Washingtons, and another shield now defaced.

Laurence Washington died in 1583-4, leaving this estate to his eldest son, Robert, whose son, Laurence of Sulgrave and Brington, died on December 13th, 1616, and was succeeded by his eldest son, Sir William Washington. The fourth son, Laurence Washington, Fellow of Brasenose College, Oxford, had a son, John, who was the great-grandfather of George Washington.

Laurence being a common name in the family, its frequent occurrence led to some confusion in the pedigrees, but there is no doubt that Laurence Washington, of Oxford, was a direct descendant of the old Mayor of Northampton, and that his eldest son, John, who was born in England about 1633-4, emigrated to Virginia, and had a son, Laurence, who died there in 1697. His second son, Augustine, was the father of George Washington, the first President of the United States.

Although shorn of nearly everything that denotes the dwelling of an English family of rank, Sulgrave yet retains some marks of its former state. It was the home of an important county family allied to the ducal house of Buckingham, and the powerful family of Spencer. One of the Washingtons was Governor of the city of Worcester during the time of the civil wars of Charles I., and held that city during its first siege. His daughter was buried at Wickhamford, near Evesham, and the Washington arms appear on her tomb in the chancel of the church of that place. His wife was the daughter of Sir John Packington of Westwood, in Worcestershire, and this fact gives us a good idea of the importance of the family in the seventeenth century. Like most of the nobility in the Midlands they first owed their wealth to the industry of wool-stapling, and although enriched by the dissolution of the monasteries, their gains at the expense of religious houses appear to have been rather a curse than a blessing. The civil wars further impoverished the family, and the only chance they had of retrieving their fortunes lay in the direction of emigration. Transplanted to new soil the energy of the family was renewed, so that the scion of an English squire was enabled to become a founder of one of the greatest nations of the world, greater that Rome, and as yet only in its infancy.

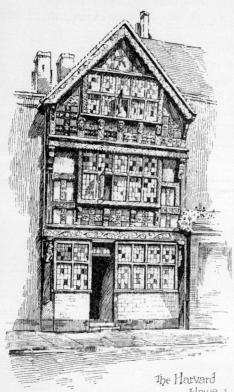

The Harvard House

It is a remarkable fact that this district supplied not only a first President of the United States, but also the founder of one of the greatest universities. At Stratford-on-Avon a handsomely carved timber-framed house bears upon one of its stout oak beams the initials T.R. 1596. A.R., recording that Thomas Rogers and his wife built, or beautified, the house in that year. Their daughter Katherine married Robert Harvard, and their son, John Harvard, having emigrated to America, founded Harvard University; he himself may have visited his grandfather, who died here and was buried, according to the Registers of Stratford-on-Avon, on August 31st, 1639.

The house is well preserved, one of the finest of many fine ancient houses in the town. Every part of the front is elaborately carved with ornaments either conventional or heraldic.

Note.—Another point on the East and West Junction Railway from which Sulgrave may be reached is Blakesley Station (30 miles from Stratford-on-Avon). Sulgrave is about four miles from the Red Lion Inn at Blakesley, where a carriage may be hired.

CHAPTER XL

AROUND MEON HILL

"Of all the hills I know, let Meon first take place."—DRAYTON.

ONE of the most conspicuous hills in the landscape around Stratford is the flat-topped Meon. It rises like a truncated cone above the plane. Its top is fortified so strongly, and its position is so important, that one becomes aware from observation only that at one time Meon ranked as a great fortress of a bygone race.

The Romans usually chose a low-lying spot near a stream of water for their fortified camps; while the ruder Celts, unable to match the Romans in many ways, could equal them in engineering feats. These hardy warriors usually chose for their strong positions a hill-top, and were able when necessary to obtain water by boring.

Meon appears to have been a stronghold of the Dobuni, the people who lived in Gloucestershire, and whose country bordered on that of the Cornavii. These people were a warlike race, and appear to have been at constant feud with their neighbours: and, although they have left no record beyond their earthworks and their sepulchres, it is known that the Romans had some trouble in dealing with them. The remains of Celtic fastnesses are to be found on both sides of the Avon, which in those days formed a natural boundary between the territories of the tribes. The

probabilities are that the river was much wider then
than it is now, spreading out in places into lagoons and
marshes, which have since been drained.   Some of these
marshes were doubtless dry in summer time, and afforded
excellent grazing ground for the flocks and herds of the
Britons.

The Romans extended their power over the whole
district, constructed their great roads through it;
founded cities, places like Gloucester, Cirencester, and
Worcester.   Their camps were numerous, and the remains of important ones, such as that at Chesterton, are
scattered about the country.   Warwick itself appears
to have been well defended by the Romans, and at
Stratford one would expect to find at least the remains
of a camp if nothing more.   Time and the hand of
the agricultural labourer have obliterated many traces
of military works of the earlier people, and of the
conquerors of this land.   The hill fortresses have
escaped some of these destroying agencies : Meon being
one of the best preserved earthworks in the district.
The hillside affords a pleasant site for villages ; several
cluster about its foot : Quinton, with its tapering church
spire, Admington, Clopton, recalling memories of one
of the greatest local families, and Mickleton, most
important of all.

Like those in many other hillside places the houses
in Mickleton are built of stone, and differ from the
typical midland cottages ; but certainly they are more
substantial, if not quite so picturesque as the black and
white, thatched homesteads.   The village has not yet
been spoilt by summer holiday makers, there being no
river near, and the railway some little distance away ;
yet few places have so many delightful spots within
easy reach.

x

To the east of Mickleton is an ill-kept road leading
to Hidcote, a road always covered with loose stones
from the quarries near the village. It is an up-hill
ride, but the view we shall soon obtain is well worth
the energy required to negotiate it. A short way up,
and at right angles to the road, is a lovely hillside path,
overhung with trees, while below the undergrowth
is varied and luxuriant. Cattle having no access here,
fine specimens of beech, with their branches and evenly
spreading off-shoots reaching to within a few inches
of the ground, may be seen in perfection. The scene
from this path is magnificent, and on a clear day the
eye may wander over portions of several counties.
There is another of these deep valleys, running parallel
with, and on the left hand side of the road; Kiftsgate
Court, a house that is visible for miles around, stands
on a hill on the other side of this valley.

If we wish to see the stone quarries we may climb
higher still, where the traveller must perforce push
his iron steed, and turn first to the left, and then to
the right. We are now on a by-path, and still climb
higher on a road impossible to ride upon. We soon
reach a height where stone walls replace the hedge-
rows, and the landscape looks bleak and bare, but the
prospect of the Cotswold Hills and the intervening
valleys is always beautiful, and especially so when the
setting sun gilds the distant hills.

It is in one of the deep combes among the hills that the
weird sounds known locally as the " Mickleton Hooter "
used to be heard, sounds of dread with nothing seen.
Hard by the track of an old Roman road may yet be
distinguished, but it is not at all clear whether in
the rustic mind the sound is supposed to have any
connection with the ancient Romans.

The church at Mickleton is rather a fine one, with tower and handsome spire : it has many interesting associations, especially with the Overbury family, several of whom are buried here. The connection between the Overburys and Shakespeare, as far as at present known, is very slight. The name appears on one of the documents in the Chancery proceedings of Shakespeare *v.* Lambert, for the recovery of the Ardens' lands at Wilmcote, Overbury being the solicitor for Lambert, though at the present time it is hard to tell whether it was Sir Nicholas, or his son, Sir Thomas, who was concerned in this case.

The Overburys were long settled in the district : they mated with many well-known local families, and the records of their baptisms, burials, and marriages are to be found in the registers of several parishes round Meon.

Young Thomas Overbury, a youth of more than common intellect and learning, attached himself to Robert Carr, one of the favourites of James I. While Carr's ambition prompted him to seek titles and dignities, Overbury preferred to be the favourite's adviser, and to busy himself in the direction of state affairs. Alas! he became an obstacle in the path of an ambitious, wicked woman, whose fiendish mind devised all kinds of means to procure his death. Overbury was a gentleman of respectable family and rearing, and would have scorned to avail himself of the means which were used for his destruction. The Earl of Northampton, whose estates at Compton Wynyates may be said to have made him a neighbour of the Overburys, played off his niece, the Countess of Essex, upon Robert Carr, the favourite. The wicked Countess befooled Carr, but so long as the faithful Overbury lived, her interest with her lover could not be paramount.

The story of Overbury's imprisonment in the Tower and how he was poisoned by eating jellies sent him by the Countess, is an oft-told tale : a tragedy which, had it taken place earlier, might have suggested to Shakespeare some of his tragic scenes. These events, however, happened a little later than the period in which the plays were written.

The case of Sir Thomas Overbury was only one among many desperate acts which disfigured the reigns of Elizabeth and James 1. The facts were fairly well known at the time, and must have formed a subject of conversation for the Poet and his friends, some of the chief actors being their near neighbours.

Of course Overbury's case was too delicate a matter for Shakespeare to view directly, and the events happened too late in his life for him to have used. Still they are examples of the manners of the time which the dramatist has so wonderfully portrayed in his dramas.

There are still members of the Overbury family living among us, bearing out Burke's assertion that among the professional men and shopkeepers of our country towns, we may now look for the representatives of our oldest and most honourable families.

After the murder of Sir Thomas Overbury his friends and partizans did all in their power to bring the murderers to justice, but it was some little time before this end could be accomplished. Ben Jonson was one of Overbury's friends and admirers, and Field, the friend and fellow actor of Shakespeare, was another. Owing to the exertions of Nat Field several editions of Overbury's poem, "The Wife," were published, and in the later editions of these some verses, eulogistic of the author, were contributed by Ben Jonson and others, including someone whose initials were "W. S." It has been supposed that this was Shakespeare himself, and if so the lines upon Sir Thomas Overbury would be some of the last he wrote. In a matter of this kind it is impossible to say with certainty that the lines were, or were not written by Shakespeare. They may have been written by him, but they do not altogether recall his style. As they are little known, they are here appended for the reader to form his own judgment: the copy is taken from the tenth edition, published in 1756, but they were apparently written in 1615-16.

> " So many moons, so many times gone round,
> And rose from hell, and darkness underground.
> And yet till now this darkened deed of hell
> Not brought to light? O tardy heav'n! yet tell
> If murder lays him down to sleep with lust
> Or no?[1] reveal, as thou art true and just,
> The secrets of this unjust, secure act.
> And what our fears make us suspect, compact
> With greater deeds of mischief,[2] for alone
> We think not this, and do suspect yet one,
> To which compared, this but a falling star,[3]
> That a bright firmament of fire.[4] Thy care
> We see takes meaner things; it times the world;
> The signs at random thro' the Zodiac hurl'd;
> The stars wild wand'rings, and the glib quick hinges
> Which turn both poles: and all the vi'lent changes
> It over-looks, which trouble th' endless course
> Of the high firmament. By thy blest force
> Do hoary winter-frosts make forests bare,
> And straight to groves again their shades repair.
> By thee doth Autumns, Lyon's flaming mane,
> Ripen the fruits; and the full ear sustain

---

[1] The Earl of Rochester and the Countess of Essex.
[2] The supposed murder of Prince Henry.
[3] Overbury.   [4] Prince Henry.

Her burden'd powers.   O being, still the same,
Ruling so much, and under whom the frame
Of this vast world weigh'd, all his orbs doth guide.
Why are thy cares of men no more apply'd?
Or if: why seem'st thou sleeping to the good,
And guarding to the ill? as if the brood
Of best things still must chance take in command,
And not thy providence? and her blind hand
Thy benefits erroneously disburse:
Which so let fall, ne'er fall but to the worse?
Whence so great crimes commit the greater sort,
And boldest acts of shame blaze in the court,
Where buffoons worship in their rise of state,
Those filthy Scarabs,[1] whom they serve and hate.
Sure things mere backward: there, honour disgrac'd,
And virtue laid by fraud, and poison, waste.
The adulterer up like human, and so sainted;
And females modesty (as females) painted,
Lost in all real worth.   What shall we say?
Things so far out of frame, as if the day
Were come wherein another Phæton
Stol'n into Phœbus wain, had all misgone
A clean contrary way.   O powerful God,
Right all amiss, and set the wonted period
Of goodness in his place again: this deed
Be usher to bring forth the mask, and weed
Where under blacker things lie hid perhap,
And yet have hope to make a safe escape.[2]
Of this make known, why such an instrument
As Weston, a poor serving-man, should rent
The frame of this sad good man's life?   Did he
Stand with this court bred, learned Overb'ry
In strife for an Ambass'dorship?   No, no,
His orb held no such light.   What did he owe
The prophet malice for composing this,
This Cynosura in neat Pœsis:
How great and good men ought, and all, to chuse
A chaste, fit, noble Wife, and the abuse

---

[1] Beetles.
[2] Gervase Elways, the Lieutenant of the Tower, was not then taken up.

Of strumpets friendly shadowing in the same.
Was this his fault? or doth there lie a flame
Yet in the embers not unrak'd, for which
He died so falsely? Heav'n we do beseech
Unlock the secret, and bring all to view,
That law may purge the blood, lust made untrue."

W. S.

CHAPTER XLI

A STUDENT of church architecture will find the neighbourhood of Stratford-on-Avon a very interesting field for his investigations. Unlike many other districts in England where the building material is not so durable as in the Midlands, many old churches remain to this day but little altered structurally since their foundation. There are good specimens of Saxon work, several beautiful little Norman churches, a great deal of graceful Early English work, some few examples of the rich Decorated period of Gothic, and more of the Perpendicular work of the fifteenth century. Coming to a later period we find churches of seventeenth century date, like that at Compton Wynyates, and a perfect specimen of a Georgian church, eighteenth century, at Billesley. A volume might well be devoted to the churches of Warwickshire, but in the present chapter we can only indicate the most salient features of a few churches in the immediate neighbourhood.

ALVESTON. (Two miles)

The village of Alveston, locally called "Auson," has two churches, one a modern structure built in 1830, close to the high-road from Stratford to Charlecote, too new to interest a visitor; the other, now disused, is situated on the west side of the lane leading to the river. The chancel alone is standing, the nave of the church having been destroyed many years ago: the foundations are visible beneath the grass, and the chancel itself appears to have been rebuilt in the Georgian period. The gravestones in the churchyard are time-worn and neglected; village children, finding the abandoned burial-place a convenient playground, have left their mark here.

A door has been placed at the west end of the chancel, and is now the only way into the church. Two carved heads of ancient doorways, the sole remnants of the Norman church, the one placed over the west door, the other built into the exterior of the south wall, are certainly most curious: both appear to have been carved in Campden stone. The one over the west door is a tympanum whereon in low relief are represented two quadrupeds fighting, both beasts have enormous tails, which, curling between their legs, stand erect over their backs. Over the beast to the left is another, and smaller, quadruped; a large bird appears to have settled over the back of the beast on the right: while in mid air between the two is another bird, possibly a dove. The tympanum built into the south wall is composed of four stones. At the top, in the centre, is an interlaced pattern forming circles; on each side, on a separate stone, is the representation of an animal, possibly a lamb, since one hoof is visible, but the tail is treated quite conventionally: it curls between the legs, and coming out over the back, ends in a *fleur-de-lys*. On a long stone beneath these smaller ones the carving is much defaced, but in the centre there appears to have been a representation of a bird, while on the left are more interlaced circles, and on the right an imperfect and very curious jumble of interlaced work. The tympanum is now supported upon two brackets, rudely carved, and evidently formerly capitals of two columns, one on either side of the doorway. These carvings bear a resemblance to those at Ribbesford-on-Severn, and would appear to belong to the Norman period, though they may be survivals of much earlier work.

The interior, now practically cleared of its ancient ecclesiastical furniture, retains the remains of an interesting monument, an altar tomb to Nicholas Lane who died in July 1595. The tomb has been taken to pieces, and parts of it built into the north wall. Nicholas Lane is represented wearing the dress of a gentleman of the time of Elizabeth; a short ruff, a doublet, trunk hose, stockings, and round-toed shoes; a belt round his waist has a dagger attached to it on the left side. There are also the kneeling figures of three sons and a daughter, and an inscription on a metal plate fixed above the figure. There is a tablet to Captain Newsham Peers who died in 1743 of wounds received at the battle of Dettingen: another memorial to Mr William Hiron and his mother is of some interest on account of the unfortunate death of this gentleman who was murdered by Littleham Bridge. (See page 50.) An old wooden reading-desk, and a painting of the Royal arms of one of the Georges completes the brief list of furniture.

An ancient, and very picturesque timber-framed house, with overhanging upper storey, abuts on the south-east corner of the churchyard: it may have been the presbytery for the vicar of the parish. It is only right to add that the fences and gate of the ancient churchyard are in excellent order, and that of late years all that is possible has been done to protect the monuments of past generations of Alveston folk.

CHARLECOTE

A bow-shot from the park gates of Charlecote House stands the picturesque modern church. The old building was a very small one, surmounted at the west end by a little wooden bell-cote. There appears to have been no feature of interest beyond an ancient cylindrical font, probably of the Norman period, and the fine tombs of the Lucy family. The latter have been carefully preserved, and are now placed in a mortuary chapel separated from the chancel by an oak screen.

The first tomb, under the wheel window, is that of Sir Thomas Lucy, knight, and his wife, Joyce. This was the Sir Thomas supposed to have been lampooned by William Shakespeare. He died July 7th, 1600, and his wife, February 10th, 1595. Beneath the tomb on panels are the kneeling figures of his son, Thomas, and his daughter, Anne. Upon the opposite side of the chapel is the monument to this son Thomas, who was knighted by Queen Elizabeth during his father's lifetime. He died in 1605 and had six sons and eight daughters. This second Sir Thomas was twice married; his second wife, the Lady Constance Lucy, is represented in a kneeling attitude by the side of the tomb. Both figures were originally painted; the lady's effigy still retains the colour of the garments, but only traces of colour remain on the knight's armour.

The effigy of the third Sir Thomas Lucy and his wife, Alice, daughter of Thomas Spencer of Claverdon, rest beneath a canopy supported by four black marble columns. This Sir Thomas died September 10th, 1640, the lady died in 1648. It is probably to the latter's good taste that we owe this monument, the work of a Roman sculptor, Bernini. Under the arcade on the left Sir Thomas is represented on horseback, and on the right are a number of books.

TREDINGTON

Tredington has a fine parish church, one of the largest in the neighbourhood, the mother church of Shipston and Newbold. It is particularly fortunate in retaining many of its ancient features, especially much carved oak, though the hand of the restorer has been busy both within and without its walls: in fact the church has been completely restored. This, however, has brought to light some interesting traces of the original Norman building. Unfortunately, in 1844, the plaster was stripped off the walls, and in the process the ancient mural paintings were almost entirely destroyed. A fragment on the west wall of the south aisle, just sufficient to indicate the former splendour of the edifice, has escaped the hand of the spoiler.

One interesting feature which was revealed at the restoration of the church was a row of clerestory windows, a portion of the original church built by the Normans. One window is Saxon in character, and probably earlier than the others. Many of the so-called Saxon buildings in England were really built after the Norman invasion, but being the work of Saxon masons they have the characteristics of the native style. A well-known example is the tower of S. Michael's Church in the Corn Market at Oxford, built about 1070-80, when Robert D'Oili, a Norman baron, lived at Oxford Castle. This tower has quoins forming long-and-short-work and balusters, or mid-wall shafts to the windows. A Norman Baron doubtless employed the masons in the district to build this church, and their work is essentially Saxon, though done in the Norman period.

Tredington Church consists of chancel, nave, with north and south aisles, tower at the west end, and porch with a parvise over.[1] The chancel has a vestry on the north side, and is separated from the nave by a handsome rood screen, despoiled of its gallery, though the door and stairway leading to it are still in situ; the latter, however, is partly blocked up.

Along both walls of the spacious chancel a stone seat runs, and upon the floor are two ancient brasses commemorating priests. One is to Richard Cassey, Canon of York, in 1427. He is clothed in processional vestments; a surplice, with cassock under, the almuce, and the cope. The figure is erect, and the hands in attitude of prayer. Below the figure are two shields, both bearing a chevron between three hawks' heads erased for Cassey. Between the shields is a trefoil leaf, slipped, bearing these words, "Ad laudé Dei" (To the praise of God). Mr Cecil T. Davis in his notes on Worcestershire brasses, states " that Richard Cassey was appointed by Henry V. prebend of Osbaldwick in the Cathedral of York, 25 Oct. 1414. He was succeeded by Robert Gilbert, 15 Dec. 1427: it is therefore probable that Richard Cassey died in 1427." The inscription is given by Dr Nash as imperfect. The

---

[1] Parvise is a term applied in the sixteenth century to the little chamber over the porch. This room may sometimes have been the dwelling-place of a chantry priest, an anchorite, or even of the vicar. At Tredington the room is at present only a dark space over the door.

other brass represents Henry Sampson, rector, 1482. He is vested in cassock, surplice, and almuce, a fur tippet with ermine tails round the lower edge. He is kneeling and turned to the right. Below is an inscription engraved on brass in Latin which may be translated:—"Here lies Master Henry Sampson, formerly Rector of this church, who died on the 17th day of the month of November in the year of the Lord, 1482. To whose soul may God be merciful. Amen." Mr Cecil T. Davis also mentions another brass as lying loose in the box in the vestry. It was part of the brass of William Barnes, Esq., 1651, and his wife, Alice, who was daughter of Thomas Middlemore of Edgbaston.

In the nave the oak benches with carved ends are handsome, and somewhat unusual in form. There is a lectern with two chained books upon it, and a fine, massive oak chest with five stout hinges in the vestry. The pulpit is Jacobean, with good oak panelling, and sounding board. There are indications in the north aisle that there was formerly a chapel there.

The exterior of the church is beautiful, the tower and spire very graceful, and the Norman doorway on the south side extremely fine. In the north door, embedded in the wood, may still be seen some bullets which are said to have been fired at the church during the civil wars of Charles I.'s time. The rectory house has been rebuilt; it was within living memory one of the finest parsonages in the country: a beautiful Gothic edifice.

In addition to the interesting church the village of Tredington possesses many features of interest to artists and archæologists, and at present is not much visited, being off the beaten track of excursionists, though close to the main road from Stratford to Shipston. In conclusion it may be mentioned that Tredington is in Worcestershire, though almost surrounded by Warwickshire.

MORETON MORRELL.   (Eight miles)

The little Early English church at Moreton Morrell has few important features. The upper storey of the tower is repaired with brick, and the east window has been restored. In the vestry is a rough and massive chest with three fastenings, and a curious padlock. Besides the registers of the parish it contains a pewter chalice and paten, and a rare specimen of a "pitch pipe," to which in former times the parson and the choir attuned their voices. Around the roof of the nave are some shields of arms, newly painted. One bell dates from 1609, and the other two from 1616. The tower, situated at the west end of the church, has a fine archway opening into the nave. There is a new wooden porch on the north side. In the churchyard a curious and ancient carved stone is worthy of notice ; it is part of a Norman tympanum.

There are two inscriptions and a monument in the chancel of the church of seventeenth century date.

NEWBOLD PACEY.   (Seven miles)

Newbold Pacey Church has been rebuilt recently. The chief fragments of Norman structure are the north and south doorways, the north being ornamented with cable and billet mouldings.

BIDFORD. (Seven miles)

The exterior of Bidford Church presents a venerable and interesting appearance; the restored interior has little to recommend it. The tower evidently is very ancient, resembling a bastion rather than an ecclesiastical tower; indeed the position of the church on a high bank above the river, near the ancient bridge, rendered it of some importance as a military post. The massive base of the tower, and the rugged masonry, tell their own tale of age. The chancel is of thirteenth century date; the nave has been rebuilt. There are one or two monuments in the church, notably that to Dorothy Skipworth, who died in 1655. The communion plate was given in 1665 by the Duchess of Dudley: it is very handsome, and is supposed to be of Spanish workmanship.

ATHERSTONE-ON-STOUR. (Three miles)

A handsome new church built from designs by Mr John Cotton of Oxford. It has a tower and spire of rather unusual design, forming a pleasing feature in the landscape. The old church had fallen into such a dilapidated state that it was necessary to remove it altogether.

LUDDINGTON. (Three miles)

Three miles to the west of Stratford, on the north side of the river, stands the picturesque modern church of Luddington. This, like the church at Atherstone-on-Stour, was designed by Mr John Cotton. It superseded the ancient chapel of ease to Stratford, a tiny edifice with a bell-cote at the west end. Here, according to an old tradition, the marriage of Anne Hathaway and William Shakespeare was solemnised. The old chapel was destroyed by fire, but the foundations may still be traced in the centre of the village, near a blacksmith's shop. In the churchyard of the new church a few wrought stones from the old edifice are preserved, and the original font may still be seen there. An ancient chained book is now in the church.

HAMPTON LUCY. (Five miles)

A fine specimen of modern ecclesiastical architecture may be seen at Hampton Lucy. Though an ancient foundation there is practically nothing of the old church left since the rebuilding in 1822-26, and the enlargement by Sir Gilbert Scott in 1858. The tower and nave are poor specimens, but the chancel is a good example of Sir Gilbert Scott's adaptation of French Gothic; and the effect, when seen from a distance, is imposing. The ancient tombs of the Lucys, as before stated, adorn the little church at Charlecote. Some of the more recent members of the family, however, are commemorated here. There is some interesting, though modern, heraldic glass in the chancel windows. The church is dedicated to S. Peter.

PILLERTON HERSEY. (Eight miles)

There are two Pillertons, Pillerton Priors and Pillerton Hersey. The former lies on the main road between Stratford and Banbury. There was formerly a Benedictine Priory here, of which nothing now remains. Pillerton Hersey, so named from the owner of the manor in the time of Richard I., lies off the main road to the north. The church is a fine specimen of Gothic architecture of various dates. It consists of a chancel, nave with north and south aisles, and has a tower at the west end. The chancel is one of the finest examples of Early English or thirteenth century work in this neighbourhood. The windows are of the graceful lancet type. The interior of the chancel is now bare, except for the furniture of the sanctuary. In the south wall there is a recess, or ambrey, with a piscina adjoining it of unusual type, formerly supported by three shafts; only the centre one now remains. On the north side is another ambrey, with a shaft in the centre. There is a blocked-up lepers' window, and an Early English doorway on the south side. The nave and south aisle are of fourteenth century work, altered and modified in the fifteenth. The north aisle is entirely modern. The tower has a lofty arch opening into the nave. The roof of the nave is very finely carved, and dates from the fifteenth century. An ancient stone coffin lid may be seen in the churchyard near the south door of the church. On either side of the altar rails are rings for the attachment of the Lenten veil.

There are three bells; upon one is the following inscription:—" Be yt known to all that doth mee see that Newcome of Leicester made mee, 1602." The other two bells are by Henry Bagley; the one has an inscription in Latin, " Henricus Bagley me fecit, 1672." The other is dated 1668, " Henry Bagley made me." In the quatrefoil in the head of the east window are the royal arms of England with the initials E.R. above: and in a small vestry on the north of the chancel some old glass bears the inscription:—" Thinke and thanke God, 1574," with a Tudor rose above it.

WELLESBOURNE HASTINGS.   (Five miles)

The church at Wellesbourne is of Norman foundation, though little of the original church remains beyond
a fine arch now, on the north side of the chancel, but
formerly the entrance from the nave.   Unfortunately
the church was restored at a period when little care
was taken to preserve ancient characteristics.   There
is a plain tower of Perpendicular date at the west end ;
the interior of the building has been completely renovated.   The only ancient monument is an interesting
brass to the memory of Sir Thomas le Straunge, the
last member of a family holding the manor from the
time of Richard II. to that of Henry VI.   Sir Thomas
was Constable of Ireland, and from documents in the
State Paper Office appears to have rendered service
to the King on several occasions.   He was an ancestor
of the Mordaunts of Walton.   The inscription upon
the brass states that he died in 1426.   There is an
ancient custom retained at Wellesbourne, namely that
of ringing the bells at six o'clock in the morning on
S. Thomas' Day.

WESTON SANDS, otherwise WESTON-ON-A
(Four miles)

This tiny river-side village, once a place of more
importance that at present, is situated in Gloucestershire.   The church has recently been thoroughly
repaired and re-roofed.   It consists of a chancel, nave,
and tower of Perpendicular style.   Formerly there was
a chapel on the south side, apparently somewhat
similar to that at Wixford.   The foundations and
arches, through which it was approached from the

nave, alone remain. There is, however, a curious double hagioscope, or squint, in the south wall of the chancel. Supposing this to be in its original position, it enabled the congregation in the south chapel to obtain a view of the celebrant at the high altar. The church, though small, has many points of interest. In a window on the north side, nearest the tower, many quarries of ancient painted glass remain, whereon the Cooksey badge, a cock-boat with a table, is here repeated many times. This badge is found in the church windows of Huddington and Himbolton in Worcestershire, and seems to have been adopted by the Wintours, one of whom married the heiress of Cooksey. In the chancel there are two handsome monumental brasses to the Grevilles of Milcote Castle, ancestors of the present Earl of Warwick. The walls of the nave have traces of wall-painting in conventional designs, but unfortunately these decorations have been covered with many coats of whitewash, and are visible only here and there. The windows on the north side are flat headed, of six lights, cusped. The nave is parapeted. Some ancient tiles with shields of arms of former lords of Milcote, ancestors of the Grevilles, are now placed near the font. The living has been held for several generations by members of the Davenport family.

Weston, being a very primitive and interesting old place, is well worth a visit.

ALDERMINSTER. (Five miles)

Five miles from Stratford, on the west side of the road leading to Shipston, may be seen the massive and picturesque church of Alderminster, a cruciform structure with central tower. The Reformation and the restorer have left little of interest within the church ; it was restored about the year 1660, and again recently, but a Norman doorway and several deeply splayed circular-headed windows of Norman date attest the age of the building. The tower is handsome, and many of the windows are in the graceful style of the thirteenth century, but the restoration is so complete that it is difficult to determine what the church was like before the extensive reparations were made.

SNITTERFIELD. (Four miles)

This village on the hills to the north of Stratford, where Shakespeare's grandfather, father, and uncles held farms, possesses a very fine thirteenth century church, of which the inhabitants have reason to be proud. It stands embowered by trees on a bank above the road, and presents an appearance, externally at least, but little altered since the Shakespeares of old worshipped therein. It consists of a spacious and lofty chancel, with a small modern vestry on the north side, a nave with north and south aisles, and a tower at the west end. The tower is very massive, the lower portion dating from the thirteenth century, but the upper storeys were rebuilt in the fifteenth, and the joining of the masonry is clearly visible on the exterior of the west window, the lower half being richly moulded in the thirteenth century style. The windows resemble those at Solihull, but without the cuspings. On the exterior of the south wall of the nave, between two of the clerestory windows, an old sun-dial is still in position. The church has been so much restored that although its handsome proportions are still manifest, all the ancient ecclesiastical furniture has disappeared except

some elaborately carved oak stalls, and the old communion rail with turned balusters and carved front.
From the remains of an ambrey in the south aisle
we are able to locate the positions of one of the
altars; and near it a small window to the memory of a
member of the Attye family is interesting by the representation of two war medals painted beneath the
inscription, and the arms of the family emblazoned
in the head of the window.   The Attyes own Ingon
Grange.   In the vestry adjoining the tower a number
of old hatchments have been preserved.

Beneath the tower is a massive and boldly carved
font with grotesque heads projecting from below the
bowl.   The arcade on the south is supported by finely
moulded columns, that on the north has columns of
much plainer detail.   Both chancel arch and tower
arch are very lofty, and add great dignity to the appearance of the church.   One can only regret that the
restoration of the chancel was conducted in a modernising
spirit, and that the pavement, costly no doubt, but
quite out of keeping with the rest of the chnrch, was
substituted for the ancient one worn by the feet of many
generations of Snitterfield folk.   It was here that
Shakespeare's ancestors and relatives, and the Poet
himself, must frequently have worshipped.

Aston Cantlow.   (Five miles)

Aston Cantlow is one of the prettiest Warwickshire
villages, with a most interesting church, but being
rather off the beaten track, some two and a half miles
westward of the road from Birmingham to Stratford,
it is seldom visited, and remains a quaint old-world
place.   The outcrop of the blue lias of Wilmcote

continues for some distance towards this village in a range of low hills; owing to this formation the district is peculiarly picturesque, and interesting to both botanists and geologists. It is no less attractive to the archæologist, who will find some slight remains of a castle, a fine old church, and a fairly perfect specimen of a guild house.

The church of S. John the Baptist is surrounded by a well-kept churchyard, and consists of a tower, nave, chancel, and north aisle. The tower is of four storeys, dating from various periods, the lower portion appears to be very ancient; the ground floor being entered from the nave by a small arch of Early English date. The first storey has a small round-headed window, deeply splayed within, apparently of Norman construction; the second storey has three lancet windows with plain pointed heads in the Early English style; while the third storey, the belfry, is pierced on the four sides with large openings having double-arched heads of fifteenth century work. John Hannett, in "The Forest of Arden," records that the church was restored, the south wall of the nave rebuilt, and new seats provided in the year 1851. The unusually large chancel fortunately to a great extent has escaped the hands of the restorer; it retains the fine original roof and decorated windows, but the south wall is considerably out of the perpendicular, and would be better if it were supported by a buttress. The east window, formerly a very plain one, has been altered, and new tracery inserted; this, however, being very well done, harmonises with the ancient work.

Opening out of the north side of the chancel by two arches is the chapel of the Guild of the Blessed Virgin, where there is now a second altar. The east window of this chapel is extremely handsome, and has been well restored; it formerly contained some fragments of stained glass, now in the north window. On the north wall of the chancel is an ancient ambrey, refitted, and on the south wall is a restored sedilia of the Early English period with a piscina and a credence table above it. There are also in the sanctuary two chairs made from old bench ends, similar to those still to be seen in situ in the Lady Chapel. Two old candlesticks of wood, said to be elevation candlesticks, are here preserved; these were formerly placed upon the lower steps of the altar to support two large candles lighted at the elevation of the host. The octagonal font is somewhat unusual in its decorations, having carved sides with boldly cut quatrefoils. Each angle is supported by a corbel carved to represent grotesque heads. There are various fragments of carved stone in the church, some possibly of Norman workmanship.

At the west end of the north aisle is a curious turret containing a newel staircase with a fifteenth century carving representing the head of a lady in an elaborate head-dress; this terminates the newel. Apparently the stair leads to the roof of the aisle. There are several fine old oak chests and a book box in the vestry under the tower. There is also in the tower an ancient and very primitive church bier. The bells are five in number: one ancient, belonging to the class called "Royal head bells," from the distinguishing mark of heads of a king and queen at various intervals between the letters of the inscription. There are only other four bells of this kind known in the county. These examples are noted in the Rev. H. T. Tilley's paper on bells read before the Midland Institute, Archæo-

Burton Dasset Beacon

logical Section. The Latin inscriptions are generally
ingenious, and intended to be poetical: as Mr Tilley
remarks, "By a liberal use of racks and thumbscrews,
etc., I think some of these legends might be tortured
into being hexameters." In this case the inscription
reads as follows:—"AD LAUDEM CLARE MICHAELIS
DO RESONARE." The other four bells are dated
respectively, 1621, 1622, 1625, 1685.

The ancient church plate consists of a chalice and
paten with a hall mark used from 1595 to 1618; the
cup and cover are elegant. There is a pewter flagon
of good London workmanship. The pulpit of carved
oak of fifteenth century work is handsome and well
preserved.

Over the blocked-up north door, with its hood
mouldings in the Early English style, a niche may be
noticed. Obviously this is not in its original position,
and it is most likely that it was formerly within the
church since the rude piece of carving under the
canopy seems to suggest an Easter Sepulchre, though
undoubtedly of very unusual form. The carving represents a bed with someone lying in it, the clothes
coming up to the chin. Across the coverlid is something that may be intended to represent a child in
swaddling clothes, and at the foot of the bed is a
man's head. It is supposed that this is a rude representation of the Nativity; the Virgin Mary, and the
infant Christ, and S. Joseph being thus portrayed.

BISHOPTON.   (Two miles)

From very early times the hamlet of Bishopton has
been an important member of the parish of Stratford-
on-Avon. Its name, associating it with the bishop,

appears to point to a period when the bishop had his ton or enclosure here. The village is situated on low lying ground at the foot of a hill; it had a chapel, the site of which is still pointed out in a field near the Great Western Railway. Nothing now remains above ground in the "Chapel Close" to identify the spot, but a tree growing in the midst of the field is said to mark the position of the chancel. About the year 1830, or possibly a little later, a new chapel was built on higher ground. Apparently the only fragments of the old church removed to the new one are the font, the bell, and the communion table. The font is a very curious one; the bowl is somewhat mutilated, the base upon which it rests is octagonal. At the foot of this octagonal base are four grotesque heads projecting as if intended for brackets to support small columns. These heads appear to be rather early in character, but four sides of the column have shallow carvings of the Perpendicular period. There are two plain shields, a rosette, and a cusped panel with a rude representation of Aaron's staff. The communion table is of oak, small but massive, and with well-turned legs: it is now used as a vestry table.

The new church is a plain comfortable structure, built in imitation of the first period of pointed Gothic; and it is possible that the west door may have been copied from a doorway in the original chapel, since a newspaper account of the opening of the church, when the Rev. I. W. Trow was perpetual curate of the hamlet, states that "the entrance door is believed to be of the date of the twelfth century, and to have belonged to the former chapel as far back as the reign of King John." This, however, is obviously a mistake, for the doorway is a modern one.

In a drawing of the old chapel a doorway of Norman character is shown, and the chapel bears a general resemblance to that at Luddington; indeed, both were small buildings intended only to meet the requirements of the few inhabitants of these hamlets.

CLIFFORD CHAMBERS. (Two miles)

Clifford has one of the most ancient and interesting of the smaller churches in the district. It is of Saxon foundation. The north and south doors of the nave have circular heads of an early type. Some authorities suppose these to be of Saxon workmanship. The north door is now blocked up. The church consists of a chancel, nave, tower, and modern vestry. The building underwent a thorough repair in 1885-86, Mr John Cotton being the architect. The work was most satisfactorily done, every care being taken to preserve the ancient features of the building. The original church had a chancel arch of early form, with a circular head and very narrow opening. This was removed, and a wider arch substituted. The tower is Perpendicular, but the foundations are probably of earlier date. A gargoyle on the western side is carved to represent the muzzled bear, the badge of the Earls of Warwick. The windows of the nave are also Perpendicular in style; those on the south side of the chancel belong to the Decorated period, but the east window has fifteenth century tracery restored.

The roof is entirely modern, of unusual and handsome design. The font is an early one of peculiar shape, being seven-sided; it is thought to be Saxon. There is a low side window, and a curiously carved pilaster near the pulpit; this pulpit is of oak, with handsome Jacobean carving. The vestry contains a large chest, very massive, and wrought out of the trunk of a tree. It is iron bound and furnished with rings to facilitate its transport, like a military chest.

The monuments of the Rainsfords have been placed upon the north wall of the chancel; and consist of two fine brasses (1583), one with the figure of Hercules Rainsford and his wife, with their children beneath, and the armorial bearings of the knight and his lady above. The shield above the head of the lady has been lost. Another shield bearing the arms of Marrow has been recently found in the manor house, and is now fixed upon the wall of the chancel. Over the vestry is the brass of Elizabeth Marrow (1601). An extremely handsome monument of another Rainsford and his wife is now placed on the north side of the sanctuary. The monument is of alabaster, elaborately carved ; the kneeling figures of the knight and his lady are placed on either side of a faldstool, and are fine specimens of the armour and costumes of the period. In the east window some good stained glass of unusual design has been inserted to commemorate the father and mother of the present rector. Several tablets on the wall bear inscriptions to the memory of former residents here, especially to the Annesleys, lords of the manor, and hereditary trustees of the British Museum. Beneath a great chestnut tree on the west side of the churchyard a plain stone marks the resting-place of a former queen of the gipsies.

BEARLEY. (About five miles from Stratford)

The village of Bearley, built on high ground, to the north of the road from Stratford to Birmingham, consists of only a few houses. The manor house is a quaint old building; the rectory has been rebuilt. In keeping with the village is the tiny church, with its ivy-covered belfry. It consists merely of a nave without aisles, and a small chancel, and is entered by a doorway in the western wall of the tower. Some few years ago the church was entirely rebuilt, in imitation of early thirteenth century architecture. Two blocked-up doorways, the one on the north, the other on the south side of the nave, are a little puzzling. From the capitals of two columns on the north side it would appear most likely that the doorways originally had semicircular heads of Norman work, but the shafts of the columns have disappeared, and the heads of the arches are now pointed; it is likely that when the church was rebuilt the stones of the arches were reinserted in this form. The church is dedicated to S. Mary.

ILMINGTON.   (Eight miles)

Should anyone wish to go to an out-of-the-way place, he cannot do better than betake himself to Ilmington, which lies on the hillside overlooking the vale of the Red Horse. Meon Hill is separated from it by a valley, and the road ascends from the Stour until the village is reached, and then climbs upwards for some distance towards Compton Scorpion.

The church consists of a nave, western tower, north and south transepts, and a chancel with a small vestry on the north side. A considerable portion of the church appears to be of the Norman period, including part of the tower, the south doorway, some of the north wall of the nave, and the chancel arch. Most of the windows of the chancel, and also a priest's doorway on the south side are of Early English date. The church was considerably restored about 1840, and a fine archway leading from the massive tower to the nave was then bricked up. On the exterior of the north wall of the chancel the lid of a stone coffin with an effigy upon it has been fixed upright against the masonry. In the south porch there is a holy water stoup, and in the church there are other remains which would repay careful investigation. Upon the walls and floor may be noticed monuments to the Brents, Cannings, Overburys, and Palmers. Richard Palmer married the daughter of Nicholas Overbury of that family of Borton, one of whom was the famous Sir Thomas who fell a victim to the malice of the Countess of Essex in the time of James I. There is a stone sedilia of three seats on the south side of the chancel, and in the vestry an ancient and very massive parish chest. In the churchyard may yet be seen the steps of the ancient preaching cross.

INDEX

ALCESTER, 259-262.
Alderminster, 340.
Alveston, 50, 328.
Annesley, 350.
Arden, Forest of, 296-306.
,, Mary, Cottage of, 16-25.
Ardens, The, 6-10, 11-25.
Armin, Robert, 131.
Arne, Dr, 160.
Aston Cantlow, 9, 10.
,, ,, Church, 342.
Aston - juxta - Birmingham, 11-15.
Atherstone-on-Stour, 336.
Avonbank, 75.
Avon, River, 177-191.
Augustine, Legend of, 66.

BALSALL TEMPLE, 302.
Barford, 181.
Barson, 285.
Bearley, 350.
Beauchamp Chapel, 207.
Beaudesert, 254, 300.
Benson, F. R., 173, 174.
Berkeley Castle, 280.
Berkswell, 305.
Bidford, 122, 336.
Bishopton, 347.
Blacklow Hill, 217.
Brailes, 235.
Brian, Sir Guy de, 290.
Brington, 315.

Broadway, 242, 283, 284.
,, Tower, 283.
Brooke, Lord, 271.
Broom, 124.

CAMPDEN, Chipping, 237-245.
Canlelupe, 255.
Carrington, 298.
Carr, Robert, 323.
Cassey, Richard, 333.
Catesby, 302.
Celebrations, Shakespeare, 157-176.
Chandos, Lord, Players of, 131, 137.
Charlecote, 50-61.
,, Church, 331.
Charles II., 118.
Clarence, Duke of, 292.
Cleeve, 127.
Clent, 246.
Clifford Chambers, 91-100.
,, ,, Church, 349.
Clopton House, 110, 111.
Cloptons, Monuments of, 85.
Compton, Long, 65-68.
,, Wynyates, 229-236.
Cooksey Badge, 340.
Cotswold Hills, 322.
Cotton, John, 336, 349.
Coughton Court, 127, 262.
Crab Tree, Shakespeare's, 114.
Craik, Mrs, 295.
Cupboard, Shakespeare's, 30.

Davenant, 69.
Davenport, 340.
Davis, C. T., 333, 334.
De Clares, 290.
Deer-Hunting, 55, 56.
Devereux, 13, 266.
Dingles, The, 27.
Dursley, 280.

Edge Hill, Battle of, 278, 279.
Edstone Hall, 105-107.
Elizabeth, Queen, 54, 55, 234; at Worcester, 49.
Essex, Earl of, 323.
Ettington, Lower, 263-270.
    „   Upper, 64, 230.
Evesham, 131, 186.
    „   Abbey, 284.
    „   Murder at, in 1583, 134.
Exhall, 129.

Faucit, Helen, 86, 172.
Fawkes, Guy, 111.
Fitz-Hamon, 290.
Flower, C. E., 172, 173.
    „   E., 284.
    „   E. F., 167.
    „   R. F., 86,
Folk-lore, 224-228.

Garrick, David, 157.
Gaveston, Piers, 217, 256.
Ghosts, 224-228.
Giffard, Godfrey, 307.
Gilbert, Robert, 333.
Grafton, Temple, 45, 46, 129.
Grant, John, 111.
Greene, Thomas, 73.
Grendon, 70.
Greswoldes, 304.
Greville, Fulk, 260.
Grevilles, of Milcote, 340.

Guild Accounts, 312.
    „   Chapel, 312.
    „   „   Frescoes, 312.
Guild of Stratford, 307-314.
Gunpowder Plot, 109, 262.
Guy, Earl of Warwick, 6, 192-196.
Guy's Cliffe, 217.

Hacket, Marion, 101.
Halford Bridge, 263-270.
Hampton-in-Arden, 305.
Hampton Lucy, 337.
Harewell, 299.
Harrison, Kidnapping of, 237-245.
Harvard, John, 318.
    „   House, 318.
Hathaway, Anne, 38-49, 337.
Hawes, 304.
Henley-in-Arden, 254-258, 300.
Henrietta Maria, Queen, 274.
Hertford, Marquis of, 261.
Hill, The, 28.
Hillborough, 130.
Hiron, W., 50, 330.
Hodgson, Sir Arthur, 85, 175.
Hoitt, John, 299.

Ichnield Street, 259.
Ilmington, 351.

Jordan, John, 60, 115.
Jubilee, Queen Victoria's, 174.
    „   Shakespeare, 157.

Kenelm, S., 218, 246-250.
Kenilworth, 214-223.
Keyte, Sir William, 227.
Knowle, 2, 3, 301.

Langbain's account of Shakespeare, 74.
Lapworth, 301.
Leicester, Earl of, 208, 211, 221.

Leicester's Hospital, Warwick, 210-213.
London, Journey to, 62-70.
Loxley, 251-253.
    „   Witch at, 227.
Lucy, Sir Thomas, lampoon on, 59.
Lucys' Monuments, 331.
    „   The, 50-61.
Luddington, 336.

MARRAWAY, 27.
Marston, Broad, 122.
    „   Long, 117.
Martin, Lady (see Faucit).
    „   Sir Theodore, 86.
Masoncroft, 168.
Meon Hill, 320.
Mickleton, 321-323.
Mickleton Hooter, 226.
Middlehill Park, 284.
Middlemore, 268.
Miller, Jack, 131, 138, 139.
Montfort, Peter de, 255, 300.
    „   Simon de, 256.
Moreton Morrell, 335.
Mustard, 285.

NEVILLES, The, 199.
New Place, 76-78, 268.
Northampton, Earl of, 323.

OLDEDICHE, 1-5.
Olditch, 1-5.
Overbury, 237, 323-327, 352.
Oxhill, 233.

PALMER, R., 352.
Pebworth, 121.
Perks " of the Hill," 280.
Pershore, 133.
Pillerton, 337.

Portraits of Shakespeare, 145-156.
Priests' Hiding Hole, 2, 127, 128.
Puff " of Barson," 285.

QUINTON, 321.

RADWAY, 277.
Raleigh, Sir Walter, 110.
Raynsford, 96, 98, 350.
Red Horse Hotel, 276.
Relics, Shakespearean, 140-144.
Robin Hood, 251.
Roche, Walter, 95.
Rogers, Thomas, 318.
Rokewood, 111.
Rupert, Prince, 275-278.

SALFORD PRIORS, 127.
Sampson, H., 334.
Sandells, Fulk, 44.
Sauser, Nicholas, 307.
Shakespeare, John, of Clifford, 96.
    „   William, pedigree, 5;
    birthplace of, 71, 72; relics of,
    140-144; portraits of, 145-
    156; celebrations, 157-176;
    verses attributed to, 325;
    marriage, 42-49; deer-stealing,
    50-59; at Oxford, 69; last
    years of, 77.
Shakespeares of Dursley, 280.
Sherbourne, 178.
Shirleys, The, 64, 263-270.
Shottery, 36-41.
Smythe, Sir Francis, 298.
Snitterfield, 26-35.
    „   Bushes, 112.
    „   Church, 341.
Solihull, 303.
Somervile, 13, 105-108.
    „   William, 107, 299.
Southam Family, 252.

Stoneleigh Abbey, 217.
Stratford-on-Avon, Battle of, 271-276.
Stratford-on-Avon Church, 81-90.
Sudeley, 249.
Sulgrave, 316.
Sullivan, Barry, 172.

TEMPLE BALSALL, 302.
Tercentenary Celebration, 166.
Tewkesbury, 187, 285.
    ,,   Abbey, 285-295.
Throckmortons, 6, 262.
Tombs, Mr, 119.
Totness, Earl of, 85, 110.
Tredington, 332.

UNDERHILL, 265-268.

VISOR, of Wincot, 280.

WAKEMAN, Abbot, 291.

Warwick, 192-213.
    ,,   Leicester's Hospital, 210-213.
Warwick, S. Mary's Church, 204-209.
Warwickshire Song, 160.
Washington, George, pedigree of, 317.
Washingtons, 315-319.
Welford, 185, 186.
Wellesbourne, 339.
Weston-on-Avon, 339.
Whateley, Anne (see Hathaway).
Wilmcote, 16-25.
Winchcombe, Legend of, 246-250.
Wincot, 101-104, 280.
Wixford, 124.
Woldiche (see Olditch).
Wootton Wawen, 107, 297.
Worcester, 42-49.

YARRINGTON, Andrew, 182.

TURNBULL AND SPEARS, PRINTERS, EDINBURGH.